# CREATING HEAVEN ON EARTH

Aloha
Anne C Clark

# CREATING HEAVEN ON EARTH

## My Journey from the Devastation of My Life into the Heaven in My Heart

*"The miracle is, the more I surrendered into the pure love, the more tragedy turned to grace."*

ANNE CELESTE

Sharira Press

Sharira Press
P.O. Box 669
Pahala, HI 96777



ISBN 978-0-9975869-0-9

Printed in the United States of America



DISCLAIMER:
Some names have been changed to protect the privacy of individuals.

PHOTO CREDITS:
Part One—Jeanette Hirt; Part Two—David Neshem; Part Three—David Neshem; Part Four—Anne Celeste; Part Five—unknown tourist; Part Six—iStock.com/Lenar Musin; Part Seven—Musasa Marimba Ensemble, photographer unknown; Part Eight—iStock.com/ Wildroze; Part Nine—iStock Photos/ Justin Horrocks; Part Ten—iStock Photos/Jay Spooner; Part Eleven—Anne Celeste; Author photo—Timothy Teague

## THE STORY OF SHARIRA

### Transforming Physical Experience into Spiritual Essence

*Our life is a sacred opportunity to transform*
*our fleeting physical experience*
*into enduring spiritual essence.*
*Essence is our truest identity.*
*It is all that remains when our bodies and this physical world pass away.*

*Every event we encounter offers us the opportunity*
*to build life-giving, enduring qualities.*
*Each experience is a choice—to create life through unity,*
*living in pure love and truth,*
*or to deny life with separation, conditioned responses, and illusion.*
*Each moment, we are given a fresh opportunity to choose.*

*If we live our life following the highest within us,*
*we refine coal into diamond,*
*becoming pure, clear, shining light,*
*perfectly crystallized in form.*

*In the Tibetan Buddhist tradition,*
*the Rinpoches are precious ones,*
*greatly attained.*
*Their bodies are burned at death.*

*In their ashes, their heart disciples find sharira, precious pearls.*
*Sharira are literally physical pearls. They are honored as sacred reliquaries.*

*Through deep and abiding spiritual presence,*
*these precious ones have crystallized*
*their life, their essence,*
*into pearls.*

*May this inspire us.*

*For David*
*The beloved one*
*with whom I live within*
*the Beloved One*

# Contents

## ACKNOWLEDGMENTS

*I wish to thank the individuals whose stories make up this book.*

*And I especially wish to thank the dear ones who gave greatly of themselves to help me recover from severe illness.*

*In order of their appearance in my life:*
*Barbara Swanson*
*Joe Salvato*
*Adrian Gregor*
*Sidi al-Jamal*
*and Jules Blazys*

*A special thanks to Katherine Salvato, who is smiling somewhere in heaven.*

# Author's Welcome

THIS BOOK WAS BORN of delight.

The momentum for it came as my friends in Chicago asked me about life in Hawaii, and I found myself telling story after story. Their enjoyment and enthusiasm were contagious, and I began to write down the stories I told. Since I'm pretty talkative, the stories grew into this book.

It is a delicious little taste of the islands—a collection of moments, really—some beautiful, some touching, others fascinating . . . all hopefully delightful. My private name for the book is *Deliciousness Itself: The Yummy Story of How I Came to the Islands.*[1] It has been a great deal of fun to write.

It is a Cinderella story, and a true one, for I lived it. It is a story of how I overcame great tragedy and illness—the devastation of my life, really—to fall into the arms of love: first the deep, pure love, the Unity that we call God, held within my spiritual heart, and then the arms of my beloved husband David and the warm embrace of Hawaii. I had to learn how to enter the heaven in my heart before I could experience heaven on earth. I had to learn how to constantly surrender my limited self into the pure love at the core of my heart.

Anyone can learn to do this—that is why it is important for me to share my story. What I learned is that the more deeply I surrendered into the pure love, the more my life opened in blessing. I want to share this with you. It can offer you so much. Can you imagine what your life would be like if the deep dream that moves through your heart were fulfilled?

In my case, the blessings have been extraordinary. By medical odds, I shouldn't even be recovered; most people who were as deeply ill as I was do not recover. And what are the chances that I would write an inspired book of everything my heart held of a true love . . . and then walk right into my very own story?

My story unfolds in the way I came to know the islands, how they opened for me, through my daily life here. I have told it as if I am entertaining you, my friend and guest, and we are traveling the island, talking. (And you can't get a word in edgewise!)

These stories hold hope and happiness. When I tell people the stories, especially women, their eyes light up—whether they are twenty-two or seventy-two. Their hearts open to what just might be possible for themselves. I hope that you will read this book knowing that the deep dream in your heart and soul can be fulfilled in a way far more beautiful than you now imagine. That is the way the deep, pure love, the Unity, works when we join it.

So let's open this book up like a box of chocolates and enjoy this delicious little story.

And by the way, you *can* get a word in edgewise—I'd love to hear from you and learn how you liked this book. Just contact me at anne@anneceleste.com.

Aloha!

Anne Celeste
Aina Lani Retreat, Hawaii
April 2016

# Introduction

## Aloha

***A wreath of flowers for you as we begin . . .***

I WISH THAT I could carry you to Hawaii this moment, and that you could be encompassed within its flowing grace and beauty.

So let's pretend that you are visiting me on the Big Island. And that you too feel gentlest, balmy breezes sweeping across the ocean as they softly caress you . . . and that you see shimmering, golden sunlight sparkling on waves of azure, cresting and tumbling, rolling in an endless rhythm. Imagine the delight of radiant tropical flowers tumbling all around us in brilliant purples, reds, oranges . . . near trees laden with luscious fruits, gently bowing in the breeze . . . all held within the enveloping love that is the islands, with their offering of goodness and well-being, so freely given.

And so imagine with me that I am placing a lei of plumeria flowers, luscious and fragrant, on your shoulders.

As I place this lei upon your shoulders, may the flowers of Hawaii fill the air around you, and may their fragrance intoxicate you so that you relax into the essence of aloha and begin to dream with me the dream your heart holds of the islands . . .

*Let the soft, lapping waves by the shore carry you*
*into a timeless now,*
*where all that exists is the beauty of this moment*
*Let the sweet island breezes caress you*
*and gently carry away all that is not love*
*Let the goodness of the golden sun penetrate you,*
*warming deeply*
*Breathe deep of the island's love and let it fill you*
*Relax into its goodness . . . just bask . . .*

And now listen to an old Hawaiian song, a love song to nature, as all the ancient songs were. Let it paint for you a picture of pure blue waves glistening in the sparkling sun . . . of softest rain and gentle morning dew glittering like diamonds on giant taro leaves . . . of the mighty mountain Mauna Kea, shining majestic in the mist . . . "Kaulana, Kawaihae" . . . [2]

This book is my song to Hawaii. It is my gift to you. It is the lei I place on your shoulders, with blessings of aloha.

# PART ONE

# FLYING INTO A WHOLE NEW LIFE JUST WAITING FOR ME TO ARRIVE

*Sip some homemade Tahitian limeade, and I'll tell you how the story goes*

A photo of me taken when the story begins

# 1 Flying from Years of Tragedy . . . Right into the Fulfillment of My Life

***As I touched Hawaiian earth for the first time, a commanding voice told me that I was home now***

I had no idea what was waiting for me when the plane landed in Honolulu that summer day. Even from the plane, the easy breeziness of the island began working its magic. A thrill of excitement raced through me. After all, this would likely be my one and only trip to Hawaii.

I would never even have visited Hawaii, except that my sisters had asked me to join them on the family vacation. It was unusual for them to invite me along. And it was even more unusual for me to go to an island. I had barely been to an island in my entire life. I was a mountain person, and every vacation I got, I headed deep into Colorado's mountains to ski and hike.

Hawaii wasn't even on my radar.

But all that was about to change with my next heartbeats.

As I was taking my first steps on Hawaiian earth, something very big and very deep welled up from the depths of my heart. It spilled out in huge tears that filled my eyes. My heart streamed out, "I'm finally here! Thank God, I'm finally here!" My whole heart and soul poured into those words.

What was this? I had no idea where this was coming from. It was so unknown until this very moment, and yet so very long awaited, so deep within me, that it was as if I had been waiting for this moment for years. Perhaps my entire lifetime.

After all, I was a mountain person, had always been, and had barely been to the beach in decades. So what was this?

In the next moment, more unfolded. My youngest sister, always in charge, told me to stand "here" while she and my nephew gathered the luggage. Okay. So I stood "here." I was away from the crowd around the baggage carousel, and quiet. And a very strong and deeply authoritative inner voice came through me, saying in measured pulses, "You're home now . . . You're Hawaiian . . . You belong here . . . Your entire life will change now." I still remember the words exactly as I heard them, because I felt them very deep within me.

I was swept along with the commanding voice, just listening for a few moments, absorbing, when suddenly I realized that I was hearing something. I thought for a moment that I was simply picking up the thoughts of the people getting their luggage; almost everyone wants to live in Hawaii. But then I focused my awareness and asked, "Who *are* you?" of the voice.

And the voice answered authoritatively, "You may call me the Spirit of the Islands."

What was this? I just listened. I had no idea what this meant.

I'm used to receiving inner guidance. I've lived my life by it. I'm deeply intuitive and have had a wonderful array of skills of subtle perception all my adult life. But even though I've taught many, many people how to develop their intuition over the decades, I'm not allowed to know everything that's happening. Sometimes I'm kept in the dark. Our soul does not always allow us to see what is ahead of us. Sometimes it's because what is coming is simply too big.

And this *was* simply too big. And so very, very different from what I had known for the past fourteen years. My life had been devastated in that time. I had lost my family, my true work, my home, Colorado, my savings, and then my marriage. In fact, I'd lost my entire way of life, all the ways I had known and valued myself. And after all this devastation, I had become staggeringly debilitated with severe illness, bedbound and then housebound for many years by severe chronic fatigue syndrome. It had taken many, many years of unrelenting effort just to make a partial recovery. And I had just recovered from cancer and major spinal surgery. My health was still quite impaired. So this was a special trip indeed, and a special day, August 6, 2005. I was lucky to be able to travel.

And now here I was in Hawaii, being told that my entire life was about to change.

As the week unfolded, I kept wondering what the voice meant.

I learned that the "Spirit of the Islands" is well known among the islanders and that each island also has its own unique spirit. Interesting, confirming.

In the next few days, I became very sick with a terrible cough and congestion in my lungs. I would have to leave early. After two false starts and two airline change fees, I finally booked a flight out for Sunday evening from Kauai through Honolulu, and back to Chicago. Little did I know that somewhere in Hawaii, a man named David was changing his flight to that same Sunday evening flight to Chicago.

And I didn't really pay much attention to the dream I woke with that Saturday morning before my flight home. I dreamt that I met a man, whom I hugged; and in our hug, he knew. In that hug, it was understood that it was just a matter of time before we married.

I had no idea what I had walked into when my feet touched Hawaiian earth.

# 2 How I Got Here... Or, How I Met David

***The only thing I had to do to live in Hawaii was fall in love***

It was so simple, really.

I met David in the Honolulu airport on my return flight home from Hawaii. It was Sunday night, and the flight got into Chicago the next morning after dawn. So it was Monday morning when he asked me for our first date. And it was a mere week later, on the following Monday morning, that he was telling me he felt like he was looking at his wife. I felt the same way. There was no question that we would marry.

We knew immediately.

I had waited seventeen years; David had waited ten.

How did this wonder happen?

Sip some homemade Tahitian limeade, and I'll tell you how the story goes. Everyone wants to know how we met, so I will tell you. And everyone always wants to hear the long version, so I'll tell you that too.

It was in the Honolulu airport, I believe gate 14, waiting for a Northwest flight bound for Minneapolis.

It was early evening, and I looked just the opposite of how I would have liked to have looked for the occasion of meeting my husband, the one with whom I would share the greatest love of my life. I was sweaty from waiting three hours in the Kauai airport without air conditioning, still coughing, without makeup, my hair pulled back, and worst of all, in my glasses! Charming.

I came and sat right between two men, one in a golden-colored long-sleeved tee. I didn't really notice them, and proceeded to open my Michener's *Hawaii,* a book I'd just bought at the Kauai airport to get me through the long night flight home. I was munching macadamia nut cookies, my dinner.

In a few minutes the announcer said, "All passengers leaving for Phoenix, depart at gate 14." I wondered if I was at the right gate, because that was the gate for my flight to Minneapolis—and my flight was leaving in just a few minutes. Was I at the right gate?

The man in the golden shirt on my right was also surprised by the announcer. Turning to me, he asked the same question I was thinking: "Am I at the right gate? I'm going to Minneapolis."

We began to talk. He lived in Hawaii, he told me, and he was visiting the mainland. "Actually, though, I'm not going to Minneapolis—I'm headed to Chicago." Just like me. Not remarkable then, but looking back, that Minneapolis flight connected to other cities all over the Midwest.

"But I'm not going to the city. I'm going to Schaumburg." A suburb fairly close to mine.

And then he continued, "Actually, I won't spend much time in Schaumburg, either. I'll be spending my time in Lake Geneva, Wisconsin, this coming weekend." Another coincidence—that's where I spent every weekend. But at the time, these coincidences were nothing more than the casual conversation of two people, each on their own journey.

That led to a brief conversation about healers on Kauai as we moved through the line to our plane. Then David asked if he could come talk with me on the flight. Yes! As soon as I got on the flight, I flew into the bathroom and put on my contacts and makeup.

What I loved about David that evening was the way he always stayed in touch, touching in with me throughout the whole flight. And his kindness—he was very kind to me, trying to get me into first class with him, among other things.

One thing that particularly endeared him to me was how he asked if he could take me out the coming Thursday evening. When he asked, I had answered, "Yes, I'd like that." And then later, walking together to our second flight, he asked again, "Are you sure you want to go out with me?" After all, we had only just met. His humility was touching. Arresting. Refreshing.

By 10:30 p.m., he came back to my seat to see if we could talk, and we stood in the bulkhead talking until midnight. And of course I hugged him. (The famous hug of my dream.) But I didn't realize it yet; I didn't realize what was unfolding. My soul kept it from my awareness.

I had been telling him that I worked a great deal with the spiritual heart center in my practices and classes, and that you could tell how open and connected to the Unity people's hearts were when they hugged you. So of course, I had to demonstrate. I opened my heart center and let all the love in the universe flow through me to David, through his heart. Two years later, David told me that it was in that hug that he knew.

Thursday night came, and we talked and walked along Naperville's Riverwalk. When he came back for breakfast the next morning, he brought my favorite fruit, raspberries. I had never told him I love them. By noon I realized that I felt complete with this man. Complete! I had never felt that before, never even thought of being complete with someone before.

He hugged me, and in his hug I knew that here was the man who could give me his heart and his soul. That was what I had been waiting for. His hug told me, "Yes, this is the one."

We spent the following Saturday together, taking a tour boat on Lake Geneva. And as we sat there in the breezes that swept off the lake, it was hard for me to imagine that a man I had met just the past weekend in Honolulu could be with me now, where I spent every weekend, in Lake Geneva, Wisconsin. And that he could also answer one of my biggest questions about Hawaii: what is it like to hike the rugged Na Pali Coast of Kauai? David had done it. And his adventure fascinated me.

We camped out that weekend in a tent, while fireworks went off. (Outside and inside the tent!) Later a huge storm came, and lightning and thunder flashed while our little tent gradually took on water, which gradually made its way into our sleeping bags. We scurried to bail ourselves out. But we were happy campers.

The next morning David awoke from a profound message dream about us. I had been waiting for a man who could share his inner life with me.

By Monday, as we both drove our separate cars out of Lake Geneva and back into Illinois, I wondered, "What happens next?" David hadn't said anything about "next." He'd be back in Hawaii in a few days, five thousand miles away. I picked up my cell and called him, up ahead in his SUV. And that's when he said, "I feel like I'm looking at my wife in my rear view mirror."

And so I came home and immediately began getting ready to move to Hawaii. It felt as if a deep dream had come true for me, a dream so deep it had no words, no image . . . a dream that had been living in me my entire life, unknown.

The name "David" means "beloved."

I had found my beloved.

# 3 I Decide to Leave Everything and Live on an Island

***Lisle, Illinois, or the Big Island? Let me think about it . . .***

So in a matter of a weekend, I knew I was leaving Illinois and heading for Hawaii. I had, in effect, gone through the dating phase and the engagement phase and was planning my marriage—all in a weekend—and no one even knew that I had met David yet.

It was like throwing everything up in the air and letting it land. It was the only way I could get to the island—I knew my life would be so different that I would have to totally re-form it once I got there, anyway.

And there was more. This meant I would have to clean out my basement. Oh no! Not *The Basement*! Anything but *The Basement*.

That meant all the years of accumulated lifestyle that my basement represented—archives of family photos dating back to tintypes from the mid-1800s, and everything I had accumulated in fifty-some years of living. The dread task was upon me.

I didn't see how I could do it all. The pressure of all this was so overwhelming and so sudden that I remember tripping as I walked into Whole Foods, literally falling on my face on the concrete walkway. Ouch! An outer representation of the inner turmoil.

So I started to clean the basement. I worked for weeks and weeks. And then my friend Chris came, and *we* cleaned the basement for one more week. And then David came to live with me, and *we* cleaned the basement for many more weeks. Box after box left for Good Will and garbage—and there was always more. *The Basement* went on for six relentless and grueling months. But finally the last box was packed away. *The Basement* was clean.

It took so long that David even wondered if I was ever going to be arriving in Hawaii. I had told David that first weekend, "I will swim to your boat." (This, after the Hawaiian custom of beautiful and innocent young island girls swimming out naked to meet the sailors' boats in Captain Cook's expedition.)

In my case, it took so long to "swim" to his boat that David wondered if I was doing the crawl.

But I made it.

# 4 What He Told Me About His House . . .

***I have to say, he told me so!***

From my cozy, well-appointed little townhome in suburban Lisle, Illinois, the phone conversation went something like this . . .

> "My house has plywood floors . . ."
>
> "That's okay!"
>
> "And I painted them for you today. I picked a nice new color, very fresh. That way the house will look really good for you. I took all the furniture out to paint the floors."

And the next conversation went something like this . . .

> "I have screens, not real windows . . . that's how we live here in the islands . . ."
>
> "That's okay, it's an island home!"

And the next phone call . . .

> "I should tell you I have only cold water . . ."
>
> "Oh . . . O-kay. What about the shower?"
>
> "Oh, I have hot water for that; that's in the outdoor bathhouse. I don't have an indoor bathroom. That's also how we live here in the islands. It's nice, taking a shower out in nature."
>
> "Ohh kay . . ."

And finally, the last confession . . .

> "I should tell you that there are bees living in my house. They've somehow made a home in the living room wall. But they really don't buzz around too badly."

# 5 And I Still Came!

***As we circled over the winding shoreline of the island beaches, I knew that when I got off the plane, my life would change forever***

Within a week or two of meeting, I was on the plane to visit David in Hawaii. I knew I was going to be with my husband. I did not know yet what made him laugh; I didn't really know yet how his mind worked. But I did know, very surely and very soundly, that we were joined in our hearts and souls. And now we would have to see what it was like on the level of our personalities and our daily life together.

David greeted me with a sumptuously fragrant aloha lei, the perfume of my new life, and a lover's kiss to match. Then we went on to dinner in downtown Hilo, the first time I had ever seen the town that was to become the place I would shop every week for groceries. In the night, it looked like something out of Alaska—big warehouse-looking buildings, plain and worn, with weathered paint. It felt like I was in a very rugged outpost, like I might imagine an Alaskan fishing village.

We were so excited and happy to be together. Our eyes were shining and our hearts were singing, brimming with happiness. It felt as if we had been best friends for so long that we had been laughing together since kindergarten. Dinner was so happy, filled with endless laughter.

David introduced me to tom kha soup—exquisitely good and wonderfully warming, the dense richness of coconut milk making a savory Thai version of soothing chicken noodle soup. In it floated the colors of spring—green lemongrass and deep-green kaffir lime leaves, red tomato and chili, and brown ginger-like galangal—such deep and rich flavors, exquisitely turned together in a broth, exotic and new. A taste of my new life.

Then began the long drive home as we traveled under the starry canopy of Hawaiian sky, through the balmy night air. Along the way we drove through lush rain forest, rising up into the crisp mountain air of the little village called Volcano. We stopped at Volcano National Park to get coffee. I remember gazing out into Kilauea Crater in the total darkness, trying to imagine what the volcano must look like in the day, when it was steaming.

A couple of steamy kisses to match our coffee, and we continued on into the night, down miles and miles of darkness, guided only by the light of endlessly star-filled skies, now passing through dry desert.

As we drove further on into the night, we entered the valley. The first thing I remember about the long road back into the valley was being surrounded by tall, tall trees shadowed in dapplings of darkness and moonlight, under moon and stars. The valley was deep and rich, lush with green in the silent stillness of dark.

And the scent! The most beguiling night air greeted us. Rich, sensuous perfume floated out through the valley and the night, offering tender sweetness in the moonlight, the magic of blooming night jasmine and white ginger.

On the winding road back, David stopped the car for a moment and returned with a stem of glorious white ginger for me, voluptuously, extravagantly fragrant, the scent I had become enchanted with on Kauai. (Only I never told him.) The fragrance was intoxicating. It matched the excitement of the night.

One more turn down the road, and we arrived at his land, driving up over the knoll and through the big gate, traveling the winding path past the gray stone statue of Kwan Yin under the banana grove that led to his door.

He had a padlock lock on his small front door! Island bachelor style. By the light of a flashlight, he turned the key.

That night as we slept, our room was perfumed with the heady scent of night-blooming jasmine by the bedroom. I was stunned with this, as it was a scene that I had written in a book, an inspired love story of all that love can be. When I wrote it, I had been trying to create the most romantic love scene possible, and I had intuitively hit upon jasmine, later confirming that jasmine indeed blooms at night. I was amazed that once again, I had walked into my book. I had already walked into my book when I met David, and we immediately knew we belonged together. And now the story was unfolding into the pages of my life once again.

That night we slept under an open sleeping bag on his bed, with the island breezes flowing through the bedroom. Happy campers, once again.

In the morning, the golden dawn streamed through our bedroom window, lighting the hills before us. And with that dawn, a glowing radiance rose for me, the radiance of an entirely new life.

# 6 I Meet an Island Boy's Home . . .

***It was everything he promised—and more!***

And in the morning sun, I saw the delight of his home—funky-fun bachelor style—with more sun than I could imagine streaming through the big, tall windows, and balmy breezes flowing throughout the house.

His home was all open and spacious, and it filled me with sheer joy and a wonderful sense of play. Island style. It was glorious. Especially since I had spent every day of my last seventeen years wishing for more sunlight and airflow in my tiny little townhome. Never mind that it was decidedly funky—this was fun.

David's home was part of nature. It was open and free, and a livingness flowed and streamed through his home. All of nature was just outside the window. Like breakfast, for instance.

For our breakfast that first morning, there was fresh papaya, which I watched David pick right off the tree literally four feet away, just outside the breakfast window. The papayas were hanging up twenty feet in their perch, so David used a long pole with a wire basket atop to catch them. He cut them in half and then squeezed Tahitian lime juice, also from his land, on them . . . yummm. Island exquisite.

After breakfast, he walked out on his land, carrying what looked like a big machete. He returned with a five-foot bunch of bananas, maybe one hundred fresh bananas in all. "Day-O!"[3] I discovered he had planted tens of banana trees on his land, over one hundred in all. Banana Dave! I will always remember the image of his sandals, with his cane knife leaning against the wall, and the big five-foot-long bunch of bananas alongside.

The kitchen was definitely primitive, or I guess we should say "island style." The gleaming terrazzo marble countertop was, in this case, an old door through which a small sink had been punched.

The water was, of course, only cold, as promised. But of course, we're "island style."

It was everything he said it would be, and more. As my eyes scanned the kitchen, I saw that there were no cupboards, top or bottom—only three boards which had been placed against the original white shack wall of the flower packing shed that his home had once been. They held an eclectic array of dishes, absolutely none of which I wanted to touch.

Immediately I began redesigning the kitchen in my mind. After all, being fresh from the suburbs of Chicago, with hundreds of *Divine Design* shows under my belt, I was always designing makeovers.

And just as soon as I left on my return flight to Chicago, David made the kitchen comfortable for me—with fresh new hot water, a few cabinets, and a sink countertop, just as I had wanted. All the comforts![4]

His outdoor bathhouse was a real delight, a sensual pleasure. Open to the beautiful forest, it allowed the soft breezes to flow through the shower, a delightful experience. The shower was made of beautifully rustic stone tiles, with rounded turquoise pebbles underfoot to massage your feet as you showered.

One quick balmy, breezy shower, and we were off for my first tour of the island.

# 7 I Discover the Real Hawaii . . . A Most Splendid Week

***These fruits were there for the taking—so soft and luscious that I could open them with my hands and eat them as I walked***

While I was on vacation with my family in Kauai, I had wanted to see the real Hawaii. I wanted to understand what life had been like for the native Hawaiians, and to get immersed in an experience of the deep nature of Hawaii. The elegant resort we stayed at was wonderfully luxurious and extravagantly beautiful, but it didn't allow for that.

So I was thrilled to get to see David's version of Hawaii. By that time, he had been on the island nine years. Always the nature adventurer, he knew just where to take me. It was my miracle week, a most splendid week. That week changed my life.

David took me on a whirlwind tour of the island. In that windswept week, we scooted around the island in his little white Cabrio convertible, traveling across the vast range of experience that is the Big Island. I remember the wind so softly and beautifully, caressingly flowing that it felt like the wind was carrying us as we breezed from waterfall to ocean to volcano, one breathtaking sight after another.

Every day began with golden sunlight pouring through the windows. And every day I was amazed with the abundance and goodness of nature here. The sheer immensity and power of its life force and vitality were remarkable. Everywhere, plants thrived almost beyond belief. Visiting Akaka Falls, which tumbles down over four hundred feet, I saw plants that I used to have in my first corporate office cubbyhole—little pots of pothos—now growing not two feet long but three stories high, entwining their way up tall tropical trees.

David showed me hundreds of different plants on his land and told me how little attention they needed to grow, and how fast they grew. He showed me a tapioca plant. And I thought it came in a box! Oranges grew as big as grapefruits and were so luscious, they dripped orange juice down my arm as I ate them. Hibiscus, so rare and precious in Chicago, were growing all over his land. One large tree was covered with hundreds of fluffy pink blossoms, double in size.

And all of this extravagance was offered so gently, like an island breeze, in such abundance and awe-inspiring beauty.

On our tour of the Hilo side, we drove past deep gorges sheltered by sweeping cliffs—the cliffs rising as tall as two thousand feet high—covered with cascades of lush green. Through the gorges flowed inlets of ocean waters, sweeping deep back between the cliffs. Waterfalls spilled down the heights amidst gorgeous red-orange blossoms in profusion all along the cliffs. Amazing.

We saw trees blooming all over the island—beautiful lavender blossoms cascading voluptuously down from jacaranda trees, pink plumeria lining the streets of Kona, fragrancing the air with their heady perfume, and trees studded with purple orchid flowers, beguilingly delicate. There were so many flowering trees. David told me that almost all the trees bloom at one time or another in Hawaii. Even the oak trees on his land bloom golden in their season. For someone used to the sedate maple and oak trees of Chicago, this was quite amazing.

I gazed out over the remarkable expanse of Wai Pi'o Valley on the north side of the island, and tears came into my eyes. Truly one of the most beautiful places in all the world, it is awe-inspiring and deeply touching . . . breathtakingly beautiful. Here again, deeply verdant cliffs curved six miles inland, sheltering golden-green patches of taro fields, cascading waterfalls, and a black sand beach with rugged surfing waves. It's easy to see how this was one of the most sacred places in all of Hawaii, the Valley of the Kings. "Amazing" was all I could say, once again.

We swam at Hapuna Beach, a gorgeous stretch of luscious white sand beach in front of the glamorous Hapuna Prince resort. We watched giant sea turtles basking at Punalu'u Beach, the famous black sand beach close to David's home.

We drove through parts of the island that looked just like Ireland—the Parker Ranch area up north, with its beautiful cloud-swept rolling hills and grazing cattle. We swept past fragrant forests of eucalyptus that reminded me of California. And we visited places that looked just like the surface of the moon, all naked black with twisting lava, where gnarled and gray, stunted ohia trees valiantly grew up through all that dense black rock.

We ran up to Hawi on the windswept northwestern corner of the island. The little town was a delight, just a tiny mix of eclectic artisan island shops, the fun and friendly Coffee Mill that served as a community hangout, an exquisite bakery, and a sleepy little island-style inn. It rained that evening, and I got to experience what rain is like on the island—warm, gentle, and soft, something all the locals just walk through until they eventually dry off. David laughed at me wanting an umbrella. City girl.

By mid-week I had used the word "amazing" so many times I became self-conscious about it and tried to come up with different words to describe my experience. But I could not find the words.

Kona-side, sitting by the ocean at breakfast, David taught me to see fish in the crystalline pure, deep-blue waves. As the surf rolled up into a crest of clear aquamarine before us, he asked me, "Can you see the fish in the wave?" As far as I was concerned, there *were* no fish in that wave.

But he told me where to look—right in the center of the aquamarine part, as the wave is cresting. As soon as I did this, a whole new view opened, and I immediately saw an entire school of brilliant yellow tangs, each about half a foot long. Wow!

With David's help, I began to realize that everywhere around us were schools of fish. He taught me how to see the turtles out in the water—their little turtle arms look just like shark fins as they flap up. Very cute! We saw parrot fish shimmering in the most enticingly brilliant colors of rich turquoise, radiant green, and magenta, colors so bright they were almost electric.

I was delighted the first evening, when David took me out on the far terraces of his land to pick pink and yellow hibiscus flowers to place in a vase for dinner. In Chicago, hibiscus are very exotic, and you're lucky if you can get them to grow. Here we just walked out on the land and picked them for a casual dinner.

We visited a neighbor, and she offered me a choice of tea—rose hip, mint, or chamomile. I chose mint. And I was surprised when she didn't take out a box of teabags—she went out to her garden.

One of David's friends, Pat, brought over a salad from her garden. I had never had a salad like that. It was bursting with vitality, overflowing with about eight different kinds of greens fresh from the earth. She casually sliced a lusciously ripe avocado and fresh, plump red tomato into it as we talked at the start of dinner, then dressed it with her own papaya dressing. It was an ambrosia of a green salad, and yet done so casually and commonly that I knew it was a way of life here.

And then there was the fruit. Breakfast fruit kept coming from the trees on our land—bananas, oranges, grapefruits, tangerines, papayas, and the curious pomelo, a citrus that tastes like grapefruit but is much bigger—one as big as a basketball.

I got to explore our valley. I took a short walk just around the corner to the gemlike red and gold Buddhist temple sheltered within the valley forest. There I was amazed to see a tall tree surrounded by about twenty massively big, round, shiny green things lying on the ground by the side of the road. These looked like the Haas avocados I knew, except for their perfectly round shape and five-inch diameter. I picked one of these up and brought it back to the house, asking David, "What's this?" He explained to me that it was indeed an avocado, the kind he calls a "cannonball." He went on to tell me that avocados here grow in different shapes and sizes, at least fifty varieties in all.

After a few days, I ventured deeper into the valley for a walk on my own and discovered delightful surprises as I walked—all kinds of fruits, abundant and luscious, that had simply fallen from the trees. A guava fell from the tree as I walked by. Plop! It split open as it hit the asphalt road. Purple lilikoi dangled invitingly from vines that curled up koa trees . . . yummy. An avocado rolled down into the road to greet me. Bananas grew alongside the road all through the valley.

These fruits were there for the taking—so soft and luscious that I could open them with my hands and eat them as I walked. How freely given. How deliciously wonderful.

David took me for a walk around his valley, all the way to the back reaches and into a neighbor friend's orchard. There I saw tens of trees of all description, with abundant fruit just lying on the ground. And most of it was being eaten by the birds, the very well-fed birds.

Surely this was Eden.

# 8 Feeling Full

***Realizing that this is why my suburban friends (and I) were running into malls***

When I first arrived, I felt full. Just simply living on this vibrant and life-giving land filled me . . . it was so alive.

One morning as I woke to the goldened terraces in the dawning sun, I felt so full and complete that I suddenly received an entirely different view of life in the suburbs, from which I had just emerged. I realized that the reason people flock to the malls every weekend is because they're trying to get full, trying to get this feeling that nature provides so abundantly and easily in its pure state. At least, that was certainly true for me.

And no mall had ever compared for me to the glories of nature. I had always noticed how draining shopping is after just a few hours, where the same time spent in a forest is invigorating and renewing. I had long ago realized that in nature, everything is held in unity. Shopping centers are filled with the discord of many disruptive thoughts. But in nature, everything is moving in one great harmony. And this inherent harmony within nature enables us to join that same flow, if we are open. Joining this underlying harmony allows us to touch the energy, joy, and peace that is always within nature, and always deep within us.

I had never lived in wild nature before, only vacationed within it. Living within its unity, I began to experience that wild nature completes us. It fulfills us. And that alone is enough for deep and abiding contentment. Physical objects cannot offer this sustenance; they don't carry life force, unless they are made by loving hands or imbued with love.

Here on our land, the dark night sky was so clear that it was studded with twinkling stars, and we could see the starry spiral of the Milky Way. We could see shooting stars gleam across the sky any night. And when the moon was full, it was unlike anything I had ever seen—it lit the land with an intensity almost as strong as daylight, all in a silvered glow.

Fruit from the trees just kept coming. Avocados rolled out to greet us most mornings, bananas were just in the grove outside, and fresh orange juice was on the top terraces, waiting to be picked and squeezed.

And David told me that when it rained heavily in our valley, the rim encompassing the valley ran with eleven waterfalls. We could even see one from his home.

What wonder was here.

# 9 Feeling Crazy

***What am I doing on an island . . . in the middle of nowhere?***

And yet I also felt a little crazy when I first arrived. What am I doing out here in the middle of nowhere, on a lone island, all alone in the Pacific? I was like a plant that had been uprooted and transplanted, without any roots. I felt bereft and lonely, away from all my friends and family, and all that held meaning for me.

After all, it's all happening back on the mainland, right?

What I didn't know then was that I would gradually grow into a different way of looking at that. After several years, and many trips back and forth, my view was to completely reverse itself.

# 10 Islands Call You . . .

***"In your heart, you'll hear it call you . . ."***

There is a line in the song "Bali Ha'i" from Rodger and Hammerstein's *South Pacific* that goes like this:

Bali Ha'i may call you,
Any night, any day,
In your heart, you'll hear it call you:
'Come away . . . Come away.'

Islands call you.

We have a neighbor in the valley whom I will call Charla. She was just casually vacationing here about ten years ago for the first time in a home she and her husband had rented in the valley.

The first morning when she awoke, she went out on the balcony at dawn. There, she heard the words "This is your earth home." Sudden, unexpected—but rivetingly true.

That same morning, she talked with her husband, and he agreed. Within the year after that morning, they had purchased the home with the balcony, sold their home in the Seattle area, and shipped a container load with all their belongings over to Hawaii.

It was that simple. They fell in love with the island, and created community here, often inviting a stream of people to stay on their land, sharing food and warm conversation in their kitchen. They are much loved, and part of the island community they helped create. It became very hard for them to go back to the mainland, even for a few weeks.

It happens all the time.

I remember meeting a cashier in our Ross for Less store in Hilo. She said that when she first vacationed on the island, she fell in love with it. "I went home and just cried for three months." She went on, "That's how long it took me to get back here to live."

I've heard that story many times.

Islands call you.

# PART TWO

# COMING HOME

*I came home . . . to a dream so deep it had no words, no image*

I had wanted to live with a man in the woods
David, me, and the woods

# 11 Where I Came to Live

***Imagine yourself living in the most remote place on earth . . .***

Imagine yourself living in the most remote inhabited place on earth. That would be Hawaii, a mere speck floating in the Pacific Ocean, over twenty-four hundred miles from its nearest neighbors, California and the Marquesas Islands.

Now imagine that the island you live on has the fewest people on it per square mile. That would be the Big Island.

And now imagine that you live on the most isolated part of that island. That would be the southernmost part.

This is where I came to live.

Miles and miles away from almost any sign of civilization, in deep nature, pure silence, and perfect peace. And endless beauty! It is a beauty that beckons from every joyful sweep of magenta bougainvillea to every pure, crystal-blue wave, and every gold-glowing sunset.

Around us are only endless acres of open land, edged by lapping ocean waves. This part of the island is the least touched in all of Hawaii—eighty miles of shoreline left in its natural pristine state, clear and free, as close to native as any part of Hawaii will ever be, as close to pure as any part of this earth can ever be.

Windswept by island breezes, goldened with endless shimmering sunlight, an expansive openness beckons here as far as you can see . . . endlessly . . . sweeping up across the long mountain, Mauna Loa, with its gold-green meadows, to the far-as-you-can-see white-capped sea that holds all the island within the rhythm of its waves. This is the Hawaii I know.

This is where the first Tahitians landed, awed by the volcano's red, fiery power. So reverent were they that they named this island Hawa'iki, the place known only in their legends, the place of their gods.

There are almost no people living here. You can travel this whole section of island and sometimes barely see another car. No homes mar the ocean view, and miles and miles of open land sweep by on the mauka side, with a few sleepy little sugarcane towns along the way.

There are lookouts where you can see eighty miles of coastline in one glance . . . sweeping, magnificent views of ocean spray lapping up at lava rock, dancing in the exhilarating trade winds. A few years ago, from one of these lookouts, David could see red molten lava pouring into the ocean at night from forty miles' distance, its red vaporous fountain shooting like fireworks into the darkened sky.

The southern portion of the Big Island is pure, so very pure. It is protected by a huge swath of preserve lands and national forests that extend clear across the island from west to east, half a million acres in all. This band of forests keeps the entire south pristine.

There is only one highway circling the island, and of only two lanes for almost all of it. In the south on this lone road, there are no traffic lights, no street lights, no stop signs, no radio reception. Even cell reception is intermittent.

The only thing to accompany you along the roads in this part of the island are the splendid, sweeping views by day, and the soft gleaming radiance of stars and moon by night.

It is a magnificent way of living.

This is where I came to live.

# 12 David . . . A Man of Peace, Living in Harmony with Nature

### *I had wanted to live with a man in the deep woods*

As you can tell, I am a great lover of nature, and the deeper, the purer and wilder, the better. A solace comes over me, a great sense of well-being, and a sure and deep knowing, as I walk in a forest, held within its grace. Deep forests hold deep wisdom.

But how was I to express this in the far west suburbs of Chicago?

My answer was a nearby forest preserve in which I would hike at dawn, rays of the morning sun streaming through the trees on the trail ahead, shining down beams of light that lit my path while I heard commuter cars whiz by on the expressway, oblivious to this quiet sanctuary.

I'd stay as long as I could, going off the designated paths, following the deer trails into the secret forest, sitting in hiding places while hikers and bikers moved by, unaware. Hidden within leafy branches, I would read, pray, and meditate. I'd tramp through brambles to get at secret wild blueberries, a delight of early summer. I'd walk miles and miles and miles. As I lived with the woods like this, I began to dream that I lived in a little house in the woods, hidden away, and that life was simple, so very simple.

And then I dreamt of living with a man in the deep woods. Enter, David.

Meanwhile, David was in Hawaii, over five thousand miles away, living in the deep woods of the Big Island. He spent most of his day outside, planting, mowing, and working his land. Out in his far fields, sometimes he wondered what would happen if he were to die out there all alone one day. Would anyone even know? Enter, Anne.

David is a man fully at home in nature. All his life, he has lived and worked out of doors. He told me that it has only been recently that he began spending much time indoors at all; home for him used to be only the place he would sleep and eat. He used to work his land from sunup to sundown, and even beyond. I understand that. The land has a captivating quality, it does that to you. You want to stay longer.

David has a sense of nature, an attunement to its way that is instinctive. His senses travel out broadly into any natural area. He instinctively knows the terrain, and especially where to find water. This must be how he finds remarkable pieces of land in just one day, because he has done this effortlessly his entire life. He senses the livingness of the land, the cycles and rhythms of nature, the swell and break of the waves, the changes in weather before they arrive.

David has a bond with the land. It's an affinity as intimate as any relationship with a person. He feels the land as an extension of himself. As he walks on the earth, he is part of it, and it is part of him.

But most of all, all his life, David has had a kinship with water.

From his earliest childhood, David remembers being mesmerized by water, the way it moved, the way it drew life to itself, the deer and bear who came to drink along its edges, the silvery quick fish that wriggled in its cold depths. Life took on a great deal more meaning for him around water.

At age eight, when his family moved to a point on Puget Sound, magic happened. He came alive. Now his world was filled with blue bays and green fir forests, wild and waiting to be discovered. He loved it.

An inlet lapped up right by his house at the mouth of the bay—perfect for a boy's first fishing outings. David taught himself to fish, reeling in saltwater trout as big as two feet. They were soon in his skillet for dinner and next morning's breakfast.

That bay was a wonder to him—its saltwater felt so good against his skin, and its waters and shores held endless adventure. Swimming in its waters at night, he was captivated by the way the waters glowed with green phosphorescence any time he moved, magical shimmers that obeyed his every motion.

That bay became his science lab. When the tide ran out, he'd walk the wet shore, watching big clams called geoducks, "gooey ducks", eight inches long, squirt water up in the air as they zipped several feet down into the sand for protection from his steps. He discovered an array of starfish in reds, purples, and oranges. He'd dig for butter clams, oysters, and mussels, and go crabbing. Electric eels would hide out under the rocks he'd flip over.

With his friends, he'd have jellyfish fights with the unfortunate invertebrates who were left on the shore, slimy fun. By the light of the moon, they'd watch for sharks swimming stealthily, their dorsal fins cutting a tell-tale line in the moon's reflection on the waters. Then they'd catch them. Adventure was as endless as their imagination, and what each day brought to the water and the shore.

He was out on the water every day. And within all this exploring, something deeper was growing—an intimacy with nature, a sensing of its ways.

By the time he was ten years old, his father had given him an eight-foot pram. Now he had oars, and the bay was his oyster, so to speak. The call of the wilderness beckoned! Bent on exploring, in no time he rowed far out into the bay, watching fish weave through seagrass meadows in the deep, clear waters. He saw a pod of orca whales, thirty of them, rising up in waves of power, one after another after another. David watched, spellbound.

He soon transformed his pram into a sailboat, rigging an oar as a mast, and steering the sail to catch the wind and turn the boat. How naturally sailing came to him.

Now he sailed away, ten miles to another point on another bay, where the waters were deeper and colder, the forests wilder. Immediately, he slipped his line into the cold depths, like always, when suddenly, "Bam!" A cod wrestled him on the other end. This was new. This fish fought back. It put up a strong fight, and after a contest of wills, David had caught his first cod—a five-pound monster. Very exciting stuff for a young boy.

By age eleven, he was waterskiing, and proud of how effortlessly he could ski with only one ski. He and his three friends would save up their money, then motor across the bay for a gallon jug of A&W root beer, a great treat.

Always, the water beckoned.

David loved to spend all day fishing in the streams of the deep, wild forests all around him. With his younger brother Randy, he'd spend all day wandering the streams, upstream all morning, then downstream all afternoon, in search of trout. These freshwater trout were hard to catch, and besides that, the beaver ponds were challenging—shallow, with logs—making it a real challenge to find trout and to keep his line untangled at the same time.

Other times, he'd explore the forest lakes alone. Sometimes, he'd get lost way back in the wilds at a secret, hidden lake. He'd hike in with a rubber raft in the early morning and watch the steam rising off the water, savoring the joy of being alone in the great forest, hidden from the world. Blue heron would fly away, and osprey would tend their big nests way up in the tall trees, while gentle deer drank on the shoreline. He knew the bears were there too; he could sense them, though they kept out of sight.

By age fourteen, he went on his biggest adventure yet—motoring out to Blake Island, more than fifty miles away, with two other boys to camp out for an entire week, all alone, on this wild and deserted island. It was spooky, too—an old mansion stood in ruins, empty and abandoned, with the spine-tingling thrill and terror of ghosts lingering in the dark.

As he grew, he became accomplished in all the ways of water—sailing, surfing, windsurfing, snorkeling, and diving. Water has always been a big part of his life. Which is interesting, because Taoists revere water: *What is of all things most yielding?*[5]

David is rather Taoist in his way. Taoists emphasize harmony, moving with the way of nature. When they make herbal formulas, they make them in ways that work with the forces of life. So for example, an herb to give greater energy is made from plants harvested when they are building force—when the sun is rising, and in the springtime. It likely would be taken at this time, too. This artful following of "the way" of nature is something our culture has yet to recognize, value, and learn.

Taoists move with the flow, the life force, never pushing, always sensing, and moving in harmony with what is happening, becoming part of all around them. A dance with energy. The way a skillful aikido martial artist moves backward when their opponent moves forward to strike them, gathering force from their opponent's movement, enabling them to thrust forward with greater power. Aikido means "way of harmony with energy." It flows as it moves. So does David.

A Taoist way is gentle. It does not push or force. It moves "with." It is a moving, flowing compassion and humility. It is wise. It gathers force as it moves. And it is quiet. Unseen.

For those caught up in achieving, and striving to get somewhere before someone else does, it does not make any sense at all, and seems quite foolish. The Tao is silent. Artful. The way of action which is actionless. People like David are often misunderstood.

Harmony is how David moves with nature. He moves in trust. And so nature moves with him. Many times, in his adventures, he has been in situations of risk and has emerged unscathed, held by some grace, beyond harm. This is one expression of living within the state of being that is unity, harmony.

A ready example is his hike on the Na Pali Coast on our northernmost island, Kauai. The Na Pali Coast is tough stuff. You hike along a narrow cliff that hangs two thousand feet above the ocean, with a fall straight down to the narrow strip of beach below.

As the trail begins, it looks just like a normal hike, as far as you can see. But past this early section, the trail narrows sharply, and you discover yourself perched high above on a steep cliff with only twenty-four inches of trail between you and the two-thousand-foot sheer drop. If you pass someone, you touch shoulders. And it goes on for eleven miles. When it's muddy from rain, it's high risk, and people chance losing their lives. Our neighbor, an ultra-experienced hiker, nearly lost his life as he slipped and fell over the cliff one year. Only one small tree saved his life. He grabbed it on the way down.

So David began this demanding two-day hike with no food, no special preparation at all. Unprepared? Of course, you could see it that way if you use the usual linear method of planning and preparing.

But consider a different view. Consider "being in harmony" instead. David was in accord with himself. Along the way, he found a guava, and made his first meal of that. But he had no food for the night, or the next days. What would he do? He trekked on.

Once again, his sense of timing was perfect. Before dinner he ran into a couple hiking. They were to have been part of a much bigger hiking party, but no one else showed. And now they were left with all this extra food, and the weight of it to carry.

No problem! He paid the couple and continued on his way. Not only did David not pack meals, but they were catered in for him. As he continued his hike, he experienced the many delights of those who make it all the way in—showering under a huge waterfall, swimming into big wet caves, and exploring areas that look just like Jurassic Park. He had a great time.

I have seen this again and again with him. It's instinct. Harmony. Moving *with*. Besides, he also knew that if things got really bad he could hop a Zodiac boat out.

Have you ever heard of Peace Pilgrim? She began walking for peace at age forty-four, taking the name "Peace." She gave up all her former life and identity, right down to her name. She walked with only three possessions—a comb, a toothbrush, and a pencil. The only clothes she possessed were on her back. She had no money, no home, and she taught herself to sleep outside in all kinds of weather. Her mission was to spread the way of peace. She did not eat or receive shelter unless someone provided it for her. Yet she almost always had food; her longest time without was three days.

She walked tens of thousands of miles over twenty-eight years, sharing peace and teaching peace. All this, in good health, always. In fact, her health increased as she grew older. She was in stunningly good health at the end of her robust life, when a collision took her life. If you see a photo of her in her elder years, you will see a transcendent glow about her. She had become peace.

Her inner peace was reflected in the way of her life. Her way was simple. She moved in graceful harmony, holding the presence of peace.

I see David in this way. Peace, without conflict.

The wise one lives as flowing water.

# 13 Welcome to Banana Heights! "Day-O!"

### *I get to know our land*

On one of our first walks on the land, David began to point out to me all the different bananas he had growing. They were all over the land, growing in big groves. He introduced me to each kind, and I was amazed at the different varieties—I had thought there were only a couple types. I counted how many bananas were growing, and I was amazed.

So I affectionately began to call our land "Banana Heights", because there are over two thousand bananas hanging from trees on our land at any given time—and in ten varieties. So when you enter our foyer, you'll see an honorary painting of a banana tree. "Day-O!"

David planted all of these bananas when he arrived, over one hundred of them. Some are so small, they fit into the palm of your hand—like apple bananas, most everyone's favorite, deliciously sweet and substantial. Then there are the Cuban reds—small bananas again, but this time a burgundy-skinned variety with a rosy, sparkly, iridescent cast to the banana fruit itself. And of course, we have Williams bananas, which grow in long tiered clusters of about two hundred—the kind you buy in the grocery store, big and basic. The list goes on and on.

Their flavor right off the tree is so much fuller than what you get from the store—an explosion of sweet in your mouth, sparkling with a fresh-picked tang. Definitely divine. They make irresistible banana cream pie, and the most delicious banana bread you have ever tasted.

Bananas grow in an amazing way. You know the way you buy them in the grocery store? Well, that group of bananas is called a "hand." On the tree, about six to eight of these hands make a full circle around a hanging stalk. Then, these circles stack in tiers, climbing up the stalk, running anywhere from three to five tiers, and sometimes even up to seven in all. A big bunch like this will have a couple hundred bananas—an amazing amount, and it weighs a ton.

Picking bananas is always fun. Little boys love the excitement of following David on a banana hunt on our land. David goes out with his cane knife, which looks somewhat like a machete, to find a cluster that is ripe and dangling high up in a tree. Little boys have to crane their necks way back to see it, a long way up from their short, three- to four-foot height.

Some expect David to climb the twelve to twenty feet up the banana stalk to cut down the bunch. But instead he slices through the big thick banana trunk just a couple feet off the ground. Whack! Whack! Whack! In the next moment, the huge stalk careens down, and at its end, bananas splay all around.

The bunch that comes down is inevitably at least half as big as the youngest onlooker. Wow!

More fresh banana bread, anyone?

# 14 One Hundred Shades of Green . . . The View from Our Land

***A living tapestry of green, brought to life each day by wind and sun***

One day soon after I returned to Chicago, I asked David what he was doing. He said he was looking out over "one hundred shades of green." What a perfect phrase to describe the lushness of our land and its valley. Here is what he was seeing:

Our land weaves out in waves and waves of green, as your eye cascades up the five terraces that flow down to the house. If you're just passing by, it simply looks like a lot of green. But if you take a moment and use your artist's eye, you begin to see shade upon shade of green, tumbling together in the wind, brought to life by beguiling breezes that wander through each leaf and blade.

Casting your eyes up, you catch the tall, tall trees invigorated by the exhilarating trade winds, their leaves dancing its rhythm. High above are silver oak, their tops crowned with golden flowers in the spring, weaving with the melody of the breeze. Alongside them sway slender eucalyptus, weaving together, branches crossing, groaning in the wind.

On the highest terraces, regal bamboo drift lazily to and fro, reaching some thirty feet up to the sky, their tall, spiky tops frolicking playfully as the trades tease them. They bring a touch of bright spring green and glorious spikes of tall gold bamboo canes to the tapestry. Cackling myna birds busily gather here at dusk by the hundreds to say goodbye to the day.

The wide leaf fronds of the bananas fill the land's canvas with sturdy forest green, growing everywhere. They share the heights with the bamboo, some growing up to thirty feet high, with leaves as long as a man. Not bad for a plant whose trunks are no sturdier than mere cellulose. Red cardinals and black and white mynas light on the tops of the banana bunches, taking turns feasting on the fruit as it ripens in the sun.

A giant avocado tree stands tall, and every once in a while a soft thud announces another fresh-fallen fruit. Our neighborhood dogs make it a point to trot over in the morning to get first pick of any fresh-fallen avos. And by the way, so do the birds, and the cats. We've gotta be fast to get our pick.

And every morning, the golden sun wakes it all up, casting its shimmer across the sweeps of green. Birds come to life, calling from the trees with their blessing of birdsongs. As the sun rises further across the terraces, the diamond dew drops disappear and the bees emerge, busily buzzing among the flowers. Throughout the day, orange butterflies light around the gardens, and sometimes, an iridescent-blue dragonfly darts by. Pheasants warble and cackle as they strut around the land.

The entire scene is a living, breathing tapestry, warm and humming, green and golden. It is a choreography of life that arises anew each morning, dancing with the wind, playing in the sun.

# 15 The Story of Our Land

***Looking at our land today, you would never guess how it all began . . .***

The story of our land goes all the way back to the story of ancient Hawaii. But before I tell you that story, I'll you how David found this land.

David came to Hawaii after a time of personal tragedy and heartbreak. Searching at that time, he was guided to come to Hawaii. He chose Maui because that was what he knew; he been there several times before. But as he stayed on Maui, it didn't feel right, and he found himself drawn to the Big Island. He hoped that perhaps he could buy land there, but he wasn't sure there would be any left—after all, islands are very small places.

Because of his situation at the time, he knew that if he was going to find land on the Big Island, he had just one day in which to do it. Rather an impossible mission. But remember, David moves in harmony.

So he discovered this beautiful valley, and this precious piece of land in that one day. And ever since that time, it has been the right fit.

How did he do it? Instinctively, of course, as he always finds beautiful pieces of land. Following his intuition, he got off the plane in Kona and began driving south. He was amazed to see huge tracts of land opening up, all around the island. He didn't stop for almost half the island, and when he did, it was because he saw an agricultural company that reminded him of the type he used to work with when he owned his orange grove.

He walked in, asking the manager if there was any land for sale in the area. The manager answered that yes, his father had acreage for sale in the valley.

So David drove back into the valley. The day he came into the valley was a magical day. Brilliant sun sparkled gold across the entire sweep of valley. It was a halcyon day. Just the kind of day that people decide to buy land.

As he drove back the long road into the valley, he gazed out over the golden-green expanse of meadow stretching up the mountains. Then the road swung round, and he entered the valley under a canopy of trees that gently overarched his way. He followed the road as it wound its way through the valley, driving right past the parcel without realizing it, and all the way back deep into the valley.

There, he beheld amazing sweeps of lush meadow and verdant forested cliffs, the great cliffs that surround and shelter the valley in a comforting crescent. He got out of his car, breathed deep, and took it all in. All around, he heard the remarkable sound of crickets—a great chorus rising through the valley. Within this sound, he heard the subtle universal sound. It was a spiritual practice he had learned when he practiced yoga. The tone was so clear and pure, so powerful, that he knew this was where he belonged.

Excited, he got right back into his car, drove back, and told the manager that he wanted to buy the land. But David was talking about the wrong parcel. So they drove out together to view the right parcel.

What David saw when he looked at the right parcel of land was sugar cane—masses and masses of cane grasses, growing from twelve to twenty feet tall, rustling and swaying in the breezes. All he could see was cane grass—nothing else. He had no idea that the land was terraced in five levels and that on each of those terraces, hidden in the tall sugarcane grasses, were the remains of thirty-two dilapidated greenhouses. Nor did he know that he would spend the next several years hauling unending truckloads of their debris away. It was all that remained of the flower farm that once thrived here.

The only other thing he saw that day was a dilapidated old green shack—all that remained of the packing shed for the carnations.

Clearly, this was his land. Immediately he said, "I'll take it!" That very day he signed the contract, and set out to make the land his own.

David felt elated, and deeply happy. He knew this was his place to be. And with that, he began an entirely new way of life. It all sounds so simple. But in reality, it took a great deal of courage to take that step. And it took a great deal of sacrifice. David always says, "It's a choice."

The man from whom David bought this land is Masa Kai, an old Japanese gentleman. Photos of him from this time show him to be a genial and pleasant-looking Japanese man with a round face and white hair. Here, he had lived with his family for many years, tending to their flower farm.

Masa Kai acquired this land in a most remarkable way. It is said that he got it for free. As the story is told, four Japanese men came to the valley to homestead under the Homestead Act of 1911. They divided this beautiful valley into four slices.

Can you imagine being *given* an entire valley? But that seems to be just what happened.

And even before that, in the late 1800's, this entire valley and all the fertile lands of the Ka'u district were planted in cane by the sugar cane plantations, thousands upon thousands of acres, for miles around. Three small sugarcane towns sprang up—Pahala, Na'alehu, and Wai'ohinu.

It was back in 1878 that the Pahala plantation began production, and as "King Sugar" boomed, so did this entire region. Ultimately, this very wild area was tamed with sugar cane. It became home to the largest sugar mill in the world, boasting its own bustling railway and port. The little cane towns, so quiet and sleepy now, once were a lively melting pot of workers and their families.

The workers arrived in a steady stream. First, the Chinese. Then, the Portuguese. By 1886, the Japanese were working the fields. Finally, in 1906, Filipinos joined the work crews.

This was the era when the only transportation on the island was by horse, and when bumpy roads traversed lava rock, making travel quite difficult. So the plantation built camps in the valley and surrounding areas to house the plantation workers and their families. The camps were organized by nation of origin, and each had about a dozen homes with its own little store. Each camp made a community together, a place where the families could share the everyday happenings of their lives and celebrate their traditions and faith. People who reminisce about life in these tiny villages remember fondly that it was a good life, a simple life.

It appears that there were at least three camps in our valley where workers lived. Our survey plat maps show a Japanese camp called the Iseri camp. There is an old Japanese cemetery in the valley from those days, and the old 1902 Nicheren Shu Japanese Temple still stands. I believe there were other camps in the valley, which would have been Chinese, Portuguese, or Filipino. They were disbanded sometime in the 1960s, when transportation allowed workers to move to town. At that time, most of the camp houses and buildings in the valley were transported down to the little sugarcane town.

But back to Masa Kai's story. He and the other three men were the first individuals who had ever owned this land and valley. This is quite remarkable by mainland standards, where land was privately deeded, and subdivided and subdivided for generations by the time of Hawaii's homesteading. Their pieces of land were shaped in the traditional Hawaiian land shape—one big, long pie slice running from mauka to makai, mountain top to ocean.

Before 1848, no one had ever owned land in Hawaii. It was natural, just the way it had been created. And it was shared by all.

We have to go all the way back to the first Polynesians who settled Hawaii almost 1600 years ago to understand this. It was about that time that the first Polynesians landed in Hawaii, bringing their outriggers up on shores very close to our land. Tahitians, they brought with them one very important belief about land. They believed that earth was immortal. Humans were mortal.

And so it followed that land could not be owned. The land was older than humans, and eternal, so how could anyone even consider owning it? The right and true relationship was that people belonged to the earth, the earth did not belong to people. Hawaiians had no sense of ownership of land.

And so their relationship to the earth was that of custodians and stewards. To this day, there remains an enormous love and respect for the "aina," the land, in Hawaii.

The ancient Hawaiian land practices reflected this integrity and respect. Land was apportioned for use in ways that preserved, protected, and renewed its resources. Practices that depleted resources were forbidden, or "kapu." There was no concept of profiting from land or exploiting it. An example of one such conservation practice would be the fish ponds that were kept stocked, through the use of a clever design by which fish could enter the pond through a little hole, but grew too large to leave the pond, and so could be caught later for food.

Everyone was welcome and entitled to the abundant gifts of land and sea. To achieve this, land was divided into broad pie slices, called "moku," running from ocean to mountain. This allowed each tribe to have a slice of the bounty of Hawaii, from mountain to ocean. The upper reaches of the moku held the finest koa trees, massive enough to become complete hulls for outriggers. Here lived the birds whose precious feathers were captured by feather catchers to adorn the robes of the great chiefs, the ali'i. The mid-moku land grew taro, breadfruit, sweet potato, and banana. Here were pigs, so important to Hawaiian life, as well as goats and wild cattle. And the ocean moku areas held fish ponds and the bounty of ocean fish and seaweed, as well as salt and coconuts. The moku were very large. The entire island of Oahu, for example, about six hundred square miles, was divided into just six moku.

The large moku were then subdivided into narrower slices, called "ahupua'a," named for the sacrificial pigs ("pua'a") that were used, along with lava rock stones, as boundary markers. Today, as you travel the island, you can see sections of the ancient stone walls still standing, remnants of this tribal way of life. Each ahupua'a was given its own name. The old sugar cane town of Wai'ohinu is named for its ahupua'a, "shiny waters."

All ahupua'a were stewarded by an ali'i, or tribal chief. The entire kingdom's lands were stewarded by the great chief, or king, of Hawaii, who determined how they were distributed.

All this changed when Captain Cook "discovered" the islands. Over several generations, foreigners, usually Americans with business interests, petitioned the king to allow them to take title and ownership of the land. King Kamehameha I remained firm in his conviction that no Hawaiian lands should be sold. But by the third generation, his grandson King Kamehameha III gave in, and signed the Great Mahele of 1848.[6] From that point on, land was divided and titled, no longer stewarded tribally.

As so often happens, many native Hawaiians were disenfranchised from their lands at that time, and the history of development of the Hawaiian lands began. Many sacred and historic sites have been lost to development. Today, the Kona Inn stands where the great ancient heiau, or temple, stood, its ancient stones dismantled and reassembled into the Kona Bay breakwater wall. King Kamehameha's historic living area is covered by a hotel of the same name. And the exquisite beauty of the Kona Bay shoreline is hidden by a long string of luxury homes, hotels, eateries, and retail stores, many built largely since 1980.

Couldn't the beautiful shoreline of Kona Bay have been preserved for public use? The buildings could have been set back one quarter mile, in the way Chicago's lakefront was preserved with parks. Then, both ancient heritage and modern enterprise could remain side by side, and everyone could enjoy the beautiful view and use of Kona's oceanfront. It would preserve ancient Hawaiian heritage alongside contemporary structures, human development within natural beauty and history.

Yet despite all this development, the awesome beauty and power of the Big Island remains. Its magnificent aina still deeply nurtures body, mind, and soul.

It is as the ancient Tahitians always knew. The land remains. Its power sustains.

# 16 Above, a Spiral Flight of Doves

***And below, cascading waterfalls of flowers in gem-bursts of amethyst, ruby, and coral***

One day, shortly after I arrived to stay, we were on our way to Kona on the west side of the island. As we climbed up through the winding roads, suddenly, out above us flew a huge flock of white doves. One hundred white doves rose in flight in one huge, upreaching spiral, their white-winged flight contrasting beautifully against the pure azure sky.

Rising and rising, higher and higher, within moments they crested to a breathtaking peak, then swept down and off again from whence they came. Their upsweep and dart back was over in a moment. It was mesmerizing, a living miracle.

And below, as we traveled, an array of flowers came into view, sweeping past us on either side, a bouquet offered by nature, running for a quarter mile. Cascading flower waterfalls of bougainvillea in gem-bursts of amethyst, lavender, ruby red, and coral glistened brilliant in the sun, some as high as twenty feet tall, climbing up through the trees. Orange trumpet vines studded the black lava rock walls on which they wandered. And beautiful, exquisitely tender lavender clusters on graceful jacaranda trees blossomed overhead, covering the earth in a soft lavender cloak.

Flowers beckoned from everywhere. As we drove into Kona along its ocean way, Ali'i Drive, our path was filled with the fragrance of leis, from plumeria trees blossoming in the sun. Voluptuous orange clusters covered poinciana trees, bursting out at us from side streets, stunning in their glory. All around us was joy.

What beauty was here.

# 17 The Flood of the Millennium

### *Sabine makes a narrow escape*

You've heard of hundred-year floods? Well, this was the flood of the millennium. The flood story was one of the first stories that David told me—it stood out that much, even five years after it happened.

Our valley had lived quietly in nature's peace until late in the year 2000. That November, the skies opened, and rain began to pour down, heavy and steady, hour after hour after hour. There was no warning of danger, no sense that this would be a special storm. It began just like any other storm. Yet within hours, it was clear that this was something quite different. It poured relentlessly, on and on, until the soil could take no more and the rains began to run, spreading over fields, running over roads, through woods and lava gulches, filling the entire valley with rivers of running water.

The storm began sometime in the early morning and carried on through the darkness of the moonless night. It ended just around dawn the next day.

When it was all over, the valley had been transformed, with a huge new gulch carved right down the middle of it. No road for miles around was usable. And every single bridge in the area had been destroyed, twelve in all.

In the short space of twenty-four hours, more than thirty-eight inches of rain had been officially recorded a mile or two from our valley. That amount in itself is exactly the average rainfall for an entire year in the city of Chicago. That means that the storm, a remnant of Tropical Storm Paul, dumped one and a half inches every hour for twenty-four hours.

But actually, there was more. Remember that rim that encircles our valley? Well, that rim turned this major storm into a millennial flood, because it makes the valley one giant bowl. That steady one and a half inches of rain falling every hour collected all the way down the rim's fifteen-hundred-foot height and flooded right down into the bowl that held everyone's homes.

Rich, a retired engineer in our valley, measured the rainfall on his rain gauge, and it came to a staggering sixty inches. While that's not an official measure, it does give an indication of what went on. To put that in perspective, the greatest rainfall ever recorded on earth in a twenty-four hour period was only fourteen inches more—seventy-four inches—on Réunion, a French island in the Indian Ocean, in 1952.

And all that water had to go somewhere. It tore down the lava gulches from high atop the pali cliff rim, pouring right into the valley. Those gulches, bone dry and quiet for years, now roared like a calamitous freight train. Surging waters raced down, carrying tons of massive boulders, trees, and even cars, all churning over and over each other as they roared past at breakneck speed. The earth rumbled with a fearsome noise as the giant, catastrophic torrent surged on.

The rush of water ripped out land masses and gouged wide channels across all the gulches, breaking them open twice as wide. It tore down deep into them, too—opening chasms all the way down to thirty feet in gulches that had been only three feet deep before. When it was over, the gulches were scrubbed clean, with not a plant remaining in them—a clean hiking trail had been created, stretching six miles to the beach. Devastation trail.

That night, as the storm progressed, David heard a noise like thunder. Already uneasy, he began to feel the earth rumbling. Grabbing a flashlight, he went out to check the gulch. Out into the torrent he charged, hurrying through the driving rain to the gulch. There, in his spotlight, he saw boulders the size of Volkswagens being hurled down as the torrent ripped its way through the gulch. He knew if he were to fall in, he would be dead instantly, tumbled with the boulders, lost in the mass of rock heading steadily, wildly down to the ocean.

People in the small sugarcane town five miles away said it felt as if earthquakes were erupting all night long as the huge boulders tumbled over each other and down through the gulches, moving right past the little town toward the ocean. Other neighbors in the valley said it sounded like the steady roar of a freight train that could not stop.

Everett, a handsome, strong outdoorsman in the Hemingway

tradition, spent the entire night trembling. His architect-designed home catapults out over a major gulch in the valley. The lava gulch under his home, which had always been dry, that night became a raging torrent of floodwaters, growing wider and wider in the dark as the night went on, creeping steadily toward the foundations of his home, threatening to engulf his entire home, pick it up, and sweep it downstream into the ocean. The earth shook with the constant pounding of the boulders.

Everett wanted to get to safety, but there was nowhere he could escape. He was trapped. It was dark. He was alone. There were no phones, no one to even talk with. He was alone in the dark with an end-of-the-world cataclysm creeping steadily toward him. As the cold, dark waters surged below, they rose rapidly, rising closer and closer to the footings of his home. Everett feared for his life, afraid of being washed downstream with the boulders.

He wasn't alone. That night, throughout the entire valley, the power went out. The phones went out. The water supply lines were washed away. Not one of the twenty families in the valley could communicate with one another. Everyone was on their own in the pitch dark, with earth trembling, and waters rising all around them, while terrifying noise sounded throughout the valley.

The storm continued. High up on the rim, Sabine slept in her teeny, little home perched more than a third of a mile up the pali cliff, in the depths of the valley. Her boyfriend, Kanoa was with her, luckily. He didn't always stay, but for some reason that night he did, even though they had no idea what was headed their way. There hadn't been any real warning about the magnitude of what awaited them.

Before bed, Kanoa had roped Sabine's new Toyota pickup to a tree, just in case, because the water was so strong and moving so fast. Even as he secured the rope, the water was so high that it was running under the hood.

Sabine was restless and uneasy that evening, but she went to bed and finally fell asleep. Then, at about 4:00 a.m., she awoke to a loud, smashing "thud!" in the kitchen.

Hurrying up to see what had happened, she realized that the small building behind her house had been picked up and smashed into the backside kitchen door by the surging waters. In doing so it had sealed the door to her home. Her escape route was frozen shut. She was locked in, with waters rising rapidly.

She and Kanoa stood in the dark kitchen with the flood water swirling around their calves, rapidly rising toward their knees. Their flashlight showed water pressing against the windows outside, already halfway up the window. The door was useless. They didn't dare open a window.

They were trapped by the water, sealed into their fate. Kanoa looked at Sabine and said flatly, "That's it."

But a few panicked moments later, they realized one escape route was still left—the front porch railing on the front of the house. The porch was higher, lifesavingly higher, than the rest of the house. With the backside of the home acting like a dam, the porch's floodwaters were lower.

But could they get out in time? Could they find their way in the pitch dark? The rising water was now above their knees. They had to move fast. The only option open to them was to creep out. And so they crept, very carefully, through cold, rising waters and total darkness, creeping out further and further onto the porch railing. Little by little, they made it.

Sabine's memory stops there. It was too traumatic. All she remembers is holding hands with Kanoa and walking to the driveway with a flashlight. She remembers water running so strongly that it was hurling boulders all around. Somehow, they got down the drive and onto their neighbor's land.

There, they waited out the storm in the open, shivering. As the storm raged, Sabine thought about her home. What would be left of it? She had no idea what was happening to her home or her brand-new Toyota truck in the rampage. All that would have to wait until the light of day.

They waited through the last hours of darkness. By early dawn, the tremendous storm began subsiding, wave by wave.

When dawn came, Sabine and Kanoa were okay. They looked at each other in the dawn light and laughed giddily, thankful to be alive. They had made it. They stood outside, surrounded by a brand-new waterfall, looking up at a gigantic mountain of boulders in a valley gulch, feeling just like dwarves. All around lay destruction. "It was unbelievable," Sabine says; there are no words to describe it. It had all happened in the twinkling of an eye.

When the dawn came, Everett was still intact, though shaken. He had made it through the night. His home had withstood the onslaught. And now, as he looked out, he saw that his home cantilevered over a much wider gulch. He had been so lucky. One more night, and he would have been carried away.

When the dawn came, some neighbors found their homes sitting on isolated little islands, with all the earth swept away around them. Waterfalls flooded over the entire length of the crescent rim.

But the dawn came. The rains stopped. The flood waters receded as fast as they had come. The gulches emptied. And then, the sun came out. It was a clear, new day. Everyone was alive. No one was hurt.

Sabine and Kanoa walked out, and all around them, they saw a new valley. The pouring rains had brought tumultuous damage in their wake. The torrent had deposited a mass of boulders that was fifteen feet high and one hundred feet wide—running a full quarter mile long through the valley. It deposited two acres of boulders in one neighbor's yard alone.

The flood waters had opened an entirely new gorge of a gulch, twenty to thirty feet deep and nearly forty feet wide. The whole scene was amazing. Had it rained one more day, the waterfall rim of the valley would have looked like Niagara Falls.

Now, it was time for Sabine to see what remained of her home and truck. She didn't want to look at it. But taking courage, she made herself go back up. She was afraid to look at her home as she and Kanoa began walking up her long drive, so Kanoa did the looking. As they got closer, Kanoa yelled out, "It's still there!" Her home was still standing.

In the next second, they could see that her Toyota was still standing, too. It was safe. It had survived on its own little island, everything around it washed away. A miracle.

Excited by her luck, Sabine got into her truck and started the engine. Miraculously, it started the very first time. Later, they would add rocks around the edges of the truck's island and drive her Toyota out of there.

Next, though, was the house. Already, Sabine could see that the flood waters had literally picked up her home and moved it back and to the left, so that her bedroom now hung out precariously over the new gulch. Sabine hesitated; it would be hard to see all the damage inside.

Sabine gathered her courage once again and stepped inside. Her eyes quickly scanned the wreckage. Surprise! It wasn't nearly as bad as it might have been. The floor was filled with mud, yes, and the carpet was rotten. But her piano in the bedroom? By some miracle, the water had made a circle around it and never touched it. How lucky she was.

Her house still standing, her truck safe, and now her piano—it was day of miracles for Sabine. And the greatest miracle of all was that she and Kanoa were still alive, for she knew that had her home been hit by rising waters earlier in the night, they probably wouldn't have had a chance in the brunt of the storm.

It was a miracle all around in the valley. Everyone was safe. Still stunned, yes, and adjusting to the new light, but heartily grateful and glad to be alive.

David's little girl, visiting, had slept through the night, totally oblivious to all the adults' concerns. She awoke from her sleep, saw the great water outside, and happily put on her swimsuit, running out to swim in the new pool in the front yard.

It was three days before anyone could get out. Water had to be brought in. But over the next months and years, government agencies carried away all the mountains of boulders. They built temporary emergency roads and then restored the old roads to better condition than before. They fixed the twelve bridges, making them far stronger and better engineered than they had ever been.

And gradually, the valley restored itself. And as the days progressed one by one, the valley settled down, once again, to live nestled in nature's peace, in beauty and harmony.

And after a while, it was as if nothing had ever happened.

# 18 I Soon Began to Realize That This Was an Island of Extremes

## *Meeting people of every description . . . in the same day*

Islands give you a chance to meet people you would never meet on the intersections of life in the city. In fact, islands give you a chance to meet people unlike *any* you would have met at city intersections.

It's made me realize how very homogenous we all were in the Chicago suburbs. And I thought we were all so different. Here, you might meet a bear tracker from Alaska, an Alaska salmon fisherman, a Hilton heiress, a retired professor of environmental studies who hikes thousands of miles each summer on the nation's trail system, a woman whose home almost slipped down the rim of the valley during an enormous flood, a woman who breeds exotic animals, a woman who is a military pilot, and a couple who speak Tibetan and have a Buddhist temple and Buddhist lama living on their land. And these are just the neighbors.

Almost as soon as I came to the island, I began to realize that I was meeting people every day who represented both ends of the spectrum of living.

This was brought home very dramatically to me on one of my first days on the island. On that day, within the space of several hours, I met a beautiful woman in flowing island clothes who lives in a tent. In fact, much of her life, she has lived in a tent in places all around the world. Within the hour, I also met a very successful realtor broker, a woman who lives on the ocean in a multimillion-dollar home that looks out over a vast expanse of wide, blue ocean on a sunny sweep of green Hawaiian coast. The difference could not have been more extreme.

A few days later, I met a master boat maker, a man sought out for his mastery and expertise in building fine ships. But looking at him, you would never know it—he was missing literally every other tooth, and his hair was a wild, white frazzle, like Einstein's. He and his girlfriend were creating an eclectic, artistic home of found materials on rugged lava lands.

Literally a few hours later, David and I ran into an old friend of his that he hadn't seen in about fifteen years in Costco. This man is ruggedly handsome, with a physique right out of Paul Bunyan. A master homebuilder, he has built some of the finest timber frame homes in luxury ski resorts. He was excited, talking about how he had just purchased a very expensive lot up in Kohala, and was going to build an equally expensive home on it to sell to build up his retirement nest egg.

Both ends of the spectrum, and once again, all in the same day.

Sometimes it seems that no one on the island seems to be living a "normal" life. Perhaps that's because people who come to an island must, by definition, be independent, adventurous, and creative souls.

I remember meeting a woman in the aisles of a Kona bookstore who was shocked to learn that I live on the south part of the island. She lives in the very suburban area around Kona, the only part of the island that's suburban. She stepped back, took a good look at me, and said, "My, you really *are* an adventurer, aren't you?" I had never actually thought of myself in that way, but from her perspective, I certainly was.

We know people who make their living courting danger by fishing in the open waters of the ocean—both the warm waters of Hawaii, where they catch fish like ono and ahi tuna, and in the frigidly cold, life-threatening waters of Alaska, where they bring in the salmon every summer.

I know a woman who salmon fishes with her husband in the treacherous, icy waters of the Bering Strait. They spend weeks in gray—gray skies blending opaquely into gray sea—all under the summer Alaskan sun, which means that daylight lasts until 1:00 a.m. and starts again a mere three hours later. They often get only one half hour of sleep in twenty-four hours, as their fishing boat and body rhythms pitch and sway with the perpetual sun and lurching waves. Sometimes the seas roll as high as fifty feet, creating a wall of wave five stories high that slams the boat up and down.

And yet this woman makes Chinese hot and sour soup, bakes warming bread, and keeps the cabin cozy. She is the only woman for miles and miles around. She even gathers blueberries in the tundra before they sail, harvesting a very diminutive version of them in their frigid environment—the plants only manage four inches of height and two or three berries each.

I know a sturdy woman of eighty who, at seventy years of age, exchanged her tony Honolulu penthouse for a tiny, little home in our valley, living with an outside "spa" (aka bathroom) and managing acres of coffee and macadamia nut trees. She's gone now, but her gazebo still stands outside, built especially for the grand piano she always hoped to play, a memorial to her spirit.

And I thought people in DuPage County, west of Chicago, were different from one another. What I thought were great differences between people's life situations in DuPage County were really quite homogenous. Then, the difference between working in IT at Lucent or IBM sounded different. From this perspective, it seems as if all we were discussing was a difference in belt buckles.

Where else could I meet a woman who travels the ancient Silk Road, buying exquisite, intricately woven silk cloth of beauty far beyond any silk I have ever seen? Where could I meet a man who deals in the treasures of ancient Tibet, centuries-old antiques from the monasteries that were destroyed when China took over Tibet? Or a retiree who makes his living creating beautiful gourd art in the ancient Hawaiian way, selling each one for thousands?

Where could I meet people who dive off cliffs for fun or swim the treacherous ocean shore rocks, searching for opihi, the mollusks that thrive there? Or people who hunt wild pigs for the family table? Or grow taro in water paddies, just like their ancient ancestors?

Where could I meet farmers who grow acres upon acres of burstingly healthy green vegetables on a mountainside with magnificent, sweeping views of the ocean? Or people who live down close to the ocean's shore and farm only ginger, and in three different colors? Or a family who began a vanilla farm together, and now offer vanilla tastings for tourists? Or Kona-area fishermen who hold a farmer's market of fresh-caught fish by the ocean?

And at the other extreme, where else could I see forty private jets parked north of Kona airport for the Christmas season? Or Paul Allen's mega-yacht Meduse anchored in Kona Bay?

Where else could I catch a glimpse of Michael Dell's sprawling oceanside home, all 18,500 square feet of it, looking for all the world like a small subdivision from the highway? Or one of the world's most exclusive golf experiences, the Nanea Golf Club? Built by Charles Schwab, its initiation fee runs $450,000.

Where else, indeed!

Yes, I agree—it helps to be an adventurer to live here.

# 19 Making a Home on the Island

### *Mold happens . . . or, plastic is an island girl's best friend*

There was one discovery about the island that wasn't fun at all. Mold!

Early on, I learned the hard way about mold. I had brought some favorite little leather slings with me and my pretty little watch with a leather band. In no time at all, I discovered that leather turns to mold. It took just a few weeks in the moist island breezes, even though there was no humidity. Leather doesn't work on an island. The ancient Hawaiians knew that—they wore sandals made of woven leaves. And they lived on island time, so they didn't need watches!

Also tarnished was a little set of cuticle scissors that I cherished, because they were beautifully crafted in France, and sent to me by my French pen pal in fifth grade. Metal doesn't work on the island, either, unless it is gold, silver, or stainless steel. The ancient Hawaiians had not one bit of metal in all their tools, kitchen implements, or war weapons. They used shark's teeth instead.

Paper got soggy, and greeting card envelopes sealed themselves shut before I could send them.

I learned about food, too, the hard way, of course. I would leave my home for the mainland for months and return to find that my dried mushrooms had turned to mush, the sugar had melted, and the teabags were absolutely stale. How does moisture know how to get in there?

How to deal with all this mildew, mold, rust? The answer is

exactly what the man whispered into Dustin Hoffman's ear in *The Graduate*. "Plastic!" Plastic bags, plastic boxes. Plastic! Plastic is an island girl's best friend.

Everything ends up in plastic bags and boxes here—precious photos, jewelry, even certain hardcover books. I could compete for Ms. Plastic, Hawaii, if the contest was based on usage. That would be my talent.

And as to clothes, I have many friends who have gone through the same experience. Often, we have lost clothes to tiny, little black spots of mildew that formed because of the island breezes blowing through our homes. Any tiny spot of food or organic matter can mildew—when I use a cookbook, a spot of food on my finger as I touch the cookbook page is memorialized as mold the next time I turn to that recipe. People living near the beach have to wash their already-clean clothes regularly here just to keep up with the mildew.

Very quickly, I learned the three rules of island closets—dry, light, and airy. They even sell special lights here for closets to keep them dry, and compounds called "Damp Rid" that soak up moisture in the air. Eventually, with windows (not screens), sunny closets, and dehumidifiers, we made our home safe for clothes, leather, metals—everything.

But the ancient Hawaiian islanders never had to worry about any of this. They never had such needs as "closets" in their grass huts. They probably just hung their loincloths and kapa skirts out on their spears!

# 20 When Did You Say the Container Arrives Again?

***Shopping, Big Island style***

In my first couple weeks here, I experienced something totally new to mainland eyes. In the natural foods grocery store, in the refrigerated section, was a sign: "Sorry on the parmesan. Container arrives next Thursday."

Oops! That's right—everything gets here by container. You can see containers lined up outside our major shopping centers, filled with everything that goes inside. Containers are all over the island. When people move to the Big Island, they often ship all their household goods across the Pacific in containers. And a mere ten years ago, before Lowes and Home Depot arrived, new residents used to ship entire container loads filled with all the building materials needed to construct their new homes. That's what life is like, three thousand miles away from the mainland.

So island shopping was a new experience. Different. Compared to Oak Brook, it was decidedly primitive.

If you want style, for your home or your body, it is going to come from one of four places— Macy's, Ross for Less, Home Depot, or Lowes.[7] That's it. Since I got here, we've had Target come to our island. For us, after years with only Walmart, it was like Bloomies coming to the Big Island. (Well . . . not exactly.) And until about ten years ago, there simply were not any large retail stores on the island except Walmart. (Though we do have chic little island boutiques scattered around the island in tourist areas.)

Actually, all style for the home comes from Ross. When I'm visiting with my lady friends and we spot something new in our homes, we knowingly say, "Ross, right?" Sometimes, one of us says, "Oh, I saw those. I took some time to think about it."

In fact, that's a very good point. "Thinking about it" is something that you don't get to do on an island. My friend Pat tells about a bedspread she was interested in when she was new to the island. She went home to check and think about it, then came back to buy it a few days later only to discover that it was gone. Who moved my bedspread?

When I gave her a special dish for Christmas, she had already seen it while shopping—at Ross, of course. You can't surprise anyone.

So on the island, if you decide to buy something, I suggest you buy it now. It may not be there next week. It may not even be there tomorrow. It's better to buy it, take it home, then "think about it" and see if it works, and then return it rather than lose it.

Island shopping certainly wasn't Chicago anymore. I can still remember the day, after I'd been on the island a while, when I realized that I was in the "Japanese aisle" at Walmart. I had never figured this out before. But there I was, standing surrounded by a selection of flatly white, squared dinnerware, with about twenty different rice cookers, plus rice paddles, fish steamers and plastic soup spoons. Aha!

At Costco, it was easy to realize that this wasn't Oak Brook anymore. I passed mega displays of Spam, Vienna hot dogs, corned beef hash, Portuguese sausage, and poke (raw marinated fish), favorites of the locals. Then came rows of bags of rice stacked up high, just like sandbags, monster boxes of miso, tons of seaweed, dried shrimp, and dried oyster sauce, cartons of shoyu sauce, and mega packs of chopsticks in a choice of wood or bamboo.

And then there's that other little thing—we're sitting on a volcano here. So when I came to the island, I decided that everything that I brought into my home would have to be expendable. Because, even though it's very safe, every once in a while we get a little trembler. Just so we don't forget.

So for dinnerware, I happily abandoned the idea of having another nice, new Noritake set from Marshall Fields (now Macy's) and instead had lots more fun shopping with David at Ross, of course, for hand-painted pieces from China. These were fun and colorful pieces, each painted by a different hand, sometimes even with misspelled French words in the background (trez chick, nest pas?). Eclectic and playful. We brought home lots of colorful pieces in bright island colors to mix and match. And we bought them a couple at a time, each a delight and a little treasure—like finding something in my grandma's attic. When I set the table in this eclectic style, it feels so free, so fun. Each table an eclectic expression . . . no rules . . . like a breath of fresh island air.

Shortly after we arrived to make a home here together, we discovered a store that sold imported antique furniture from Tibet and China. We went crazy. Whether or not they were authentic antiques (always debatable), they were lovely pieces. The Tibetan chests especially stole my heart—beautifully painted florals in the softly vibrant colors of Tibetan art—red, green, blue, and gold.

And how perfectly fitted to modern life those "antiques" were.

The gorgeous antique Tibetan herbal chest we purchased curiously made a fabulous CD cabinet. The authentic antique Chinese bamboo armoires were precisely the right size for TV viewing in the bedroom. Did they watch TV in ancient China too I wondered? Whether they are reworked pieces or antiques, we love them and they bring an artisan-craftedness into our home.

And regarding authentic antiques, we found something far more extraordinary on the island. I will always remember the day David first took me into a little shop in Hilo. This store was literally glowing golden inside, burnished with the luster of centuries-old pieces brought out of Tibetan monasteries.

There were massive doors twelve feet high and eight feet wide, beautifully crafted and painted in Tibetan religious themes. There were even Tibetan altars, which belong in their monasteries, one about twelve feet wide, and one the size of a small desk. Large chests, a hallmark of Tibetan furniture, were painted with magnificent and splendid scenes, truly authentic, and depicted with real artistry. Small meditation benches, centuries old, were designed with enough space to study and turn the separate pages of ancient scripture. Wooden doors and large panels made of wood each held a special painting. Tigers were often painted on the doors, symbols of strength and fearlessness. Each of these objects was a magnificent treasure for me. Each held the essence of devotion, purity, and lifelong discipline of reverence.

The entire store held an elevated and inspired sense about it, simply because of the presence of these pieces, regardless of the physical appearance of their beauty and form.

It is extremely sad to me that Tibet lost almost all its monasteries and nunneries. Only about three of six thousand remain after the Chinese occupation. Not only were these very sacred monasteries lost, but precious Tibetan monastic artifacts like altars made their way into the marketplace, when they should have been preserved. These are treasures that are part of a lineage that is over fifteen hundred years old, and they are to be treasured as symbols and artifacts of a way of life that is exceptionally pure, devoted, and reverent. For those who are sensitive, they still hold the living presence of their devout spiritual tradition. Where else do objects like this exist today?

I am sorry to say that most of these pieces have sold and can no longer be seen. They are in the homes of celebrities and wealthy people who can afford to enjoy them. Ideally, one day, some of them will be preserved in museums so they can be appreciated by all, though that will likely never happen.

But back to island shopping. Whether at Costco or Ross or exotic import stores, island shopping was part market bizarre, part ancient culture, and part island eclectic . . . definitely not Chicago or Oak Brook anymore.

# 21 Howzit, Brah?

***Da who dat, wot, wen, en wea foa talk story, yeah?***

Even as we drove around the island that first time, David told me about "pidgin," the language of the locals. It was one of the first things he told me because I would be hearing a lot of it on the island.

I still can't talk local style—it's an acquired art—but I can capture its essence for you. It has a lilting, almost lyrical sound as the words move out, reminiscent of the melodious beauty of the Hawaiian language. Yet the sentence structure is choppy and broken, with many words missing. To my ear, it's a combination of lilting beauty and broken words, impossible to speak.

For example, when I asked a lady in a local fish market to hold ahi tuna for my husband, she asked, "What time he gone come?" It reminds me of what I heard Harry Belafonte say about how he spoke during his childhood in Jamaica: "I gwine um" meant "I'm going home." I think islands do that—the words become simpler, more fluid. Easier.

"Howzit, Brah?" is the locals' island greeting. "Locals" is the name given to the people who have been on the island for generations. Originally, they were pure Hawaiian, but now they are a mix of all the peoples that came to work the land in Hawaii—Chinese, Portuguese, Japanese, Filipino, and Korean.

Though pidgin sounds a bit foreign to mainland ears, it served a very important purpose on the island. It was the way that people adapted their languages to enable them to communicate across all those cultures. It evolved using bits and pieces of each language, so that sentences often used a word from each language. That way, everybody could catch a bit of the meaning. And with its truncated form, it was easier for everyone to speak. Today, pidgin has evolved once again and now uses largely English words with a local twist.

What comes out is sort of a funny kine English, yeah?

When spoken by a true local, the phrases carry a lilt that undulates up and down, and gives the spoken word an almost musical quality. You can hear it in the recordings of Braddah Iz, Israel Kamakawiwoʻole, the late Hawaiian singer, when he speaks on his albums. Very different than mainland talk, which comes across distinctly flat by comparison. And very different from the beautiful Hawaiian language, which speaks in flowing poetry.

It is island-version English and leaves out lots of words. For instance, if we've had a big rain, a local will say, "Rain big, brah, yeah?" When a local man stopped by our home, which we were constructing, he liked it, so he said, "Come nice, brah, come nice."

Pidgin also "clips" a lot of words so they come out stunted. "The" comes out "da," as in "Da aina," meaning "the land" . . . "Jalike?" is "Do you like?" . . . "K'Den" is "Okay, then," and "Bodda You?" of course means "Pardon me, madam, but I do hope I'm not intruding?"

For a mainlander, picking up pidgin is a bit "Easy foa say, hahd foa do." So, "try fo tink local." And "If can, can. If no can, no can." Fo' shua!

So say you want some loco kine grindz, some favorite local foods, yeah? You decide to have some lau lau, a delicious local favorite. "Lau" literally means "leaf." Lau lau is an original Hawaiian wrap, taro and ti leaves, wrapped around chicken, fish, or salted pork.

It's delicious, so it's "ono" or "winnahz," as in "Hey brah, dis poke is winnahz!" In fact, it's so good, it's "brok' da mout," or "broke the mouth."

Any guy friend is a brah, the ladies are all sistahs. And for that matter, everybody is a brah, a sistah, a cuz, an auntie, or an uncle. Any time we are kind to a little local child, the little girl or boy immediately begins calling us auntie and uncle.

For locals, the entire island is family, filled with aunties and uncles—and all connected. So whatever you say or do with a local will be around the entire island on the "coconut wireless" in a matter of days.

On the island, you never do business with someone unless you "talk story" first. To mainlanders who are used to being extremely efficient in business communication, this is a total reversal because you will find yourself "talking story" for the bulk of the time and then very briefly doing the business that needs to be done. It's all done on what's called "Hawaiian time," which means, to hurrying mainlanders, slow and, sometimes, painfully slow.

"I'm pau" means "I'm done," something you might say the end of a meal, and "pau hana" means "we're done for the day." With construction workers, pau hana is like TGIF—it means a few beers on the site.

A T-shirt the locals wear says, "Aina Kea," which means "White land"—until you pronounce it, in which case you catch its other meaning: "I na kay' ah!"

K'Den, whatevahz!

# 22 Bradda Iz

***"Somewhere over the Rainbow" Hawaiian style . . . Israel Kamakawiwoʻole***

Everyone on the mainland knows Iz through his happy song "Somewhere over the Rainbow/What a Wonderful World," a melody that has made its way into movies, TV shows, and even commercials.

Yet in Hawaii, Iz is known and deeply loved as a far more

profound voice—a voice for Hawaii, the Hawaiian people, and their heritage. He stands tall as a gentle giant, playful and lovable, a giant who still lives on in Hawaiian hearts, even though he passed away in 1997.

I had never heard of Iz before my first trip to Hawaii, but my desire to hear authentic Hawaiian chant led me to him. Before I took my first trip to Hawaii, I wanted to understand the Hawaiian people. One of the best ways to understand people is through their songs and their language because it shows how they form their world. And in Hawaii, that means chant.

I looked for a CD of authentic Hawaiian chants. But when I did research at the library, all I came up with were CDs that featured songs like the "Hawaiian Wedding Song" and "Sweet Leilani," hits from the twenties and thirties. These would not do.

A helpful sales associate at Borders introduced me to Iz. And as soon as I played *Facing Future*, I was spellbound. The CD features "Hawai'i '78," a mesmerizing chant that carries the power of the Hawaiian people and mourns how they lost their way of life and their lands. It features the riveting chant, "Ua mau, ke ea o ka aina, i ka pono, o Hawai'i," which translates "The life of the land is perpetuated in righteousness." Iz continues, "Cry for the gods, cry for the people, cry for the land that was taken away. And then yet you'll find Hawaii."

Iz brought to the Hawaiian people a deepened sense of what was already building—a renaissance of ancient Hawaiian culture, the way of life that had long been banished when missionaries arrived in 1820. Hawaiian dignity resurged as the Hawaiian language, long banned, was reinstituted as an official state language in 1978, alongside English. The art of Hawaiian wave navigation, almost totally lost and yet critically important to this seafaring culture, was another part of the revival. And Iz's voice was key to the renaissance because it gave this rebirth melody, a way into the heart, and a way to join peoples together.

I fell in love with Iz. When I was in Chicago, cleaning that basement, waiting to arrive in Hawaii, I played Iz almost all the time. It was my way to be in Hawaii with David, five thousand miles away. When I had to commute on the expressways into Chicago, I'd listen to his music, and the miles would melt away.

By the way, his last name, Kamakawiwo'ole, is pronounced "Kahm ah' ka wee whoa' oh lay." It means "the fearless eye, the bold face." His name is pure Hawaiian, and that means that it's very long and flowing. Hawaiian words are open and flow with many vowels; they aren't defined and structured by consonants. And here, as in all places, the language mirrors the way of life, for Hawaii is open and free, like the Pacific breezes that flow across it.

Iz was pure Hawaiian. He spent time on Ni'ihau, the small northern Hawaiian island that is open only to Hawaiians, keeping to the old ways. So he got to experience the most authentically Hawaiian part of Hawaii. He was raised in Makaha, a very Hawaiian neighborhood on Oahu, very poor but with a great beach and surf. Iz loved the ukulele, he loved playing pranks, and he loved the beach—much more than school. His friends say he spent more time outside school than in, serenading friends under a great tree during classes. One day, he just ditched class altogether and took off for Makaha beach. There, he met a fellow truant. That day was the beginning of his band, the Makaha Sons of Ni'ihau.

The Makaha Sons played only Hawaiian music, and they soon became a local favorite. People loved the way they sang from their hearts; it was pure aloha and lots of fun. They sang all over the islands, at more and more places, and often at Punalu'u Beach, close to our home. They grew so popular, in fact, that the Makaha Sons of Ni'ihau became Hawaii's best-loved group, garnering ten Hoku Awards and creating ten best-selling albums.

Iz followed his brother Skippy as the leader of the band when Skippy died at only age twenty-eight. Iz soon became the heart of their success. But as Iz grew, his desire to express his own style, combined with his burdensome weight, which made it difficult to travel, pushed him to go out on his own at age thirty-four.

His first CD was called *Ka'Ano'I,* his middle name, which means "beloved." It amplified his success when it went platinum, becoming the most successful album in Hawaiian history. Then, Iz repeated his success again when he created Big Boy records, the most successful small recording label ever in Hawaiian music.

He began to use his voice in the cause of the Hawaiian people. He spoke out for the sovereignty movement, a political movement of native Hawaiians seeking a form of self-governance. He began to record protest songs as Bob Marley had in Jamaica. His music was a rallying cry for native Hawaiians. In his music, they heard their strength and their mana, their spiritual power.

But sadly, Iz met an untimely death. We will never know what Iz might have achieved or what more he might have contributed to the Hawaiian renaissance. This gentle giant was revitalizing Hawaiian culture and creating fans all over the world.

In Hawaii, there is an ancient, enduring belief that the amount of "mana," or spiritual power, a person carries is shown in the size of their physical body. The greater the mana, the bigger the body. This is why so many of the ali'i, the tribal chiefs, were huge physically. They needed to carry a great deal of mana to support their people and their kingdom. They even worked at this, having their stomachs massaged as they ate, so that they could take in ever more food. As a result of this tradition, today it is very common for Hawaiians to be, not just overweight, but several hundred *pounds* overweight.

As Iz grew older, he put on more and more weight, growing from a teenage weight of one hundred ninety-two pounds to a staggering eight hundred pounds. His medical doctor even estimates that Iz at one time weighed one thousand pounds. No heart, no lungs, no physical body can take that kind of weight. It pressures the organs, especially the heart. Sadly, Iz passed away at the young age of thirty-eight in 1997.

All of Hawaii mourned. The Hawaiian Senate decreed him a historic Hawaiian treasure, and his body lay in state at the state capitol, a very rare honor in Hawaii. The outpouring of aloha and grief was immense, equal to the outpourings for Hawaiian kings and queens in ages past.

Iz's ashes were spread over the ocean that he loved so much.

But Braddah Iz still lives on for Hawaiians and all who love him. Can anyone say where someone's influence ends? Iz was part of the strengthening of Hawaiian culture. He helped the ukulele make its comeback. His voice made Hawaiian music more popular around the world than ever before. In fact, the Grammy Awards now recognize Hawaiian music as its own category.

And right now, someone, somewhere in the world, is listening to

Iz sing, "Somewhere over the Rainbow." And right now, somewhere in the heavens, Iz is "Somewhere over the Rainbow", laughing his easy laugh, smiling . . . singing with the angels . . . and playing pranks behind their backs.

# 23 A Walk on Our Land Just After Dawn

***We often start our day with a morning "guacamole walk"***

In the morning, we wake to another day and the joy of gold-gleaming sun streaming across the land and through our windows. It casts its radiance on all the trees, flowers, and lush meadows, lighting them a beautiful golden green. How could we resist going outside first thing? So we often start the day with a walk on our land with our morning cup of tea.

And some days, our walk turns into a "guacamole walk". On these days, we gather fresh avocados that have tumbled down from our tree, still warm from the strong morning sun. Then up on a higher terrace, we go to our little Tahitian lime tree, always bursting with about a hundred limes on it, and we search for the limes in the tall grass under it—luscious, little yellow "eggs" that lay under their prolific tree, like the eggs in a hen's nest, waiting to be picked. Then on to our vegetable garden and what we call our "primo" cherry tomatoes. These are the best tomatoes I have ever tasted—a succulent blending of tart and sweet, shaped almost like a heart or a teardrop.

Another day of abundance and graciousness begins.

On other mornings, David goes back to the citrus grove on the far terrace and gathers up deliciously juicy oranges, when they are ripe. These are so luscious that they are almost all juice, with double the juice of their grocery store cousins.

So let's take a walk on the land together . . .

As we leave the house, you see before you the terraces, five plateaus that gracefully rise, one above the other, with the forested rim in the distance behind them. We are very lucky to have these terraces. They are made of very rich soil that the former owner bulldozed from his land above on the rim. This means that the soil is very, very rich because the many trees have lent years of leaves to it, turning the soil into a rich compost. When you see it, it is a rich, chocolate brown, beautifully dense and softly pliable. It plows down to a fine crumble. And it is very deep—over twenty feet deep—very privileged in Hawaii, where so many people have only lava rock, and the painstaking task of literally creating their own soil.

Living here has made me realize how much wealth is in good earth, for it provides and provides for us, with fruits and vegetables that give us so much vitality. One of the biggest ways I feel wealthy in my life is when I gather herbs and veggies from the garden for the evening's dinner. Such satisfaction and well-being. For me, this is true wealth.

The sky is big, beautiful, and brilliant blue, and wonderfully warming this morning, and balmy, soft-flowing island breezes gently soothe around us as we walk, while birds call to one another from the trees. This land is so sweet. It has an enchanting quality that eludes words. The bees are just getting started on their day, flying from the hive on the side of the land by the lava gulch.

As we walk, we move past the many fruit trees which David has planted over the years. Of course there are bananas all around, you already know about those. There are also many citrus trees on the far terrace. David used to have an orange grove in California, so it was natural that he would plant tangerine, orange, grapefruit, lemon and those most delicious Tahitian limes.

When people eat the fruit fresh from our trees, the first thing they notice is that the fruit is soft, and very juicy, and extra-flavorful. And then they notice some different things about the fruit in Hawaii—it's all mixed up. Here, lemons look like oranges—they can be that big and orange, too. I got a lemon from a neighbor's tree yesterday, and it was almost as big as a grapefruit. No kidding. It must have weighed about two pounds. When I sliced it in half, it took up most of a dinner plate.

Limes look like lemons—they are yellow and as big as lemons. Unless, of course, you have the kind of lime that looks like oranges . . . or the kind that looks like a normal green lime. The limes on our land are a variety called Tahitian lime, succulent and extra juicy, with a very bright flavor, just exquisite. And of course, they make the most wonderful Tahitian lime pie.

We also have a pomelo tree. A pomelo is a basketball that you eat, yellow in color. They're so sweet that you don't even need to sugar them.

Then there are the exotic fruits like cherimoya, which Mark Twain famously described as "deliciousness itself" (he was right), and sapote, both of which open to a soft, whitish custard that you eat right out of the rind. We also have guava, papaya, avocado, fig, persimmon, Hawaiian strawberry, macadamia nut, Malabar chestnut, sugar cane, and coffee.

Vibrant pink amaryllis and orange nasturtium volunteer in the backyard. It's amazing to see Christmas amaryllis growing wildly all over the back yard, at any time of year. We pick yellow, rose and coral hibiscus before dinner, for the table.

Our land is filled with trees—many bamboo, in twelve varieties, as well as several kinds of palms, and beautiful koa wood, unique to the islands and prized for the special way it glows golden through its curly grain.

Out back is a big tree in the backyard which, in a good year, is literally dripping with tangerines, little orange balls filling the branches like an overladen Christmas tree. We can see it from the whirlpool tub in the bathroom.

It's part of a small grove of citrus trees in our backyard. That grove includes a lemon tree, an orange tree, and a persimmon tree. These were planted by the old Japanese family that lived here. If you trek deeper into the little forest grove, you will come to their old shed of gray, weather-worn boards, now crumbled with age, slumping over under one of the orange trees. There used to be a massive beehive in that orange tree, and you could smell the sweet scent of honey in the air.

When I arrived, you could also see their small green bath house in which they had a traditional-style ofuro Japanese bath, but David took it down. An ofuro bath is a ritual in Japan, a deep bath in which you relax and warm yourself after washing. It is actually the precursor of our American hot tubs.

And around their home, the Japanese family had planted ti plants, whose long green leaves shoot up like a fountain off their long stalks, creating a waterfall effect. For Hawaiians, ti plants represent blessing and protection for those who live within the lands they bound.

Around back, there are lava rock formations that I love. They look like a miniature version of something out of Jurassic Park. With ferns and other tropical plants around them, it's like climbing through a little jungle on a little expedition as we walk around the back of the house.

There is also a huge mango tree in the backyard, beautifully full and rounded with luxurious leaves. It is really two trunks intertwined as one. Its branches reach out about thirty feet. Mango wood is very prized for its beauty. Its exceptionally beautiful grain curls through a variety of colors, ranging from light tan to deep shades of brown. Mango wood is about as hard as any wood gets. Our mango has never borne fruit because we are at twenty-two hundred feet, and that's a little too high in altitude for them. But when you see mangoes ripening on trees, like on the way to Kona, they drip down on their vines deliciously, beckoning you to come and take one . . . truly low-hanging fruit.

Out back, I have a prized collection of cherry tomatoes. These just "volunteered" in the backyard. One fall, after we'd been away for months on the mainland, I discovered them growing in the backyard when they were about two feet tall. Within a couple months they were massive vines, rambling around the fences we put up for them.

And across the backyard fence, our neighbor has a guava tree. Last fall, in the height of the season, while I was happily harvesting handfuls of beautiful cherry tomatoes, I was amazed to hear a soft "Thump! Thump!" every few minutes as a new guava fell to the ground.

He also has a tree back there, another tangerine tree that is filled with winding vines and "choke tangerines." That's local talk for unbelievable abundance.

Some rare days, we have "visitors"—wild turkey and wild peacock.

And we regularly entertain pheasants who wander onto our land in search of garden munchies. One rare day, two wild peacocks quietly ambled up our deck and sat in front of our French doors, looking through the large glass panes. They were quite content to just sit on the porch and enjoy themselves, making themselves part of the family.

And the other day, a flock of wild turkeys, about six in all, visited, and made raucous noises as they traipsed and gaggled about the land.

The pheasants here are a Filipino type called Kalij, and they move very quickly. They are amusing to watch because they dart very rapidly, their legs racing under them as their upper body remains perfectly still—almost as if they were moving effortlessly on a conveyor belt while their little legs are going like crazy. They get very nervous any time we get at all near and, sometimes, simply fly up into a tree. From this point, they survey our vegetable garden, waiting until no one is looking, and then they swoop down and feast on the tomatoes.

I was on a terrace yesterday, a terrace that is gently encompassed by graceful palm, fragrant ginger, tall red ti, and golden bamboo, which surround a large area of lushly soft Hawaiian grasses in the center, and I felt how sweet the land is. It's enchanting, entrancing, and always draws me back. I am falling in love with our land.

As I write this, I have been here nine months over two and a half years, and it is still a dream. Every morning, I wake filled with joy, and often at night, I can't sleep from excitement for tomorrow, just like a little kid.

What treasure is here.

# PART THREE

# EXPLORING THE NEIGHBORHOOD

*Let's go on an island adventure!*

A sea turtle at Punalu'u Beach

# 24 Hiking Kilauea Iki, a Magma Crater with a Past

***Lava fountains shot up almost twenty stories here back in 1959***

Hawaii's Kilauea Volcano is the only "drive through" volcano in the world. It's also one of the most active volcanoes in the world. So every time something explosive happens here, volcanologists from around the world rush into the park to drive through and watch it unfold. Tourists come here in flocks, too—Hawaii Volcanoes National Park is the absolute favorite attraction in all of Hawaii.

It's a great place for hiking on the island, and there's a special hike that I love to take. It's a miniature version of the big Kilauea Crater, called "Kilauea Iki." "Iki" means "baby" in Hawaiian, and Kilauea Iki offers a chance to hike through an actual lava crater in a comfortable, harmless "baby" way—without the hot lava.

It makes a great hike. It's primal and windswept, so you feel like you're living the story of creation as you trek across all that black lava. On the way, you'll walk by steaming flumes of heat rising from rocks still hot to the touch, as fine bits of rain sparkle in the sun and wisp around in the crisp, invigorating air. Looking up across the lava lake, you'll find that you are encircled in a lush, native rainforest that runs around the crater's upper rim. It's a captivating forest of giant ferns that arch twenty feet high, dwarfing you as you walk under them in a world of soft, green, mossy fronds. And birds are everywhere, high up in the trees, as many as twenty-five species, trilling and filling the rainforest with their melodious songs. It feels magical, like you've just walked into an enchanted story.

And it is magical. This is the home of Pele, goddess of fire, goddess of volcano. Ancient Hawaiians were deeply afraid of offending her. They made many offerings and prayers to appease her and to save themselves from the wrath of her fiery lava.

As you hit the trail across Pele's hardened lava lake, there's an exhilarating feeling that comes up. Primal earth! Something about the wind whipping around, all that black bare rock, and the wild serenity gives you energy. It's great fun.

Looking out past the crater, far into the distance, you can see smoke plumes rising in the sky from the Kilauea Caldera, the big volcano. With the sun on them, they shine silvery white as they billow and funnel out hundreds of feet high, releasing gases from the turbulent magma deep underground.

All that smokes reminds me that Kilauea Iki is a magma crater with a past! After all, that flat black lava once was a huge red lake of lava, roiling and surging, splattering and slumping. And this crater was once twice as deep—eight hundred feet down.

All that changed in 1959. In that year, after decades of quiet, Kilauea Iki suddenly erupted.

It happened the night of November 14, 1959. For three months, Kilauea had been sending out warnings. Thousands of quakes and tremors had rumbled through the crater. It had been gradually swelling with lava. Scientists knew that something was coming, and now, it emerged. The quakes on this day became ten times stronger, massively shaking the entire summit for five hours, throwing off boulders to make way for what was about to occur.

The show was about to begin.

Imagine a Niagara Falls of red molten lava pouring down eighty stories, running half a mile long. Amazing. Fiery lava poured out of the slopes, sending incandescent, roiling streams of burning red molten rock all the way down into the bottom of the crater. The lava glowed incandescent orange, gurgling as it slid its way into the lake. There it flowed out in rivers of lava, glowing red orange, and then quickly darkening into black as it cooled. It must have been an incredible sight.

It was like the Fourth of July, only far more awesome. Along the way, the moving lava set off sudden flares. These were flash forest fires. Flaming trees, like gigantic sparklers, hurled down into the swelling, bubbling lake of lava, where they burned bright yellow as they floated across the surface of the lake, carried by the flow until they burned out.

Vents opened up all along the slope where the lava had gushed out, and after a while, they merged to become one giant vent of flowing red lava.

And then, the main attraction appeared. A spectacular fountain of lava shot up like brilliant red-orange fireworks. It reached from fifty to nineteen hundred feet in the air—almost as high as a twenty-story building—a record for a lava fountain in Hawaii.

The light show was accompanied by deafening sound. A gigantic, rumbling roar moved with the flowing lava. People said it sounded like thunder and the pounding of fierce surf waves combined into one great, continuing explosion. The colors were primal—the incandescent red glow blasting into the sky, quickly cooling into blackened, hard cinder and spatter that rained down and piled up into tall, towering cinder cone hills. It was earth being born in tumult and fury.

The immense power of the volcano was awesome. The eruptions went on for thirty-six days. In one twenty-minute eruption, volcanic spatter stripped the entire surrounding forest instantly, leaving only darkened trunks standing eerily on blackened earth. Later, winds carried the flames still further, destroying many forests downwind.

As the eruption continued day after day, the lava lake kept growing higher and higher. Gradually, it rose higher than the vent from which the red lava had gushed. This ended the spectacular fountains, but it also began another show. The fountain's submerged spray now sent out stunning waves of red lava rippling across the lava lake. These molten waves hit the sides, splashing up in red incandescence, and rippled heavily back across the lake. Quite a show.

After every eruption, lava began to drain back into the vent from which it came, creating a dramatic vortex, whirlpooling as it was sucked back down into the crater. The rate at which it was pulled back was awesome, four times faster than the rate at which it had erupted. And the noise was deafening, as red-hot lava and massive chunks of black lava rock slid back into the vent, disappearing.

Over the next five weeks, there were seventeen separate displays of lava pouring into the crater, creating an ever-changing show. Then, finally, by December 20, it was suddenly all over. The lake had risen four hundred feet and held millions upon millions of tons of intensely hot, fresh lava. People from all around the world had come to marvel at the spectacle.

Today, the crater is almost fully cooled. While the lava lake was created in only thirty-six days, it took a full thirty-six years to cool down. When you start at 2,200° Fahrenheit, it can take a while. In fact, it's probably still not entirely cool in its core.

So when you hike over Kilauea Iki today, you can still feel the heat and you can still feel part of what happened here when earth was born in fire, and red-hot lava created the most magnificent fireworks on earth.

# 25 And Disappearing into a Lava Tube

***A river of red lava created this great hike almost five hundred years ago***

Just across the street, and through another magical canopy of fern forest, sits the Thurston Lava Tube. I love this short hike. It's so much fun! As you enter the area, you are at eye level with the tops of majestic tall ferns, soft and misty, so you have the special opportunity to actually see all the rare Hawaiian birds at eye level. It's great for snapping photos. As you walk down the stairs and through the fern forest, you can see the big black tunnel ahead, the Thurston Lava Tube. The Hawaiians call this tunnel "Nahuku."

As you enter it, you can smell the moistness in the air, and since you're likely to be the only ones in there, it's a little eerie and spooky, like walking into some secret place from the past. And this lava tube is a secret place—native Hawaiians used it for hiding things like food and, in some cases, themselves when tribes were warring.

The park has lit the tunnel, which makes the walls shine golden, and highlights all the contours and shadows for the full length, one third of a mile.

This lava tube was formed by a huge river of lava that flowed through here. As lava flows, it hardens quickly around the edges. That's what created these walls and ceiling. And even though it hardens, new liquid lava keeps flowing through the contours of the tube. When the lava is gone, the tube becomes a hollow cave.

Hawaii actually has lots of hidden lava tubes and lava caves to explore. There are many, many cave conduits on the island, one running as long as forty miles, the longest cave tube in the world. The southwestern corner of our island is honeycombed with lava caves, and many are on private lands in Ocean View. But Thurston is the best lava tube to walk through for those who aren't spelunkers—it's easy, well-lit, and safe.

The contours of the walls are a frozen moment in time, a map of the way the lava surged through here some five hundred years ago. If you use a flashlight, you can see artful patterns that minerals have left in the contours of walls. And up above, roots dangle in the wet ceiling—they're from the plants above ground. There used to be lava stalactites up there too, but souvenir collectors took them; that's why it's important to leave things intact for others.

Red-hot molten lava is flowing right now on the island, making its way to the ocean. It creates acres of new land and new lava tunnels every year. It's living earth, molten and moving, a never-ending story of creation, and of new lava tubes to explore.

## 26 Punalu'u Beach

***Black sand, green turtles, and awesome wild beauty***

Just a few minutes from our home is Punalu'u Beach, a sparkling gem on the south coast, a beach where coconut palms sway over glistening black sand and crystal-blue waters. It is a very special beach, in many ways. In fact, the Travel Channel considers it a top-ten beach in all of Hawaii.

This beach is a rare wonder, and beautiful, the best black sand beach in all of Hawaii. Pristine and rugged, it is a wild taste of the real Hawaii—the way it was when ancient Polynesians discovered this island of lava. All that intense black sand makes for a lot of dramatic beauty. And its origins are dramatic, too—it's a touch of the volcano. It was once all lava, pouring down from the mountain in fiery lava streams. When the lava hit the ocean waters, it cooled suddenly, exploding and cracking into small pieces. Then the rugged, surging waves broke it down further into the sparkling, glasslike sand that you see glistening today.

Beyond the beach, there's also plenty of lava rock all around on which to venture out near the ocean's edge amidst the intense wave action. One time, when I was standing out on the lava, all of a sudden, a humpback whale breached right in front of me, only fifty yards away. It happened so fast, and so close to me, that I could scarcely believe it.

Out on the beach, it's brisk and exhilarating—strong, clear winds flow in off the water, while brilliant white-capped waves crest against the deep Pacific blue. The ocean surf can get rugged here at times—it's invigorating!

There are many facets to Punalu'u Beach. It is the best place to see Hawaii's green sea turtles—it's their favorite nesting area on the whole island. So it's easy to see them, and most often there's at least one great big turtle up on the sand basking, oblivious to the tourists staring at it. Sometimes people see as many as ten turtles at a time.

Punalu'u is filled with history, if you know where to look. It may well be the very spot that the first Polynesians landed, when they beached their outriggers after the long journey from Tahiti. That honor is usually reserved for Ka Lae, South Point, though no one really knows for sure.

Punalu'u also holds the ruins of an ancient Hawaiian heiau, or temple. It is a hill with a flat rock temple on the top, a very simple stone structure in ruins. I like to think that this temple was used for offerings to the gods for good fishing and rains, abundant food and healing, and not the human sacrifice so often practiced.

The ancient Ali'i Trail, the King's Trail that circled the entire island, can also be seen at Punalu'u, if you hike south, out beyond the fishing boat ramp and out to the point. You can even walk the King's Trail for quite a while, hiking in ancient footsteps.

For centuries, Punalu'u was the traditional place where Hawaiians dove for freshwater. There are many bubbling springs flowing all over here. The springs are part of volcanic history too, because they are fed by mountain water running down from the volcano through lava tubes. You can feel the springs as they feed into the ocean, because suddenly the water is cold.

Punalu'u is named for those freshwater springs. The word "puna" means spring. The ancient meaning of Punalu'u is "spring dived for." Hawaiians would swim out into these ponds with gourds and then dive down deep to find the pure freshwater. There, they would slowly turn their gourd upside down, fill it with freshwater, then cover the gourd opening with their finger, and bring it back up to the surface. Hence the name.

Just behind the beach is a beautiful freshwater fish pond, with ducks gently gliding, and water lilies and water orchids blooming in delicate lavender. A Hawaiian version of Monet's *Water Lilies*.

Punalu'u Beach is for swimming or snorkeling or a lazy afternoon nap under the shade of the coconut palms. Just don't sleep under any coconuts, or you might not wake up!

Surprisingly, most of the time, the beach is very quiet, so visitors have all this rugged beauty pretty much to themselves. It's always struck me as rather remarkable to have so many world-class, beautiful beaches and to be able to enjoy them in such privacy, but that's the way it is on the Big Island. Just don't tell your friends!

# 27 Beaches . . . Any Way You Like It

***Beaches here are like ordering at Starbucks***

> How would you like your sand? White, Black, Green, or Gray?
>
> Did you want lava rock with that? (We'll throw it in for free!)
>
> What kind of wave action? Great waves, breaking left? Gentle surf for boogie boarding? Great swimming? Bathtub for babies?
>
> What kind of underwater adventure? Fantastic snorkel fish? Turtles? Dolphins? Manta rays?
>
> What water sports? Snorkel, snuba, scuba? Boogie board? Bodyboard, surfboard, paddleboard? Kayak? Outrigger? Wind surf? Billfishing?
>
> How did you want your boat ride? Sunset sail? Glass-bottom boat? Submarine? Whale watch? Manta rays? Marlin and big-game fishing? Sea caves? Volcano lava flow?
>
> People or private? Public beach? Resort beach? Secret hideaway?
>
> Maybe a little romance? Gorgeous white sand beach? Waterfall? Great sunsets? Green flash? Champagne ponds? Queen's warm pond?

You name it, we've got it on the Big Island. Now, did you want a beach umbrella with that?

It's not just "the beach" any more. No island in Hawaii offers as varied a beach experience as the Big Island. Everybody says Kauai has the best beaches because they're long, white, and gorgeous. Pretty impressive, but they're not alone. The Big Island also has some of the very most beautiful white sand beaches in the world. But the Big Island offers something else, and that is the most variety by far—from breathtaking black lava rock beaches, where big white surf splashes under swaying palms, to a beach made of semi-precious green peridot and olivine, to "secret" beaches, well-hidden and off the well-trafficked turista path.

The Big Island has over one hundred beaches, probably more than any other island, but that stands to reason because it is by far the biggest island in the chain. Big Island beaches are like shelling along a really great shell beach—there's enough variety to delight anyone.

So let's order up a beach at the drive-up window. I'll tell you where to find a great beach in any category—and you can look up the details on the web.

Let's dive right in and do some snorkeling. The Big Island has the best snorkel beaches in all Hawaii, and you will see hundreds of types of fish in its clear, warm waters. My vote for the top three begins with Ho Nau Nau. Also called "Two Step" (and much easier to pronounce), this beach gets its name because you take two big lava rock steps down into the water. For many, this is as good as it gets. While you're there, visit the Place of Refuge, one of the best ancient historic sites in Hawaii.

Also try Kealakekua Bay, where Captain Cook met his demise, another favorite snorkel spot with kayaking. Here, you kayak in bluest waters out to the snorkel area. And in Kona, at the south end of Ali'i Drive, you'll find the other top snorkel beach on the island, Kahalu'u Beach, where a protective reef makes it easy for everyone to snorkel. This is gentle snorkeling that you can walk out to, and it's minutes away from the bustle of Ali'i Drive. David says that in the years he's been here, there are less fish and more people at this beach all the time. One time, we even saw a local picking fish out for dinner.

Say you want soft white sand and world-class beaches? I'd

recommend any of the resort beaches, especially the Hapuna Prince beach. By Hawaiian law and courtesy, you're welcome to enjoy them, resort chairs and all. At the other end of the spectrum, for a stunning black sand beach afternoon, try relaxing at Punalu'u Beach, and watch the giant sea turtles bask in the sun. When it's chilly on the island (and it does get chilly in the winter), the heat absorption of the black sand makes this the warmest beach around.

For family fun, hands down, it's Magic Sands, one of the many little pocket beaches in Kona. This is an absolute favorite of families and is so named because the sand magically washes out to sea and magically washes back in with storms. Great body surfing and boogie boarding. And if you've got babies who just want to laugh in gentle waters, try Spencer Beach north of Kona.

For romantic beaches, head to the resort beaches. And if you want to snuggle under a waterfall alone together for the sheer delight of it, head to the Hilton Waikoloa and swim in their resort-designed pool. There are natural waterfalls you can swim under on the island, but it can be dangerous, so I won't recommend those.

Banyans is the favorite local Kona surf spot, and they'll let you know it's their turf. A good tourist surf spot would be Kahalu'u Beach in Kona—fun waves, and great for a picnic.

And as for those secret beaches . . . I'm just not telling!

# PART FOUR

# GETTING COMFORTABLE

*Pick a guava from the tree, and come walk the valley with me . . .*
*I'll tell you its stories*

The valley fills with the heady fragrance of ginger

# 28 Getting Those Bees Out of Our Living Room

***What to do with the huge hive of bees on the side of our home?***

Remember those bees David told me about?

Well, once I moved in, they were in *my* living room too. Every day, we had as many as twenty humming honeybees meandering around our couches, looking for the flowers. David had attempted to hold them back valiantly with duct tape over the little holes where they flew in. But even duct tape, the guy's fix-anything solution, could not fix this one. They were determined.

Every day we could hear them humming. Every day we could smell the honey. And every day the hive kept getting bigger. It had been a year now since David had first discovered the bees. That hive must be huge by now. We could hear them in the wall when we put our ears up to it . . . it was alive and humming. With busy little, stinging bees.

Somehow, we were going to have to remove them from the wall. But how? And who would do such a thing? The person who did it would have to perch up on a ladder outside, and do a juggling act with tools as he ripped off the siding—only to get an explosion of angry bees pouring out all over him. He wouldn't be able to run, he'd be stuck up there on that ladder, and he'd have to work as fast as he could, tearing out all the honeycomb to get the bees out. Yikes! And that was if everything went according to plan.

There were no volunteers at our house. David was concerned that he might be allergic to a sting. And even though I'd kept bees in Colorado, a neck injury prevented me from precarious heights, as well as using crowbars. We called around to bee keepers, and no one was interested. Maybe they'd been this way before.

Time passed. The hive grew. Now there were about thirty bees a day joining us for lunch in the living room. Then, a break happened. We heard about Daniel. Daniel was a new neighbor in the valley. Word was that he and his son had raised bees.

Daniel looked like a man from Amish country. He had very clear, sparkling blue eyes, and his face was a picture of glowing health. He had a black beard that extended about four inches below his chin, and he wore a brimmed hat. He was reserved, a man of few words. He had come to the island from Alaska. We didn't know much about him; he was quiet. Trim and slight of build, he was muscled and very strong, and he worked any job in the valley that came his way, silently and with a remarkably graceful rhythm—steady, slow, and paced, all day long.

What little we saw of him we liked. He had an intelligent sparkle to his conversation and was likeable in a quiet, country sort of way. Daniel was inevitably pleasant, no matter what was happening. He had already mowed our land as a surprise, gratis, while we were on the mainland. We knew it was an offer to open the door to paid work.

Maybe Daniel was our man. We asked him. But no, he hesitated. He'd never taken bees out of a house, he said. There were a lot of risks—he'd have to be up on a ladder dealing with a swarm of angry bees while he tried to get their home, the honeycomb, out of our home. It was a daunting task—and why should he put himself in hazard's way?

So we both stood back from the open question, and let more time play by. Meanwhile, we hired Daniel to work around our place, tearing down the old tractor shed, putting up a fence, and digging out gardens from the all the rocks in the soil.

Days passed. And while Daniel worked, he cogitated over whether or not to remove the bees. And while he worked, we got to know him. He turned out to be a most remarkable character.

More time passed. After a few weeks of silence on the subject, and with assurances that he would have decent protection, Daniel agreed to clear the bees. Daniel had decided that he wanted to start a hive. The honeycomb cache in our wall would set him up overnight with the exceptional honey from the valley.

We had our deal. Next, it was our turn to make good on our promise of protection.

None of us had a bee suit. Bee suits are those things that make you look like Neil Armstrong on the moon—a big helmet with netting and a white outfit that covers you head to toe. Our best bet on the island was an improvised "bee suit"—a thick painter's coverall that looked like it would stand up to the job. We got a wide brim hat with mosquito netting and leather gloves.

What we didn't have was a smoker—we couldn't locate one in time. Without a smoker, things were going to be challenging. In the bee business, a smoker is what saves you from getting stung. A smoker is a contraption made of a long metal can with a bellows in which you burn a bit of paper. The little smoldering fire sends out a steady stream of gentle smoke that literally pours over the disturbed, angry bees. The smoke magically and miraculously calms the bees. Under its spell, bees become extremely passive and docile. They don't sting. That's how eccentric old beekeepers can smilingly entertain horrified onlookers by wearing a swarm of bees, playing with them, even shaping the swarm to make a long, grotesque beard while everyone else is panicking for their safety.

Without a smoker, things could get dicey indeed.

Finally, the great day came to remove the bees. We went out to the sunny side of the house, where the hive was, and tried to figure out where exactly they were in the wall. They could be anywhere in a twenty-foot length of wall, and the wall itself was sixteen feet high. We chose the place where we could most hear them, and where we could smell the sweet honey wafting out in the island air. This had to be the place—didn't it?

David placed the ladder on the wall where we thought the buzzing was loudest. On the top of the ladder, he set the crowbar that Daniel would use to wrest away the siding from the bees. Putting the ladder in the wrong place, even just a few feet off, would mean that Daniel would have to start the process all over again . . . in a cover of angry bees.

Then it was Daniel's turn. Taking courage, Daniel slowly and steadily climbed up the ladder, ten feet high, armed with a SKILSAW, a nail puller, and a knife to cut the honeycomb out from the house. He moved slowly up in his awkward bee suit, veiled hat, gloves, and boots. How strange he looked in that getup climbing up on that ladder.

Once in position near the top of the ladder, Daniel went to

work. First, he sawed through the siding, cutting a strip two feet high and four feet long. He pulled the nails, and then—this was the big moment—he wrenched his crowbar under the panel of siding. *Zzzzz*! Now the bees were loose. The air filled with a cloud of angry bees pouring out from their nest. They began to buzz around Daniel, bombing him, trying to get their intruder. We all wished we had a smoker!

But the open wall didn't show much hive. This clearly wasn't the core of the hive. Aargh! Daniel would have to step down the ladder, move it over one panel of siding, and begin again. He did this in a hail of bees. They weren't going to stop. The only choice was to keep moving—as fast as he could.

Taking a deep breath, and moving with deliberate slowness and calm, Daniel went on, repositioned the ladder, and undid yet another four-foot siding panel. This time, he was right on top of the hive. Now all hell broke loose. When he pried the siding away, a torrent of hot, zinging bees funneled out, angrily attacking the air around him. Inside the wall lay the heart of the hive—it measured all of twelve feet wide, snug between the studs.

Daniel was remarkable in this hail of bees. He had only one choice—to keep moving, and he did so with remarkable calm and steadiness. He was getting stung now. Zing! Zing! They hailed in on him. It took a lot of guts and poise to stay up there on that ladder in the hell storm he unleashed.

Now the backyard was filled with bees looking for something, anything, in their chaos. In a matter of moments, they had emerged from their hive and created a huge swarm cloud, so dense it was dark, churning, and roiling with hot, angry bees buzzing around wildly.

Luckily, they swarmed about six feet away from where Daniel stood on the ladder. They buzzed madly around in their swarm, looking for home. And through it all, Daniel continued working. He was cutting out the honeycomb now, lifting out huge chunks that dripped golden nectar, placing them carefully into his five-gallon buckets. He worked on and on for what seemed an eternity. Fifteen tensely poised minutes marched by, one by one, until he had carved most of the comb out of the wall.

When it was over, Daniel l had suffered about fifteen bee stings.

His getup had protected him from the worst of it. As for the house, the better part of one wall was gone.

But Daniel had his hive. His buckets were filled to overflowing with great chunks of honeycomb, oozing golden deliciousness. The chunks would make a fine hive. And the sweet nectar of island flowers would fill his life for many years to come.

# 29 Daniel, a Study in Practicing Contentment

***How much do we really need to be happy, anyway?***

Daniel was a very interesting study in living in harmony for me.

He was very different from the men I had known in Chicago. He was slight but very graceful. Don't get me wrong, Daniel was very masculine. Though small of build—he stood only about 5'10" high—he was very strong, in a way that was quite different from how we normally think of strength. His strength came from something bigger than simply his graceful, slender body. It came from his consciousness.

Daniel had stamina that allowed him to do hard physical work from dawn to well after dusk, day after day after day. Not bad for a man in his late fifties. His favorite jobs were digging post holes and digging out all the many lava rocks from our garden soil. This is very tough, hard work. He did all this on the very simplest of foods, and all raw. His breakfast was a papaya, lunch was a big avocado from our tall tree—it took all of fifteen minutes— and dinner was a big salad. He was barely eating.

Yet he was a powerhouse of stamina and endurance. His movements were steady and rhythmic, in fact, they were flowing. This is very unusual in a laborer. Many laborers move heavily. Daniel's movements were more like the rhythm of a conscious dance, free form, slow, and meaningful. Mindful. But though his speed was admirably steady, his output was slow—only about one quarter as fast as the other construction workmen on our property. At times, this was extremely exasperating to us. But Daniel was a perpetual motion machine, working well past the time every other man was spent.

By the time we met him, he hadn't eaten sugar in twenty years and he had spent the past few years preparing his body to eat strictly raw foods. He knew a great deal about diet and health. When we asked him to join us for dinner, he refused any food that was not raw, even though it was all organic.

A New Zealander, he had come to the Big Island by way of Alaska, as many people do. He wasn't used to money, and had very little use for it. He had lived in Alaska in a spiritual community that had been created to give parents an alternative way to raise their children in a safe, wholesome environment within nature.

And it was *very* alternative—the entire community lived without any money. Most of the time, they didn't need it because their every need was satisfied by their hard-working self-sufficiency. When they did need something from the outer, moneyed world, they bartered. And if that didn't work, they sold some of their grains and crops.

It's probably the way most of our grandparents and great-grandparents worked up until the 1900s. A simple life. One of the main things that made their life so simple was not simply the lack of money and the plethora of needless things it bought. It may have been that they learned to be content with what they had.

In a word, they practiced contentment.

So Daniel lived in our valley, quite contentedly, in a tiny, little island home. And by now, you know what that means! A mere twelve by sixteen feet, his entire home was the size of a mainland bedroom or living room. It was roughly the size of Thoreau's cabin at Walden. And here Daniel came to live consciously.

This little cabin of simplicity was painted the simplest of colors. It was white, white, and white—inside, outside, siding, and trim. It had a little four-foot-wide deck, painted green, upon which climbed a whimsical orange honeysuckle. Climbing up the four steps, you discovered that there was not even a door at the front entrance—only thick, clear, vertical plastic strips that hung down across the top, making a covering. You parted these to enter.

Inside, as your eyes took in the room, you could see just enough space for simplicity—a single bed pushed into the corner on one long wall . . . a small desk with a simple wooden chair on the other . . . a row of shelves running up a third wall next to a window, with hanging space for clothes on the other side. That was it. The simple emptiness of the little house was charming.

It had actual windows in it, which as you know, isn't always expected. It was made of single-wall construction so that the walls on the inside are the construction studs with the back of the outdoor siding attached to them.

And immediately out back, running along the entire back wall of the little cabin, was a simple outdoor kitchen in the open under a tarp. An old refrigerator, a wood slab counter, and a crude sink made up his facilities. About fifty yards away was a little "necessary house" with a half-moon on it. Probably just like Thoreau, too. Nearby, an outdoor shower completed the dwelling.

Daniel lived here for free for several years in exchange for gardening and mowing. Life can be so simple here, so effortless.

It's actually quite freeing to live with almost nothing. And it is exhilarating to realize how little we really need to live well in this world. One time, long ago, I put all my possessions in storage shortly after I moved to Colorado. I remember the little thrill of happiness that ran through me when we closed the storage shed door on a household of possessions, locking everything away. I felt free, relieved of a burden. I was thrilled.

It felt so free to have all my possessions gone. It was actually a relief. It was very similar to the feeling I had when I stayed in a monk's room on the monastic campus at Mundelein Retreat Center in Chicago. I entered the small room, which had been this particular monk's entire personal world, and I felt an exhilarating sense of joy thrill through me. What more did I need?

So this was Daniel's entire world. And what more did Daniel need?

Daniel got around the island on his motorcycle and managed to live on his worker's salary of little more than ten dollars an hour. He simply did not need money, and more than that, he did not *want* money.

Daniel is what I call a Minimalist. There are many of them on our island. The ones that do it by intelligent, conscious choice are quite noble individuals. They just have a different calling than the rest of us.

There is a very rugged, handsome man of French heritage who travels the island on foot with his pack and walking stick. We often see him walking as we drive by; he doesn't want a ride. His face has the healthy ruddiness of a man who spends his days in nature. He is always clean, in strong, good health, and looks radiantly happy. He speaks with a French accent and is charming to talk with. When I talk with him, I notice the sparkling brilliance of his crystal-blue eyes and his intelligent take on the world. He is clearly living in the deep channel in which his life flows, to paraphrase our friend Thoreau again.

Another example is Daniel's girlfriend, whom he met shortly after beginning work with us. She had moved to the Big Island after losing her entire life and all her possessions to Hurricane Katrina. So why not start anew in paradise? A willing relative allowed her to pitch a tent, and this is how she put her new life together.

The Big Island has a great deal to teach about simplicity and contentment, and how little we really need to be thoroughly happy. In fact, when I think about it, the less I have, the freer and happier I am.

There is great joy in emptiness.

# 30 Extreme Packing Shed Makeover!

***Dancing on the subfloor . . . Do the Bumpout!***

And then it was time to build a home together. After all, you do remember the "island-style" home that I inherited, yes?

A few early experiences had convinced me that there would have to be some changes made.

Like the night early on when we had a couple of David's friends over in the evening for dinner. It was in February, which is one of the coldest months in our valley, and of course there were no windows, only screens. And that night was especially cold. So when the temperature hit 52°, and we were sitting in the living room over stir fry, and I was freezing, I knew there were gonna be some changes made. These folks were used to it and never even shivered, but yikes, it was *cold* for dinner that night! (And actually, that's a very low temperature for our valley; usually it gets only about as low as 58° on winter evenings.)

Then there was another thing . . . the way the soothing island breezes sealed all the mailing envelopes shut before we could use them . . . or the way any sheet of paper in the house became soggy before I could write on it. For someone who loves to write, that's a bit compelling.

Clearly, we needed a window solution.

And a floor solution. And a bathroom solution. And a kitchen solution. And on and on. We even needed a roof solution. Why, there were so many solutions needed, we'd have to redo the whole thing.

Basically, we needed a new house.

Our lovely little home had, at one time, been a packing shed. And just what is a packing shed, you may ask, and rightly so. We've all heard of carriage houses remade as homes, but this is a new one.

A packing shed is a place where flowers are prepared for market. Long ago, this land had been a flower farm, and the packing shed was where they sorted and packed the carnations. David was living in a packing shed. We were going to have to do an Extreme Packing Shed Makeover!

David was a former contractor of fine oceanside homes on the West Coast. And in my former marriage, my husband and I had built a custom passive solar home with the guidance of a superb architect from a large Denver firm, plus a solar engineer and contractors. Putting this combined experience together, we looked at David's packing shed, shook our heads, and said, "Unh unh." Somehow the packing shed just didn't cut it anymore.

So we decided to build a new home, close to part of the old home. We would attach them with a covered walkway, island style.

What we didn't realize at the time was that the project would be as much about learning about each other as it was about designing a home.

I wanted to use an architect to design the home. After all, this was a big project for which I had no background. But David had different ideas, based on watching his parents' experience.

When we met, that very first camping weekend, he told me something important as we headed to breakfast in Lake Geneva. He told me that I reminded him of his mother. And that she and his father had done everything together. They had built a very successful and happy life together, working at their own business and raising their family on the water in the Northwest. They built modular homes and owned an RV park. They figured it out themselves. And so we would do the same here. No architect. There was very little money for any of this, anyway.

Okay. But what a large task! Absolutely daunting. I didn't even know how walls get attached to floors back then. And David had always used architect's blueprints before and had never designed anything himself. Did I see warning signs here?

At that time, we'd known each other less than a year and had never done a project together. So we were very new together as a partnership, let alone an unschooled architectural design team.

I didn't realize how differently we processed things. But I soon would.

I launched into the project as I always do—plunging right in, studying it in depth. I gathered as many books as I could about housing design, creating a small library that detailed and diagramed everything from Swedish cottages and open-air Thai homes to Hawaiian glamour homes and "affordable house plans." I couldn't even begin to "grok" how to design a home. I was missing about five years of architectural schooling, for starters.

And while I was diligently pouring over endless plans, David was so nonchalant about the whole process, which concerned me. I didn't know how David's mind worked then, how he solved problems this big. So I was diligently working away at house designs, plowing ahead, trying my best, while he was apparently doing nothing. I began to wonder how we would ever put a plan together, me knowing nothing and he not really designing anything for us.

Somehow, we had to get this solved.

I got very anxious. I would lay awake at night panicked with anxiety that it wasn't going to be possible to design it ourselves. Then I'd wake up in the very early morning, get up, and work on a few more drawings to try to get something to work. Over time, my ideas began to have a cohesiveness. A home was taking shape. It was going to be like a cottage, with air flow from all four sides moving throughout the home, and lots of light, with big windowed French doors and windows that opened to the outside, letting nature fill our home.

Finally, after too many weeks of anxious graph paper designs, David snapped into action, and with his contractor's knowledge, put it all together in one beautiful, coherent design.

If you are familiar with the Myers-Briggs Type Indicator, the most widely used test for understanding personality types in the world, then you might guess by now that I am high "J," a person who makes decisions easily and quickly, loves deadlines and structure, and likes to plan and analyze.

David, on the other hand, is exactly the opposite. His style is intuitive, almost unconsciously moving through his sensing and feelings, letting things coalesce within him. He doesn't come to decisions quickly. Gradually and slowly, something from within takes form in his mind, and then, all of a sudden, so it seems, it spontaneously emerges as a wonderfully creative idea.

Unfortunately, as I lay in bed during those harrowing, anxious nights, I didn't know this. I only knew that he wasn't designing the house. And that I, being high "J," was trying to make up the difference.

But finally, there it was, a concept. It was a beautiful home done in plantation cottage style—symmetric, substantial, and sturdy—with a beautiful open-beam wood ceiling. And simple. The design was, ultimately, very simple.

So the design was done. Next, we had to have a house designer draw up the plans. We were referred to a CAD/CAM designer by a realtor friend of David's. The designer came in, high on pakalolo, which in Hawaiian means "crazy weed." David taught me to look at his dilated pupils. And he swore, literally, with every sentence. He lived to surf and designed homes to float the bills. Very impressive. Especially after my last home had been designed by the finest architectural firm in Denver.

This would not do. This was way too "island style"!

So we located a home designer who was more down to earth, if you get my drift. An architect would review the plans, stamp it, and we'd be off to permit land. And that is just what we did.

And we did it. We created a lovely looking home design all by ourselves.

Next, David had to build it. David laid the foundation with construction workers in weeks of rain and mud, while I went into Chicago in September and planned our wedding. Not that I didn't want to be around for all the construction mess and frenzy, understand (wink).

It was just that I had suddenly received an intuitive awareness that if I did not have my wedding that fall, my youngest sister would not be able to attend in an enjoyable way. She had had breast cancer by this time a ghastly thirteen years, her devoted oncologist saving her life by moving her from one chemo drug to another, before the cancer outsmarted the drug. Sadly, I understood that time was running out this time. So without mentioning my motivation, I rushed back to Chicago to create an entire wedding in one month. This way, my sister could enjoy the wedding with everyone. We could be there as a family.

Luckily, my intuition guided me effortlessly to pick the right weekend, Thanksgiving weekend, and the perfect location—the

Herrington Inn, in Geneva. When I called the hotel, the only opening they had was that one weekend. When I called my minister friend, the band, and everyone involved, it was all a go—effortlessly. No one was doing anything the Saturday after Thanksgiving. Voilà! Instant wedding.

So I whisked into Chicago for a whirlwind wedding planning tour, including one entire afternoon devoted to tasting cake and frosting samples, as well as viewing hundreds of cake designs. Though the cake extravaganza afternoon was de rigueur with our wedding inn, I can remember when ordering a wedding cake took only twenty minutes at the local bakery shop.

Having planned our wedding in record time, I returned, on a bit of a cloud, to the Big Island, and to David, and . . . a completed subfloor. We were thrilled. You could actually stand on our home now.

When I had left, it had only been a dream in the air, just a bit more than string lines tied to marker posts to delineate where the house would stand. Now it was taking on tangible, living shape. How exciting!

Why, you could even dance on it! And that's exactly what we did. We danced on the subfloor to celebrate.

Next came the walls. As David and his team began to put up the walls, we realized that—oops—we had a problem. We had redesigned the room layout a bit along the way, and now there was not enough space for the bathroom within the confines of the rectangular shape. Where could it go?

David to the rescue again. He suggested a "bump out," literally bumping out a section of one wall to make room for the bathroom as an extension. It fit perfectly. I didn't know you could do that!

And this time, we were so happy that we danced the Bump Out, bumping out our behinds together to make the point. Do the Bump Out!

And then it was time to go back to Chicago for our wedding. We stayed for the holidays and winter in Chicago—wouldn't want to miss winter in Chicago! When we came home early the next year, we had the roof put on. Finally, we were under roof.

And now we had a shell, the physical structure of what we had created on paper over all those cups of tea and coffee. It was great to see our hopes and plans come alive in such a beautiful structure.

And while we built our home, we learned a lot about each other along the way. Home construction is something that has stretched many a marriage to its breaking point. As a former contractor, David knew this and kept remarking about "what a good sport" I was.

But in our case, it was actually a great experience because we got to learn about each other much faster than had we been sane and not tackled a home together within our first year of knowing each other . . . along with my moving to Hawaii, our traveling back and forth to the mainland, and getting married.

And don't get me wrong—there were plenty of stress points. But no stress fractures. Because, ultimately, we used it as a way to learn about each other. And to learn how to love each other more.

Who needs the Myers-Briggs Type Indicator to learn about your spouse when you can design and build your own home together?

# 31 A Walk in Our Valley

### *Walking in nature's abundance*

One of my favorite times to walk in the valley is just before dusk because it is so full of fragrance. The ginger and jasmine open then. So let's take a walk together, and I'll describe it as we go. We're walking in early April, so the "fruit report" is from that time.

First, as we leave the door, we are immediately surrounded by the perfume of angel trumpets, large and beautiful trees with trumpet-shaped flowers eight inches long in pink, yellow, and white blooms.

We walk past a big banana patch so big that there are paths through it—a miniature banana jungle. And there's a big avocado tree that reaches up over one hundred twenty feet, with avos that roll down the hill toward us. Then we're at our gate. Turning left, we walk past an orchard of macadamia nut trees, all in neat rows. Kalij pheasants run and play under the trees, chortling and cackling together. As we walk, they dart through the openings in the hurricane fence to get to safety in the wild area across the street.

Walking on, we turn the corner of the mac nut orchard only to be greeted by climbing shoots of blue morning glories intertwined in small trees, growing up among the patches of yellow ginger flowers. The yellow gingers are magnificently showy—big spikes of tiny little yellow trumpets, each filled with perfume. There's a huge Albizia tree here that rises up a couple hundred feet. It stands as a stark monument, a memorial to the intensity of the lightning bolt that scarred its white trunk and charred the branches that reach up through the forest. That bolt was so strong it not only burned the tree, it also zapped the asphalt road right in front of it, buckling the center of the road. Kapow!

We walk on past several fields of horses, and then the asphalt road cuts steeply down into a big lava gulch, over which hang massive eucalyptus trees with their welcoming shade. This was one place that the deluge in the big storm of 2000 roared down. But you'd never know it today—it's covered in grasses, gently blowing in the breeze.

A bit further on, we discover a guava orchard with fruit dripping over the road. Their sweet-tart tang fills the air. Many have plopped to the ground and broken open; they are that soft. The harvest is almost over. We can pick some off the tree, open their soft yellow skin, and eat the pink fruit inside as we walk.

The late afternoon air fills with the fragrance of yellow ginger and white jasmine, floating throughout the entire valley. On special evenings, something very rare in all the world happens—the valley fills with their heady scent, and the whole valley feels enchanted, like a Shangri-La.

Another quarter mile, and up ahead I can see impatiens that have grown up five feet tall, reaching over the ferns in front of them, in their search for sunlight. As I walk, I'm gradually encompassed by a raucous chorus of thousands of myna birds perched high up in bamboo trees at dusk here. They like to visit at night, and sometimes they congregate in our bamboos, too. They aren't always here, but when they are it is a wonder. It sounds like thousands upon thousands of birds.

I walk by a koa tree near the road, and on it I see dancing a luscious lilikoi vine, laden with hanging fruit. The fruit look like large green eggs and won't be ripe for another month. But the wait will be worth it—lilikoi are a uniquely savory blend of sweet and tart, so ambrosial that they are known as passion fruit. The vine climbs up the koa tree, covering it, and then dances out on the telephone wire above the ground, doing its high wire act, its plentiful fruit dangling down from the vine. I used to come here and search for ripe lilikoi in the tall grass.

Next, a couple large lemon trees come into view. Their lemons are big, bigger than oranges. They are so big, in fact, that they fill half a dinner plate. In good citrus years, this tree overflows with lemons, as many as four to a bunch. Several have fallen on the ground where they lie, food for the bugs.

I walk past the avocado that hangs over the second gulch. The fruit is just now coming in and will offer avocados for nine months. One time, a brilliant-green, shiny, round of avocado rolled out to meet me as I walked the path here.

Another eighth of a mile brings a peach tree with small green peaches on it. These never get very big, and I've never had one of them, but they are always tempting. And just beyond them are bananas, planted right by the road, their fruit drooping for the taking. And sometimes locals do come and take a bunch.

Walking on, to my right are red poinsettias, growing eight feet high, still blooming since November. As I approach the coffee farm and the mamaki tea farm up ahead, the gentle evening rains are starting, as they often do at dusk, and I notice that the sound of raindrops is different.

On my right, the raindrops are hitting coffee plants, and their sound is a gentle ping, ping, ping as they hit the crisp, shiny leaves. On my left, the raindrops are touching mamaki tea leaves, Hawaiian nettle, and the rain here becomes a soft, fluid touch.

Past lots of acreage with sheep and cows, I cross another gulch and find a loquat bush. Its fruit is smaller than a plum and yellow like guava, ripe and delicious. Beside them grow more bananas; they grow freely all over the valley. I can see a few impatiens growing wild in the gulch below.

I'm almost home now, and I pass the tender, little red lantern plants that never fail to amaze me. They are a delight to the eye, with exquisite red-orange lantern cups dangling down, veined with deep red, and a showy, long stamen protruding like a trumpet. The detailing on them is extraordinary.

They are called Chinese lantern, or abutilon. Every time I look at them, I cannot help but reflect on how exquisitely designed they are and how this exquisite patterning pervades all of life, whether we can see it or not. As we accord with the unity in all life, we begin to see a perfect pattern running through our lives, too.

Then it's past the tree in whose branches our neighbor has planted island orchids. We glance into his orchard at allspice, ginger, and clove plants, move past one more mango tree, more coffee, more mac nuts, and I'm home.

The birds are singing their last calls of the evening, the sun is setting, and all is well, very well indeed in this magical valley.

# 32 The Pure Peace of Our Valley

***The ancient Hawaiians' entrance to Shangri-La***

Our valley is a hidden gem, a little emerald hideaway, unknown even to many who live on the island. Wildly lush and green, it is a forest tucked into a half-moon rim of verdant cliffs called "pali." The pali scale as high as perhaps two thousand feet around the valley and run with eleven waterfalls when we have big rains. We can see some of the waterfalls from our windows.

Our valley is a sacred place, mystical and magical to those who know it. To the ancient Hawaiians, the forest on the rim above the valley held the entrance to their sacred Shangri-La. At times, when clouds nestle down in the valley and their wisps lace through the green cliffs, the whole valley takes on an ethereal, otherworldly quality. It is easy to see how this was the entrance to Shangri-La.

It is often called "a magical place" by people who grow plants. In fact, these are the words of a man who should know. He has a huge palm nursery on our island, one of the largest in the world. The way plants grow here is legendary.

Yet the words I most often hear visitors use to describe the valley are "spiritual" and "sacred." The valley is known as a place of healing. Many come in confusion and crisis and leave in clarity and peace. There is great freedom in this deep nature for people to be who they truly are away from outside pressure and expectation. Returning to center always heals.

But even more, the valley allows people to be held within the great peace, the profound unity of nature, which alone and of itself can be fully healing. All healing is, at root, a return to the Unity, the divine within.

I believe that part of the healing quality here is the deep silence within which the valley is held. The silence here is so pure that it feels like whipped cream that you can cut. It's delicious. I've found that it offers a chance to stop the constant inner noise and busyness of the mind . . . to simply listen to pure silence . . . and to absorb it. Outer silence draws us inward, dropping us easily into reflection and spirit. We sense ourselves part of the Oneness of Life.

And it is so very, very silent. On the valley's thousand-some acres, there are only about twenty homes. Nary a car goes by in a day, and the ones that do, we can count, usually on two hands. No planes fly over. A helicopter flying overhead is an event; it happens once or twice a year.

David told me when I arrived that he doesn't like to play music in the house; it interrupts the beautiful sound of the silence. David hears the subtle universal sound current on our land very strongly.

When I return after walking the valley, if there is music playing in the house, I find that even fine music interrupts the pristine silence, where the only sounds are the wind rustling through the bamboo and silver oak, and the birds calling to one another.

This peace and silence flow from the purity of the valley. It is one of the purest places on earth.

Purity holds great power. This power expresses on many levels, from physical, through psychological, all the way to spirit.

To experience the power of purity on the physical level, try this simple experiment with common substances, as they affect our senses of taste and smell. Taste honey, and really savor it. Now, taste sugar and really savor it. What happened? For me, the taste of pure honey is whole and ambrosial. It has a rounded feeling to it. The taste of refined sugar is empty. Pure honey has a building quality for our bodies; it restores and is used to heal. Refined sugar has a linear, pushing, driving quality; it depletes. It is used to push tired bodies further. We become out of balance when we use it. Similarly, the fragrance of pure incense is full, rounded, and beautiful, the smell of poor incense is sharp and off-putting.

The more we refine our senses, the more we move toward purity. So it is with our lives.

This natural purity extends to everything in our way of life in the valley . . . our water, our air, our earth, our sky, our ocean.

Our valley water is some of the purest water on earth. It tastes vibrantly crystal clear and is very life-giving. It is "EPA Gold Standard," in the words of a water engineer. It does not need to be treated because nature does that quite well.

The water travels all the way down from permafrost snows high atop the volcano, Mauna Loa. It trickles gently down through the mountain, being refined and purified as it moves through the volcanic strata and ash. It is said that it travels for seventy years. And it arrives through tunnels dug by the Chinese a century ago. That is why it is so pure.

The valley air is sweet and pure and filled with fragrance . . . the beguiling scent of white ginger, the tangy sweetness of guava, and the rich, sensuous perfume of night-blooming jasmine. The scents are especially luscious during a full moon.

One of my favorite experiences here is driving into the valley by night, past the moon-shadowed tall trees, taking in the indescribable scent of night jasmine when the whole valley is filled with the scent, almost too much . . . under a canopy of twinkling, bright stars. There is no place in the world I know of that fills with fragrance like our valley.

And we have only natural light here. Which means that the rhythms of nature's light and dark are very easy to move in harmony with. Many people in the valley keep farmer's hours—to bed a bit after sundown and up with the rising sun. It is easy to follow, the rhythms of nature lead you into that kind of a pulse.

The night sky is so clear that we can see a remarkable, sparkling brilliance of stars, thousands upon thousands of stars, as if some great hand cast them out like fairy dust into the sky. The vast starry sweep of the Milky Way is visible here. Some nights, we just stand under the stars in quiet awe. Last night, we watched in delight as two shooting stars streamed across the sky.

Our good earth is rich and deep, the soil chocolate brown and sweet. When David tills the vegetable garden with the tractor, it is so deep and fine that it has to be some of the most exceptional planting soil on earth. We are very, very blessed. Soil, after all, is the basis of all life, along with water and sun. And our nurturing afternoon rains and brilliant days of sunshine make for lush gardens of vegetables and fruits.

A few miles away is the purest water, shimmering in waves of aquamarine and brilliant turquoise, stretching out to deepest sapphire, filled with schools of fish that you can see in the waves as they break—schools of bright yellow tang, gorgeous blue-green parrot fish, turtles, dolphin, whales, and so many more.

Can you imagine how pure this must be? So far away . . . so clear, so true. Purity and simplicity, silence and slowness hold great power. They hold the power of life.

This must be the way it all was, once upon a time.

# 33 Island Eyes, Aloha Feet, and Hearts So Big

***Some native Hawaiians have eyes as turquoise as the ocean***

One day when I was in Ocean View, a huge subdivision on lava lands, I came across two guys in an ATV, a favorite local form of transport. I remember needing to ask a question or something.

One of the guys, very handsome, jumped out of the ATV and proudly announced, "I'm a local boy." As they came up to me to talk, I could see that his eyes were pure turquoise. I had never seen eyes like that in my life—pure, clear turquoise. They took my breath away. They were captivating, the color of the azure ocean that surrounds our island.

I told David about it, and he explained, "Those are Hawaiian eyes, turquoise with flecks of purple." David thinks they are the result of generations and generations of a Hawaiian island people whose lives have been held within blue sky and turquoise waters.

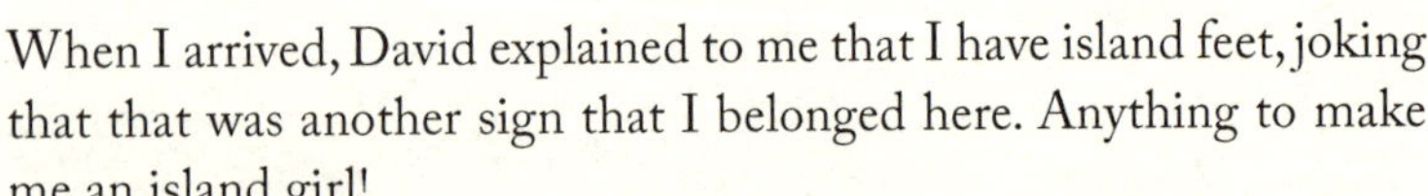

When I arrived, David explained to me that I have island feet, joking that that was another sign that I belonged here. Anything to make me an island girl!

Aloha feet are island feet, feet that are used to going barefoot. They get broad without the constraint of shoes, and the toes spread to grip the ground. Imagine being an ancient Hawaiian, tracking through sand along the beach, or wearing sandals made of ti plants, as you walk across the lava rock trails that circle the island, or wading through water-soaked fields of taro, and you get the picture of why island feet are broad with spread toes.

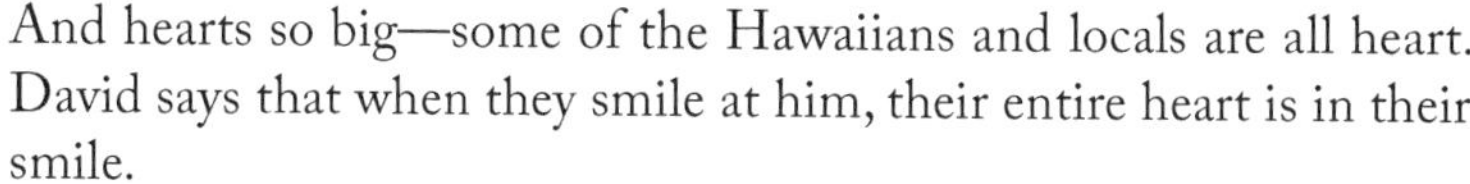

And hearts so big—some of the Hawaiians and locals are all heart. David says that when they smile at him, their entire heart is in their smile.

He has told me about big Hawaiian men, men who hold lots of mana, spiritual power, who are huge. Their hands are big enough to crush David's hand easily. Yet they take his hand in both their huge hands, in a very gentle way, far gentler than a mainland handshake. And then they bow their head to him a little, open their heart, and say, "How are you, my brother?"

It is just like Hawaii itself, David says, big and hugely powerful, and yet so very gentle in its touch.

# 34 Sabine's Dream

***She dreamt of her island home, even as a child in Germany . . . before she even knew Hawaii existed***

Sabine has a wonderful story to tell about how she came to Hawaii.[8] As a child growing up in Germany, she felt distinctly out of place. She felt so terribly constricted by all the limitations around her, the endless rules and regulations, that she rebelled whenever she could.

At night in bed, she would escape into an inner world, the world her heart held, the place she belonged. She saw herself standing in the mountains of a lush tropical land, looking out into an endlessly blue ocean. It was so very clear for her. She saw herself living together with her soul mate, surrounded by children and friends in small, cozy homes.

There was a great deal of love in this little island community, and lots of fun and play. They all lived together in harmony. They spent their days working together in the garden, cooking together, laughing, and enjoying. They were all so very happy. Radiant joy shone from their faces.

All day long, during the struggle of her young life in Germany, she looked forward to going to bed so that she could return to the magical place within her heart. Something deep within her knew where she belonged and was drawing her toward it. Just as in the song "Bali Ha'i," the island was calling her.

What began as a childhood longing for the islands then impelled her to move her in the direction of those dreams, without even knowing she was doing so.

As she grew into a young woman, she began to visit Holland, where she met a man with the most compelling green eyes she had ever seen. Instantly attracted, they fell madly in love. Sabine's heart opened into a depth of love she had never known. She felt her soul flowing through her. And she felt joyfully one with her higher self, and one with Michael.

She knew she had met her soul mate. But even so, it was not to last because their lives had to take them in different directions.

Time passed. Then she had another dream. She saw a beautiful girl with gracefully long black hair sitting with her at a picnic table in those island mountains that overlooked the ocean.

Now her life began to move in a different direction. Away at college, she searched for another love only to discover that what she found was meaningless to her. Then a brute of a man demanded that she live with him. Too afraid of him to resist, she moved in with him.

During the years she lived with him, she felt a complete captive. She was beaten and raped and felt totally powerless to do anything about it. Her fear made her powerless. She could not even tell her parents, she was so afraid. It was a living hell. And yet it taught her some enormous lessons, for during this time, she learned courage, the courage to do the things she needed to do to unlock the vision of her life.

Michael appeared now and then like a ray of hope for her, visiting her from time to time. One day, he brought with him his new girlfriend, Lea. Lea had beautiful long black hair. Once again, Sabine was immediately drawn to her. Sabine and Lea developed a loving friendship over the next months.

Meanwhile, Sabine discovered herself pregnant. And with that, the brute she lived with only grew more brutal. She felt trapped, violated, oppressed. Yet the baby she was carrying filled her with joy. So in her living hell, she grew stronger, driven by her love for her unborn child.

This love gave her the strength she needed to leave the brute and to find her own apartment. She gave birth to a beautiful boy. And then, the brute returned. And once again, Sabine could not find the strength to resist his demands that they live together again.

She stayed with him over several years. Gradually, driven by financial pressure, they sunk into their most abysmal moment of all, when the brute suggested that if he killed them all, at least they would all be free.

At that moment of her life, Lea appeared at her door, saying that her relationship with Michael had ended. Would Sabine like to accompany her to the United States? New York was where she planned to live.

Yes! Sabine immediately and secretly raised a little money, packed one bag with her bare necessities, told no one, and left. She could think of nothing except immediate escape.

When she arrived in New York to meet Lea, she discovered that their plans had changed. Lea had just met someone who invited them to housesit on the Big Island of Hawaii.

They left for Hawaii together with their babies, both born at the same time. When they arrived at their new home, it was totally dark, and Sabine could not see anything. But the next morning, she awoke to joy. She could not believe her eyes. She was in the home of her heart, exactly as she had been dreaming all her life. She was standing in a lushly beautiful tropical mountain valley, looking out over a breathtaking view of endlessly blue ocean.

Over the next months, they built the small houses she had seen as a child. They tended their garden together and cooked together, surrounded by their children, the good earth, the sun, the balmy ocean breezes, and the most brilliant stars she had ever seen.

Sabine shares her story, "Home of My Heart," on the internet as an example of manifesting, creating the life of her dreams. And indeed it is. It is a wonderful story of a dream come true.

When we see Sabine's story that way, we perceive it as the act of consciously projecting out into the world what we want or desire and then manifesting it. Mind is the builder. Thoughts are things, and thoughts create. What you think, you create. All this is very true. And mastery of a projective-creative mind, just as mastery of a receptive-intuitive mind, is very important to our spiritual development, both individually and collectively. We must all learn these skills.

Yet for me, Sabine's story is also something more, and demonstrates something deeper. When we move beyond the level of our conscious personality, with its wants and desires, and relate to ourselves as souls, then we begin to see something greater. We begin to see Sabine's home as the effortless unfolding of the destiny held within her heart and soul.

For me, it is not so much that she created it, as that she perceived it. She did not even know that Hawaii existed as a child when she dreamt it, so choosing it was not even a conscious act. It was something that welled up from deep within her. She was recognizing the seed pattern within her soul, yet unexpressed in the physical world. It was beyond her conscious choice; it appeared to her as a dream that filled her. And she never deliberately tried to find Hawaii; it found her.

When we read her story in this way, it opens understandings that make our lives more graceful. We can see several principles in her story.

Our destinies are held within us. Our destiny is never outside us, it is within us. We don't have to create it. It already exists, yet unseen. We merely need to accord with what is in our hearts and souls already. When we understand our life paths in this way, we see that we do not need to strive to reach something outside us.

Our destiny is held within the seed pattern of our soul. And our heart communicates that to us, not our conscious mind. Only the heart is large enough to apprehend this subtle seed pattern. It is not something we can consciously "figure out." The conscious mind waits upon the heart for this guidance.

Our hearts whisper this destiny to us as a longing, a deep hunger that draws us unerringly in one direction, and no other.

Yet this destiny is greater than ours alone. For it is life longing through us, longing to be and to express more fully. This destiny is the dream of life through us. And all of life, every living being, depends upon every other living being to fulfill this seed pattern.

It is our role then, not so much to work to create that destiny, as it is to open to perceive what life dreams through us, by listening deep within. It is held as a perfect pattern in the invisible. When we have perceived this pattern, then our conscious creative mind is meant to hold the pattern, and our hearts are meant to love it, until it is embodied in the physical world. All of life is guiding us to express this perfect pattern held within our souls. Everything cooperates toward this good, both open doors and closed doors, both ease and difficulty.

With this view then, we see that Sabine did not so much manifest or attract the home of her heart as that she was spiritually developed enough to perceive the seed pattern within her soul. She allowed it to move through her into expression. This seed pattern of her soul matured within her and ripened as the home of her heart. It was the dream of life through her, seeking to express itself in ever greater ways. In the fullness of time, this seed pattern became visible in the physical world.

It was Sabine's particular destiny to experience this home of her heart. That is why she was born dreaming of it.

We are all born dreaming of the seed pattern within our souls. The closer we draw to our soul, the clearer it becomes. It is the divine template within us for which we long. And we must follow that deep longing within our hearts, and nurture the seed until it blossoms in our lives.

Now, I would like to tell you the story of the dream that life dreamt through me.

# PART FIVE

# THE DEEPER STORY OF HOW I GOT HERE . . . TRANSFORMING TRAGEDY INTO GRACE

*The miracle is, the more I surrendered into the pure love,*
*the more tragedy turned to grace.*
*That's really how I got here.*

As soon as I walked onto the beach at Waikiki,
I asked a fellow tourist to take my picture

# 35 I Remember When I First Arrived in Waikiki . . .

***Everything was soft, soft . . . so very soft***

Everything was soft, so very soft . . . the air was soft . . . the white sand was soft . . . and when I stepped in the water, it too was soft—warm and inviting. So inviting that I wanted to take off my clothes right then and there!

The feeling of being part of nature this blissfully balmy was overwhelming. I belonged. I was part of this. It felt like I was floating in a balmy, loving breeze of well-being.

As soon as I walked on the beach at Waikiki, I asked a fellow tourist to take my picture. (After that message at the airport, wouldn't you?) I knew this was going to be an important time in my life, even though I didn't yet know why. And even though I hadn't had much sleep in the last thirty hours—I had been up all night preparing for this trip, and I hadn't slept on the flight—I still knew this would be a special photo.

The next morning, when my sister and I woke early to take a dawn walk through Waikiki, as we approached the beach, we saw people getting up from their night's slumber in the sand by the waves. Ten young men came out from the beach, and I even saw a young woman walk out with her quilt. These were people who had spent the night under the stars, on the sand at the ocean, just yards away from the big thoroughfare that ran through Waikiki. With its big, shiny upscale shopping area on the other side of the street, it would be similar to walking off a night's slumber on the beach and crossing onto Sixth Avenue in Manhattan. I was amazed that they felt safe sleeping there. But that's how the islands are—gentle, loving, nurturing. Later I learned that anyone can sleep along any beach in Hawaii. No one owns the beaches—not the resorts, not even the fancy homeowners.

At lunch that day, we stopped at a Waikiki institution—Hamburgers in Paradise—where they serve up "five-napkin burgers,"

burgers literally dripping with sauce, ketchup, and mustard. In this happiness, I noticed that my heart was open hugely. It felt so big. Something was happening. Something was carrying me along. And I was floating along with it . . . simply happy, relaxed, and at peace. Bliss.

This was new. So very different than what I had known for so many years before.

# 36 How Did I Get So Lucky?

***Especially after so many years of grief and tragedy***

Many people have told me that I got lucky. Yes, I got lucky, very lucky. Let me count the ways . . .

> To find a man with whom I feel complete.
>
> To find a partner after seventeen years . . . and in my mid-fifties.
>
> To fall in love so easily.
>
> To merge, heart and soul, from the very beginning . . . with no question that we would marry from our first hours together.
>
> To have it work so well together, so flowingly, ever since.

Yes, I got lucky.

> To be able to live in Hawaii, effortlessly, without ever seeking it.
>
> To be able to finally heal my body after years of devastating illness.
>
> To be able to write the many books that flow through me.

So very lucky.

> To wake each day to the joy of another sun-filled, glorious day . . . in paradise.
>
> To look so forward to each day, a precious day to grow and develop spiritually, building and refining, day upon day upon day.
>
> To anticipate so much these years and the fulfillment they will bring.
>
> To be able to live what is most important to me each day . . . doing spiritual practices, ever refining . . . in deep, pure nature . . . writing the many books I have been given to write . . . gardening . . . with my beloved husband David.

I could not have imagined that I could have all this.

Yet there was a time when my life was just the opposite. There was a time when my life was devastated. To share that story, I have to go back to when I was twenty-five, sometime in the mid-seventies, in a Chicago suburb.

# 37 The Deeper S When I Was Twen When My Soul Came Over and My Life Opened in Jo

***It began from a state of unknowing***

When I was twenty-five, my soul came over me.

In that year, my life went from "darkness to light," as the ancient Upanishad prayer petitions, "Lead us from darkness to light." I didn't know then that my life was dark—it was a normal life and apparently highly successful. I was living the life of all my peers, with a corporate career, a suburban commute, and a marriage that fit the picture. I simply was not conscious, not aware of myself as anything more than a personality functioning in the physical world.

I had always had many wonderful opportunities. I was born into a family in which I felt loved, and many doors to success and enjoyment had opened for me. Life was very easy for me. In fact, what life asked of me actually felt too simple, too boring.

More important than any of this, though, I was almost totally unknown to myself. I knew so little of myself that I didn't even have a real awareness of my feelings. I was living the formula life that was laid out for me, compliant and high-achieving.

But I was searching—for meaning, for value, for contribution. Since age eighteen, I had wanted to know the truth about life. And I wanted to find my true lifework. I had never been able to find exactly where I belonged in the world of work, yet my lifework was so important for me. None of the degrees at the university seemed to fit.

And deeper under all this, I was searching to know my true self. But that was unknown to me then. I spent my time unknown to myself, living my life from my conscious logical mind, telling myself what to be and what to do all the time. I was intensely demanding

l this constricted and limited me

omething began emerging within hing softer and kinder, something opening deep down inside. It was e, leading me, beckoning to me. ep longing within me. This longing e to express myself, to be who I truly ctured thinking of the world I lived in, with its obj shments, and striving for ever-greater outer success. It was something that instead softly and formlessly called to me, something that began quietly and ever so imperceptibly to open my heart to myself. It began to lead me in a new direction.

Something in me was getting ready to come to life. My soul was opening within me.

An authentic vision heralded my new life.

The windows on the commuter train to Chicago were dark the entire way into the loop because it was before dawn. The morning began as usual, with me sitting in a quiet seat on the train, studying sociology intensively, preparing for the Graduate Record Exam for graduate school.

The next thing I knew, I was staring at my face in the mirror of the dark train window, smiling a little smile of knowing, like the *Mona Lisa*. I had just emerged from an authentic vision. I had been transported to a different place, and I had returned, deeply satisfied and content.

In that vision, I had been in a lovely home, made of logs. Beautiful music flowed through the home. I was in a long lavender dress and pregnant. I was weaving a beautiful cloth on a loom. And there was a sense of pottery making in the background. It was lovely, enraptur-ing, and gently captivating.

It was something I had never known.

That vision, though lovely and enticing, was absolutely foreign to anything I had ever experienced. And yet, within the next two years, I would be living within that vision. The vision was accurate, both physically and symbolically. For I did live in a beautiful log home and did a bit of weaving and pottery making. The lavender dress and my pregnancy were symbols, representing the beginning of my spiritual work. The weaving was the beautiful artistry of rhythms that I perceive in life. And the music was the flow of spirit through it all.

In fact, when I actually lived in that setting, I wrote a poem called "Whole Cloth."

***Whole Cloth***

*My life weaves out like poetry,*
*first verses come unknowing.*
*And though I know not what will be,*
*the rhyme continues flowing.*
*As warp meets woof through metered time,*
*time's twinings scarce conceal*
*The patterned thread, the measured rhyme,*
*the meaning now revealed.*

Shortly after the vision, I met Sean, the man who would become my husband. My world burst open in joy! His touch in my life was so life-giving. How could I resist? It felt so healthy. I felt like a cat, wanting to bask in the warming sunshine of his love.

His love gave me the strength I needed to begin to pull myself out of my life of conformity and compliance, with its deep fear of criticism. When I asked him why he chose me, for he was a wise and wonderful seventeen years my senior, he answered, "Because I could see how hard you were trying to get out." He saw how painfully constricted I was within myself.

I had deeply mystic experiences of the unity of all life. In spontaneous ways, I entered the current of harmony that runs through all of life.

One lunchtime, I stepped out of the tall corporate building where I worked, onto the crowded streets of Chicago's Loop area at noon. But I did not step onto a busy street filled with pedestrians and cars, the glint and din of traffic, the smell of exhaust—I stepped into an experience of deep harmony, where every car and every pedestrian footstep was part of a great unfolding unity.

I was taken within the experience and enveloped in its slow unfolding harmony. I knew exactly where people would step, and where cars would move, and they did so as I watched. It was as if a secret, beautifully, perfectly choreographed symphony had been revealed in the motion of the day-to-day grind of living. Everything was unfolding with a grace far beyond what people comprehend or even dream.

I began to live on streams of my soul's grace. All the treasures of spirit held within my soul now opened within me.

A deep inner urge compelled me to take up many new things at this time. I began yoga and meditation, practices I had been wanting to do for the past several years. My dreams began to speak to me, prescient and deeply guiding. I taught myself to concentrate my mind, and soon was receiving intuitive information that I had never experienced before. I simply knew things that I had no logical, sensory way of knowing. I took college courses in counseling and learned to get in touch with my feelings and perceptions. I began doing pranayama, breath work. I aspired to be a psychic and, later, a healer. My feet were set firmly on the spiritual path.

I began to study an array of spiritual teachings that would grow and grow throughout my lifetime, as if the gates to a hitherto unknown universe had sprung open, and I walked among their riches. I played records of Gregorian chant and immediately dissolved into a clear channel, disappearing, being prayed through, effortlessly. I began to receive enormous flows of intuitive information and perceptive insight. I began to write these down, each one of them, and I have continued scribing them to this day.

At the same time, I began to receive information about people, and most especially, about the meaning and purpose of the experiences within my life. I was given a deep understanding of my spiritual life purpose. Such comfort and understanding! I sensed much deeper into the happenings of people around me, and the situations that we were involved in, and I soon began to be looked upon as someone to whom people could come for guidance and spiritual counsel.

I discovered my life's work in intuition and spirituality, and the rhythms that form our lives. No wonder I could not find my calling at the university.

I began to see light around people, and to be able to finish their sentences within my mind exactly as they would finish them, before the words came out of their mouth.

It made my life so easy. I felt that with these abilities, I could "slalom" through life; I wouldn't have to hit the posts on the course. I could ski around them in grace.

But I misunderstood. I was young. There was so much for me to evolve and become, so much balancing and clearing I would have to do. No amount of intuitive ability could prevent me from having to consciously learn the lessons my soul had chosen for me.

So in the short space of one miraculous year, my world was made new, turned upside down and inside out in the most wonderful way. I was living on inner streams of grace. I didn't know it at the time, but my soul had come over my personality. It would take me more years to be able to see it in this way. I simply knew that my whole life had changed. I had gone from night to day, darkness to light.

# 38 My Soul's Vision Came True . . .

## *And I lived the beauty it foretold*

When Sean and I first met, within our first hours of knowing each other, we decided to start a teaching ranch together, teaching psychology and spirituality somewhere in pristine nature. And so within two years of my vision, we had moved to Colorado, purchased that log home, and begun a new life together. Here, I experienced the unfoldment of the vision.

By the time I was thirty-two, I had everything I could want in life. I was married to a man I deeply loved, living on a forty-acre gentleman's ranch in Colorado, in a beautiful passive solar home that could have been in the pages of a fine homes magazine, on acres of pine, meadow, and foothills, where we gave cross-country ski parties in the snowy winters. We even had a small creek, part of the headwaters that contribute to Cherry Creek in Denver, exceptionally valuable in Colorado. I got to live like Thoreau in the woods, something I had dreamt of half my life, since age sixteen, when I first read *Walden*.

Our land was pure, and so sweet. I was so deeply rooted and at home there. I used to be able to hear a tone within the land as I approached it, driving home from the office. (Everything has subtle music, if we are subtle and still enough to perceive it.) Once, I went out and sat on a hill, wanting to get to know the land. I meditated on the land, asking it to speak. I received this flowing answer: "I was once a raging river, swirling in a sea of torment. Now my waters are the grasses." I ran to my husband and asked, "Hey, what do you think of that? Is it true?"

My husband, who was fixing fence posts, looked up from his work and said, "Well, we're living in what is called the Denver Basin. This entire area used to be under water at one time." Pointing, he said, "See those mesas all around? They were once islands, in the basin." Looking down, he said, "And look where I'm standing—I'm on an ancient sandbar."

And so it went. To live in the beauty and peace of Colorado meant everything to me. Walking in a Colorado pine forest, I felt in perfect harmony, and my guidance flowed through me like a knowing, sparkling clear mountain stream. My mind grew so still in meditation that if thought intruded, I knew it meant an unusual event would occur later in the day; its disturbance was already subtly perceptible.

I began my spiritual work alongside my corporate career, teaching people how to develop their inner guidance, and how to move in harmony with the rhythmic patterns of their lives. Though I excelled at my corporate career, it had always felt very meaningless to me. But my spiritual work filled me with joy. It gave me meaning and purpose. I loved to see my students' eyes light in delight with the discovery of the inner stream of knowing that flowed through them.

And so it went. I had absolutely everything I could have wished for. My only remaining desire was to do my spiritual work full time. The picture in my vision had been fulfilled.

But there was great learning ahead of me. Within a period of five years, this entire image of my life would be destroyed. Ruthlessly.

# 39 And Then That Beautiful Life Was Utterly Devastated

### *More tragedy than I can bear*

That pinnacle in my life was like a wave, rising to its crest, splashing up in one final triumphant crescendo. But then, waves crash. They shatter down suddenly, pounding deep into turbulent depths.

In the five years of my early thirties, I experienced so much tragedy that I began to understand what it was like to live through the bombing of Berlin in World War II.

I lost almost every living member of my family who was older than me—in five years. Almost every adult with whom I had grown up as family passed away. My dear father, who had been such a great dad, was gone suddenly to a massive heart attack; my grandmother, whom I loved so much, died gently in her sleep; and my uncle died from cancer, all within eight months. Then, my aunt and a dear great aunt passed away. And finally, in the fifth year, my mother was gone in an instant, shockingly. Six people I loved were gone, just like that. Only an uncle and aunt remained.

It felt so empty. The love that had once held me was gone . . . all those who made up my circle of family, my comfort, my belonging. The circle of people who sat around every wonderful Christmas table, and who laughed at every birthday celebration. My way of life was gone. It was staggering, shocking, and all too sudden. These were people who had never been sick, and now they were all gone. It was like a war had ravaged through my life. *Where was my family?* My siblings were all that remained.

And none of my siblings spoke about all this tragedy. For me, not being able to share and to grieve together was so painful. *No one to grieve with.* But one time, I heard a sister say, "That was before our family was decimated," in conversation, and I felt a bit of understanding from a family member.

Our income was devastated. My husband lost his high-salaried executive position and was without substantial work for many years afterward. *How would we cover our bills, especially our huge 15.75% mortgage?*

I was left, once again, to provide for all our needs on my own, this time twice my salary. I nearly exhausted myself working eighty-hour weeks, consulting alongside my corporate position, doubling my salary. *I was getting so tired; I knew I couldn't keep going like this.*

And so finally, our beautiful dream home was lost, the home in nature that I had dreamt of for half my life, and had worked toward for a quarter of my life. *Now where did we belong?*

I lost all of my savings, all I had worked for until that time, with the loss of that home. And with that, I lost my life dream of teaching from the ranch together. *What happened to the dream?*

I had to give up my spiritual teaching work, which filled me with joy. My increasing corporate responsibilities no longer allowed for that. *I thought my work was a spiritual work. How could I do my true work?* This didn't make any sense. I felt so confused.

*What was left?* It was like a war had ravaged through my life.

Finally, I had to give up living in Colorado, my joy, my home, the one place where I felt deeply rooted. And now, it too was gone. And so we returned to Chicago, financially-safe Chicago, cold and ugly to me.

With that, all my dreams were lost, gone. There was almost nothing left. My life felt shattered.

But there was more to lose. There was my marriage, my heart. No matter how hard I tried, it was slipping away.

I had always dreamt of sharing a lifework with a great man, and he was the man—brilliant, remarkably wise, phenomenally creative, deeply intuitive, and clairvoyant. I found him intensely fascinating. And handsome. Lady friends were always quietly telling me how incredibly handsome he was.

I could not imagine being with another man. From the moment we had met, I had known him. We shared memories of a distant past together, the scenes merging into a shared story of long-ago love. We were so perfectly fitted together.

Such laughter! Such joy. It was effortless and exciting. His sparkling blue eyes opened the sky for me, and his loving heart opened my life, freeing me to begin to be who I truly was.

Seventeen years my senior, he truly saw me and recognized me. It was the first time in my life that I had ever felt deeply understood. He brought me to life with his deep, keen perception of me, his constantly loving encouragement, his warm, magnanimous heart. And I so desperately wanted to come to life, to be free of my inner prison of repression. I basked in his love. It felt so healthy. It was the sun that allowed me to open the tight bud in which I held myself closed. What a gift.

I gave my whole heart to him.

When I met him at the major corporation where we worked, he had been there for twenty-one solid years. Two years later, just before we married and moved, he resigned. For the rest of our time together, he was never to hold a position steadily again. I provided for us for our entire marriage. Though he was brilliant and exceptionally capable, and even worked as a general manager at one of the largest privately-held Colorado corporations for eighteen months, he held only scattered employment for our entire marriage.

For many years, I consoled myself that his employment instability would surely end, this constant financial uncertainty that kept me so anxious would resolve, and I wouldn't have to work so very hard to pay all our bills alone. One day, I would be able to do my true lifework. He always told me it would be my turn next.

But twelve years into our marriage, my turn had never come. I was at bottom, living at a survival level emotionally, exhausted from pulling the load alone, heartsick of the empty promises. The one thing I knew for sure was that if I lived alone, I would at least have stability in my life. I had been reduced to such a desperate point that stability—emotional and financial—were more important to me than marriage.

Still, I didn't want my marriage to end. I loved him so. I had tried everything to save my marriage. I just wanted us to share our responsibilities equally. But he would not join me. I tried marriage counseling with him twice, but each time he left after the third session, while I continued on, growing stronger.

Finally, when I told him I wanted a divorce, he replied without hesitation, "You're right. I can't do this to you anymore."

How stunning.

And even then, when I signed the divorce petition, warm tears fell on the papers.

# 40 Everything Is Gone So Quickly . . . Now Where Do I Belong?

### *My body grows very cold*

My husband and I separated, pending the divorce. I fell into a year of darkness and depression. My entire life had turned dark, desperately dark. I felt like a widow. It was all black when I looked out—I could not imagine being with another man.

I felt bereft; everything that had sustained me was gone. I no longer had my spiritual teaching work, the work that gave my life meaning and purpose. My parents were gone, my brother had moved away. That left me with my two sisters, whose behavior felt so deeply hurtful to me that my counselor advised "divorcing" them. But instead, I chose to try to belong as family with them, attempting to create a loving relationship with them, allowing myself to be constantly, painfully hurt. They were my family and I loved them, I wanted to belong with them.

I was all alone.

I felt like I belonged nowhere. With no one. I felt lost. It was all dark. And my body was getting very cold, cold in a way I could not warm. I had times at the office when all my energy would just disappear, like my life force had drained out of me.

These were all signs that I was losing contact with my soul, which gave me warmth and vitality, and golden joy. Something in me was dying, deep down.

I couldn't receive the inner guidance that had always guided my life, and had given me such peace and understanding; it was too turbulent inside. There was no one to talk with, except my Colorado counselor at the other end of the phone line. I had no support from family. The only support I had was the love I was struggling to nurture for myself.

After two months of pain and darkness, I took a week's vacation into the mountains of Colorado. There in the mountain pine forest, for the first time in months, I was able to receive guidance about what had happened. Before that, I had been like a stunned animal, unable to hear my inner voice clearly. In the serenity of the mountains, I asked why this tragedy had to happen. Finally, I could hear an answer. It was only two words, but they spoke to my heart: "Something greater."

I kept going, at corporate jobs in Chicago that were intensely demanding, eighty hours of work a week. These were messy jobs, where either I established an entirely new corporate department, or resurrected substantially malfunctioning departments. My physical heart began to hurt from the burden of work. But I struggled on. I knew I was working so intensely to numb the deadening pain.

I had always had vibrant health until this time. In college, I'd been highly honored for my many contributions, and after college, I was always recognized for my outstanding corporate work, which I always did alongside one other demanding focus—studying sociology, teaching spirituality and offering spiritual counseling, or getting my MBA at Northwestern University. I was always impressed with people who had made major contributions, and I wanted to make a contribution. I loved to work and I loved to accomplish.

Now, once again, I was doing two jobs at once, this time at one new job. I had been hired to take over a department where I replaced two managers. This dropped an under-staffed department with fourteen direct reports right into my lap. We put out one large catalog a week, with screaming drop-dead deadlines. It was nothing to have three of my staffers queued up outside my office door, waiting for me to finish my phone call, another call blinking on hold, and a drop-dead deadline catalog cover on my desk. Intense. Dizzying.

In addition, I was studying for my MBA in Northwestern University's Kellogg School evening program, as well as dating, and working out. And I'd take vacations into Colorado whenever I could, to hike in summer, and ski in winter. Having lived in Colorado, I loved to ski.

I was on total output, without much coming in to me. After a year, I was lucky enough to meet a wonderful man named Joe. But I was losing my stamina; I would come home from work for an evening with Joe, and just sit and stare. My body felt wooden. My eyes had lost their light. In Traditional Chinese Medicine (TCM), these are all symptoms of liver problems. And in TCM, the liver houses the corporeal soul. Clearly, I was losing my conscious connection with my soul.

And I began to get sick. I had the flu four times that year, and when I visited my MD, he said it was just "bad luck." And this from a suburban doctor affiliated with the major hospital in the area. I now know that had he and I been more knowledgeable, we would have supported my immune system.

I kept getting a little worse and a little worse. I tried to help myself with as much rest as possible, reading about health, and taking supplements. I tried other medical doctors. I cut back on all my activities, focusing only on work. But nothing brought improvement. Instead, I kept picking up symptoms. By fall, I had acquired a cough I could not shake for months; I was constantly coughing. In TCM, the lungs relate to grief.

It became harder and harder to get to work. I used to sit on the commuter train at the station in the morning looking at the station sign that read, "Lisle, Illinois." And I would silently say, "Goodbye, Lisle." I knew that, somehow, I would not be taking the train much longer.

Inner guidance had spoken, "You will go through a gentle

transformation that will change your life entirely." Ah, the oh-so-ever-tactful words of my inner guidance.

And so began a downward spiral into terrible illness. I grew weak, terribly weak. Some days, I did not have the physical strength in the morning to get out of bed for work; I'd go in at noon. It became a major challenge just to walk the one mile from the train to my office every morning, carrying my attaché. Shooting pains would stab my right side, a place I was to later learn was my liver. Somehow I kept struggling on.

My symptoms kept increasing for over a year. None of the doctors I consulted could help me—they couldn't diagnose what was wrong with my body. I knew it might be chronic fatigue syndrome, but that would be horrible, I couldn't face that. I just kept going. Already very ill, I was not making good decisions.

No matter how much rest I got on the weekends, the terrible, painful weakness remained. Over time, I began to lose my ability to think clearly. Sometimes, my short term memory would just disappear, and I'd forget the names of my staff, people whom I had hired, trained, and worked with for over a year. I could not find the right words to say what I meant.

Finally one day at the office, I collapsed. I could go no further. My staff said my face looked green. My assistant had to bring me home, and all I could do was lie on the couch. My entire lower torso was trembling deep within. After I had rested a while, I tried to get up, but I discovered, to my horror, that I could no longer lift my body from the couch. I could no longer stand. How frightening. *What was happening to me?*

When Joe drove me to my appointment with a new MD, I slept all the way in the back seat. I was too weak to sit in the chair in the doctor's office. I had to sit on the floor, propped inside the corner walls for support, trembling with weakness. By this time, I had chronic fatigue syndrome at a very severe level.

If ever there was an inconsequential name for an extremely severe illness, it would be "chronic fatigue syndrome."[9] The name sounds innocuous, like you're feeling tired all the time. It also sounds whiney, like you're complaining. After all, in our adrenal-depleting society, almost everyone past forty feels tired. But chronic fatigue syndrome is something far worse—it is a severe, systemic illness that takes your entire life away.

My current MD, the one skillful enough to help me make a substantial recovery, considers chronic fatigue by far the most difficult illness she treats. The three illnesses she considers most difficult to treat and recover from are chronic fatigue syndrome, AIDS, and cancer—in that order.

The stage was set for that "gentle transformation" that would change my life entirely.

# 41 Yet There Was One Glimmer in the Enfolding Dark . . .

***I slipped into the Unity once again, and found myself within the hearts of everyone in the room***

Amidst all the pain and struggle of my increasing illness, I walked, unknowingly, into a deeply mystic experience. For a moment, I slipped again into the beautiful unity of love in which we are all held, unaware.

A few months before I came home ill, I was at my job and stole away at lunch to a little restaurant a block away for some peace and quiet during my lunch hour. As I walked, pains stabbed my right side again. I was really pretty miserable, but I needed some lunch.

The restaurant I chose was a little microbrewery called the Tap and Growler; it had the best food around. It was deep-toned and dark inside with brick walls, as I remember, a typically old neighborhood tavern, warm and encompassing. There were only a few other customers around, lunch was just getting underway.

I ordered my lunch and sat with my book, reading. It was just an ordinary moment in the midst of a busy day. After a while, I casually looked up as I took a breath and suddenly discovered that I was deep within the hearts of everyone in the room. I literally was fully within everyone's heart, at the same time. This was a far more expansive and deep experience of being with people than I had ever known. I was within each one of them, and understood each of one them, as if I had lived their entire life, felt their feelings, and looked through their eyes. All this knowing was held as if in a deep reservoir within me, and I could have offered each of them profound insights about their lives, had they asked.

With my next breath, my awareness pulsed out further, and I was now in the building, feeling it as if it were my body. I suddenly became aware of how old the structure was. It felt like it was about one hundred years old.[10] I sensed all that had happened here. I had never even noticed the building before when I came here for lunch.

One more breath, and I knew this consciousness was too great to be contained in my job as a catalog director. I knew I was going to grow into this way of being. This was about being with people in a much deeper and more meaningful way, a way close to the root of life.

It heralded something so much bigger than what I was living.

# 42 I Fall Deeply Ill

***And no one believes I will recover, not even my MD***

My life changed overnight. Before, I had easily shouldered the work of two people, and now I could barely support my body's own weight.

When my assistant drove me home from the office that day, I could not have imagined what lay ahead. I was to be bedridden for about four years, and largely housebound for many more, just barely functioning. I would recover enough to be able to live a half-life, and then I would get cancer. A woman would run into me with a big van, not watching where she was going, and I would have to go through major spinal surgery.

My early years with chronic fatigue syndrome (CFS) were devastating. I could barely lift my head off the pillow in the beginning. I could not sit or stand because I was literally too weak to support the weight of my own body. After the day I came home to stay, my first doctor's visit was conducted with me sitting on the floor in the corner, propped up by the two sides of the wall, shaking from the exertion. I lived my life from my bed or the living room couch, most often too weak to do anything but just lay there.

Chronic fatigue syndrome is a debilitating illness that is very complex, and complicated to treat. It is not well understood, even after decades of research. There is no cure. Most medical doctors do not understand how to treat it.

When CFS is as severe as mine was, it is fully debilitating and is recognized by the Center for Disease Control as being as disabling as other severely compromising illnesses, like multiple sclerosis, heart disease, or end-stage renal disease.

To add to the anguish, months and years of work to make small gains are often completely set back—with no ability to explain the cause.

Laura Hillenbrand, the marvelously talented author of *Seabiscuit* and *Unbroken*, has suffered with severe CFS for decades. She described the effects of taking a long car drive in a short article for the *New Yorker*. During the drive, she could sit. After the car drive, she was so severely set back that she could not move herself in bed or even speak for months. Experiences like this are very hard for most people to understand. But that is how it is with CFS.

Since mild exertion means extreme setback, it is much more difficult to recover from CFS if treatment is delayed. In my case, I shouldered an intense workload for twenty months before finding some form of treatment, and this likely brought on the extreme severity of my illness. Hauntingly, full recovery is not expected in such cases.

I remember a day, over seven years into this debilitating illness, when I was standing in the hallway of my medical doctor's office. An MD colleague was visiting in her office that day. I could hear him talking on the phone with another MD, not realizing I was near. He stated matter-of-factly, "You know that there is no recovery from CFS." It was chilling. I was simply not expected to recover.

In my first years, I could barely move from my bed. I could not even perform basic grooming a lot of the time.

Waking in the morning, at first I could not even lift my head from the pillow. Getting to the bathroom was a major challenge. I was so astoundingly, so profoundly weak. I would have to wait until I had enough strength. This would be a critical trip—one of the few times I would be able to get up today. I would need to grab my hairbrush, a glass of water, and brush my teeth in the short time I could stand. So as I lay there on my bed, waiting the necessary time for strength, I planned the sequence by which I would grab my most basic needs in the few short moments I could stand.

For many months, I could barely shower or bathe; doing so filled my body with pain. It was many months before I could sit in my stylist's chair to have my hair cut, and then my long hair was cut short so that it took no care. In the early years, I sometimes arrived for medical appointments in dirty clothing. I simply wasn't strong enough do the wash; I wasn't able to lift the bundle of clothes.

Most of the day in those early years, I could do nothing but sleep and rest. After a while, I recovered enough to be able to read in bed. I was lucky that I was able to read; many with severe chronic fatigue cannot. I read about seventy books that first year, book after book about CFS and health, recovering, healing, miracles.

It was devastating. My constant, unanswered question was, "How can I recover?" Nothing helped me recover. It was so scary. It felt so hopeless.

I collected miracle stories from my readings, put them in a notebook, and reviewed them to keep my hope alive. I collected tens of stories of miracles from history and biography. I kept searching for what would heal me. I needed a miracle. *What allowed healing to occur? How did spontaneous healings happen?*

One book in particular spoke to me, Niro Asistent Markoff's remarkable story of how she overcame AIDS, *Why I Survive AIDS.* This was before there was any treatment for AIDS, and a diagnosis of AIDS was a death sentence. Here was a woman who had actually overcome a horrific, incurable illness. How did she do it? Could I possibly hope something like that could happen for me? The bare, slender hope—*did I dare to hope?*—in the face of my body's devastation made me antsy, edgy, nervous. I could barely touch the hope. It was like reaching out to touch a hot stove—I'd touch it and pull back. I could barely face the hope. *Could I dare to hope that this illness that never got better could actually end?*

And yet I could not help trying, despite the despair. I kept a daily diary in my bed to mark my progress and to help me hope. Early entries read something like this: "Today, I could lift my head for five minutes." Day by day, little by little, I regained the capacity to hold my head up, and then to sit up. A doctor's homeopathic remedy enabled me to stand at times. But I was still desperately, profoundly, weak.

It would be years before I could reliably take short walks to the end of my block. In fact, I remember the accomplishment I felt at being able to walk up a small sidewalk incline that was barely noticeable to others. For years, I could not do it. I could not wear shoes and hope to have the strength to get up the stairs to bed.

I did not smile or laugh for two years; I did not have enough energy, and nothing was funny. I was living in pain. Talking on the phone, even for ten minutes, was exhausting, and it was all I could do in a day. A friend once asked, learning that all I could do was lie there, "Don't you get bored?" I told her that I didn't have enough life in me to get bored.

What does severe CFS feel like?

The short answer is, it feels like your entire life has been stolen away. Because there is nothing you can do on the physical level of life. It feels like constant failure, constant, unremitting failure to do even the simplest of things. In my case, I had experiences like resting hours until I was finally able to get the strength to go downstairs, stand to put pasta in a pan of water, and then quickly lie down on the couch . . . only to discover that I was no longer strong enough to get up to take the pasta out of the pan.

It feels like no life at all.

It feels like despair.

How do you describe weakness so profound, so penetrating, that it *hurts*? Deeper than bone-tired, this weakness was so profound that the slightest effort took everything I had. In the beginning, a day's goal might be writing a check, juicing carrots, or talking to someone for ten minutes on the phone. Energy was my most precious commodity, and the little increments that I got had to be budgeted extraordinarily carefully.

The illness felt like a very sick chartreuse, a malaise so encompassing, so debilitating, that I always felt worse than if I had a very bad flu, day after day after relentless day. It is so ugly to remember. I had constant nausea. I could rarely think clearly. I was crawling through my life.

I would start the day—waking up after a few scattered periods of sleep throughout the night, no more than two hours at a time (it takes energy to stay asleep)—feeling as if I had been hit by a truck, totally wiped out. It would take me hours to wake out of that. Sometimes, I would wake with pain and spasms in my lower abdomen. If I had those, I knew I would have to lie flat the entire day. Even in my fourth year, after one of these "wipe-out mornings," I would not be able to move much until mid-afternoon, and I wouldn't be able to be up at all that day. It took many years for the pains to subside.

Then another day would begin. Sick to my stomach, mind in a fog, so weak I could barely stand, pain in my abdomen, stronger pain in my legs, not sure if my mind was working well at all, I would come downstairs for breakfast. It might be noon or 2:00 p.m. before I could do this. The sunlight would sting my eyes, morning orange juice would give me an immediate, sharp headache, and I'd stand and get out my morning supplements and medicines. I'd have something to eat and then crawl back into bed for the day. As I said, I was crawling through my life.

I slept most of the day, but I always woke exhausted, never rested. My nerves burned, they were so compromised. My body was just a little bundle of severe weakness, barely able to function.

As I improved, I could sit for about an hour in the morning, a weak little bundle, sheltered in the corner of the couch. Then exhaustion would overtake me, and I'd go back to sleep, returning to bed for the day, rallying again in the evening for a bit. As I improved more, I began to meditate every morning and to do very gentle yoga, practices I had done for sixteen years.

I lived alone. Joe came every evening, though he did not stay with me through the night. And occasionally, someone would help me.

Joe was traveling abroad for business then, licensing technologies for a Fortune 50 corporation. One time, he had to go to Switzerland. He gave me the name of his hotel, in case I needed to call him. It had a name comprised of just two words like, "river" and "flower." I could not comprehend the name as he spoke it in English. We repeated it several times. I wrote it down for safekeeping and placed it on my nightstand. Even then, I kept confusing it, and when I looked for my note, I could not even find it. I literally could not retain the simple English translation of his hotel name.

I remember staring at my dresser from my bed, day after day, week after week, watching it accumulate dust, wondering, how will I ever dust it? The simple motion of moving my arms back and forth several times to do so was extremely exhausting. I could not do it.

Reading this, I imagine a caring reader asking brightly, "Well, why didn't you just have someone come in and clean?" But the reality was that I didn't have the mental capacity to think like that. I was too ill to ask for help or to organize help. And the people who were helping me spent their time getting the groceries, driving me to medical appointments, sitting with me. There was no time left for housekeeping. I don't even remember anyone talking with me about it.

Where before I had deftly shouldered enormous workloads, managing everything that came my way, now I could not figure out how to get the dresser dusted.

One thing everyone agrees with is that CFS is severe immune compromise. For over a decade, I wore turtlenecks constantly, day and night, even through the hot summer sun, to avoid any chill that might so easily devastate my feeble progress. Opening the refrigerator door, I would sneeze from the draft, a draft I had never even noticed before.

CFS affects the nervous system in many ways. In my case, my nerves were so raw that slight things made deep impressions. I remember my heart racing watching dramatic TV programs, something I had never experienced before. One time, while driving to my MD on the expressway, a truck kicked a small pebble up on the road. Ping! It hit my windshield. It was just a small, everyday thing, but for me with my shattered nerves, it was as if a grenade had gone off in front of me. I was shaken. I had to pull over to the shoulder to recover.

CFS makes nerves raw, and I was to learn that a strong, balanced nervous system equals emotional poise. In my case, with raw nerves, I had very little emotional poise. I cried very easily, became afraid, and didn't reason logically. I remember yelling at Joe for giving me Valentine's Day roses in an art gallery instead of in the privacy of my home. How I regret that. Raw nerves, shattered emotions, the terrible weakness, and the horrible, awful, unending burden of never being able to get better no matter what I did made me feel very depressed and sad. And under these emotions lay a very deep grief. My entire life had been lost.

All the ways I had known myself were gone. Where once I delighted in chasing my little niece and nephew around the house, whooping it up, roughhousing, tickling and teasing them, now they had to come to me where I lay, and I would hold them to me, teasing them by gently pinching around their ears, pretending I was a little mouse nibbling away.

CFS impairs circulation to the brain. My mind could not function. Sentences that were the least complex made my head hurt to follow them, and I could not follow them. Numbers were impossible; my mind went blank. I remember trying to figure out how to get my green bar paper into my printer, a task I did without even thinking before. Now, after trying for five minutes, I could not figure it out and had to let it go. Any math was out of the question; it would be seven years before I could do simple addition in my head again.

Looking out the window, I would get dizzy watching a bird fly by. The same thing would happen watching motion on TV. The sound of music was too much, and when I could accommodate to music, all I could do was listen to the same soothing melody over and over again.

Driving myself to my medical appointments, sometimes, I would not be able remember where I was on the expressway, though I attempted to keep reminding myself over and over what exits I had just passed, even slapping my face to help myself stay alert. When I arrived for acupuncture, checking my pulses, my acupuncturist would say that I had arrived only through sheer will; he could barely find my pulse, it was so faint. The session would begin with moxibustion to bring up my pulses enough that he could detect them.

As I improved a bit, I could take on grocery shopping myself—but just barely. The trip meant waiting for days, lying in bed, waiting to have the energy to make the two-mile trip by car to the local Jewel grocery store. It was a grueling ordeal. While grocery shopping, I would not be able to stand very long, so I would squat down on my knees, and pretend I was very carefully studying all the cans of beans on the lower shelf. Or I would lean up against a cold freezer case, and look like I was studying all those packaged chicken legs. I would have the bagger bag my groceries so that the cold items for the refrigerator were separated from the rest, because I would not be able to bring in all the bags.

After I had checked out, I would sit on the bench at the front of the store to recover. Then I would drive myself home and immediately lie down to recover from the ordeal. After about an hour, when I had a bit of strength, I could go out to the car and get the bag of groceries that belonged in the refrigerator. The others would have to wait a couple days until I had more strength.

I shopped this way for several years.

Even the simplest tasks were daunting, so daunting that I had nightmares about being able to do them. *Would I be able to get my bill paid tomorrow? How would I ever drive myself to my medical appointment?* I would have nightmares about not being able to make it to my medical appointments. And when I woke, I would be haunted with anxiety. *Would I be able to hold onto my home? Would I have enough money to pay for the medical care that I needed? How long would it take to get better? And, did I dare even dream of getting better?*

Days turned to weeks, months passed, and years slipped by. For the first years, the only way that I could see any bit of progress was by comparing my health year to year, not even season to season. And then I only saw the most minimal progress, for it was so easily set back. One time, early on, all of two years' faint progress was reversed in one month, inexplicably. No MD I saw knew how to help me.

In those years, I watched as people got heart attacks and recovered. People got cancer and recovered. My niece and nephew graduated from elementary school, and then junior high. And I still lay, desperately weak, on the couch and in my bed.

*Why couldn't I recover?* I was living a nightmare of debility. There was nothing left.

*Would I ever get better?*

# 43 I Fall to the Bottom of Despair . . .

***And nothing, absolutely nothing I try, works***

I got to know what it was like to have almost no life force in my body. It felt to me like what the moments before death must be like, when everything drains away. It was beyond weakness, such a subtle, thin state of breath and body, breath and body.

Many times, I felt like I was dying. In the early years, especially during the night, I had such strange sensations running through my body that I was often afraid I would die in the night. My body felt so very vulnerable, so strange then. And I was all alone, in the dark, afraid.

No one gave me much hope. My first MD told me later that he did not think I would make it. Though I had quality medical care weekly, there was very limited progress for the first seven years.

My life was gone.

Nothing worked. As hard as tried, I could not get better. After seven years, I was still very, very ill. Nothing I tried had really been effective enough to heal me in all that time.

And I had tried and tried and tried.

I did everything I could do to heal, on all levels—spiritual, psychological, energetic, and physical. Anyone who knows me knows that I put forth an enormous effort, do excellent work, and am highly productive. I get things done. After all, I had held profit-and-loss responsibility for a multi-million dollar corporation before. But very little was budging here.

And I tried everything. If there was any valid basis to believe that a therapy, a supplement, or a medical practitioner could help and was not risky, I tried it. From the first night I came home, I began working. That evening, I asked my friend Roger to go to the library for me and bring me books on CFS. I began reading them that very night.

From that night on, there followed a mountain of effort.

On the physical level, I had almost weekly appointments with medical doctors for many years, and weekly appointments with acupuncturists for over twelve years. I consulted medical specialists in CFS at university hospitals in Chicago and two nationally-recognized CFS experts in other states. I had such high hopes for one of these experts, an MD who had written several books on CFS, but his many medicines did nothing for me. I made no improvement with him. It was very disappointing.

In addition to medical doctors, I also saw many varied complementary health care providers, who provided everything from electrodermal testing and live blood analysis to auricular therapy, deep tissue massage, and many different forms of body and energy work. I don't even want to tell you the number of healthcare providers I saw, the number is so high.

I researched and studied all the information about CFS I could find, at least two hundred books and articles on health and healing. I used three medical models—Western medicine, homeopathy, and Traditional Chinese Medicine—to gain as big a view as possible.

I ate an exceptionally clean and careful diet, drank the purest water I could find, followed many various healing diets—vegetarian, Ayurvedic, food combining, candida, wheat-free, low-fat, allergy-free, blood type. Any possible toxic substance was avoided. My mercury fillings were replaced. I went for years without honey or sugar in any form.

There were supplements too numerous to mention, and fascinatingly exotic and earthy-smelling Chinese herbs from Chinatown that I cooked in a pot, making an herb soup that tasted like healing strength. I juiced vegetables. In my attempt to get a decent night's sleep alone, I must have tried at least forty different practices and supplements. I did practices to rebuild immunity, like regular moxibustion, a Traditional Chinese Medicine practice of burning mugwort on meridian channels to build blood and chi.

On the energetic level, I did yogic breathwork, pranayama . . . studied and practiced chi gong with three different teachers . . . took Tai Chi several times. I studied energy healing with Rosalyn Bruyere, a remarkably masterful healer and, in my experience, the finest energy healer in the country. I trained in her method of energy work. I received energy work from one of her advanced students.

As I got stronger, I could do yoga again, a practice I had previously done for sixteen years. I took advanced yoga classes. I tried to walk in the morning sun, though it was very difficult to be up that early, and whenever I could, I walked by large bodies of water to pick up energy.

I kept a careful diary and monitored my health, trying to find the correlates that would help me to recover. I had managed almost all the functions of a direct marketing business before, and I was now pressing those same skills into the task of my recovery.

On the psychological level, I received counseling and studied psychological counseling further in college classes. I changed many psychological patterns. I completed training in Hakomi, a body-centered therapy especially successful in work with the subconscious.

On the spiritual level, I tried to understand the purpose of the illness in my life. What was I to learn? As I strengthened, I once again began meditating every single morning, another practice I had done daily for sixteen years. I prayed and hoped, affirmed and visualized. I continued to do my own intuitive readings and dreamwork, as I had for decades. I worked with past lives. I consulted other intuitives and medical intuitives.

I read many spiritual texts, ancient and contemporary. I studied the practices and life views of people who had recovered from major illness and CFS to try to understand what enabled recovery from devastating illness. I wanted to learn the answer to my one constant question: *What makes a miracle?*

I kept searching for what would heal me. I needed a miracle.

*What allowed healing to occur? How did spontaneous healings happen?*

There were so many more things I did that it would fill a small book of its own.

Many of these efforts led to limited improvement. Yet even the gains I had achieved could be so easily lost in a setback. Long hoped-for, prayed-for, worked-for progress would be dashed so easily, and with it my hope. Even after six years of being home, I was set back so severely one January that I was fully bedridden and could not drive for almost a month. It took three months to stabilize.

After seven years had passed, my body still could not function reliably. I was still very weak and unsteady, and easily overcome by debility. I could not reliably sit at my computer or show up for scheduled activity beyond medical appointments. I was writing from my bed, and I had begun to teach intuition again, but I was doing it all in the constantly weak, nauseous, flu-like state that is CFS. Needless to say, I had no social life beyond my boyfriend's visits and occasional time with my family. Taken all together, all this effort, after seven years, had enabled me to make about a 10–30 percent improvement, depending on the day.

It appeared that the illness would not let me heal. And I had tried from every ounce of me to let it go.

During this time, I read a true story about a man who actually walked out of quicksand, which is impossible. He observed that as he walked in the quicksand, there was a moment in his step when he lifted a bit from the mire. By repeating this small part of his step, he gradually walked out of the entire bog and rescued himself.

Another man, thrown overboard with other passengers into the cold Atlantic at night when their ship sank, managed to survive the entire night in the water, an amazing feat. He did it by managing his breathing, slow and steady, slow and steady, all through the night. In the morning, he was the only one alive; everyone else had perished.

Surely, I thought, we can walk out of impossible mires, one tiny little step at a time, one slow and steady breath at a time. Surely, there must be a way.

I realized, within my first few months, that surrender seemed to hold an important key. Give everything over to God, and let the power flow through you.

And so I surrendered.

I created a practice of surrender. Every morning, as I lay there, I would practice surrender—first, surrendering everything on the physical level to God—my body, my home, my money, all my possessions. Then, all my relationships, all I loved. Then, all my hopes and dreams, my world views, my pictures of myself. I surrendered everything I had.

I cried and cried and cried the first two years.

I reviewed my entire life. I couldn't help it; it just flowed before my eyes as I lay there, day after day. It seemed that my whole life had come to nothing. What had I really accomplished in all my years? It felt to me like I had not been able to achieve anything. My books were still not written, and now, I had no life.

Would I never be well?

*What remains, after all those tears?* So much washed away in those tears, in those years. What was left? It certainly was not "me" as I had known me.

It felt to me like I was living a very great failure. It stung. I had always valued myself so much for what I could accomplish and contribute, and now, all that had been ripped from me. It hurt horribly. I felt stripped.

The physical world no longer worked for me. Clearly, I would have to find another way of living and of valuing myself.

One night, early on in the illness, as I was leaving the Jewel grocery store, I distinctly remember asking myself who I was now, now that

I could do nothing. I had been such a high flyer before I got sick. I had always handily done the work of two people, and that effortless capacity was something I had taken for granted.

Now this evening as I was leaving the grocery store, I reflected on the interview I had just seen of John Templeton on *Wall Street Week.* I so admired his accomplishments and integrity. I had been a great accomplisher all my life. *Who was I now, now that I could accomplish nothing?* I understood as I asked the question that I would now have to focus on being, since I no longer had a chance at doing.

But later that evening, lying on the couch, I had a remarkable awareness. I realized that even though I spent every day lying down at that time, too ill to stand, I was actually living my life ideals more fully and consistently than I had been when I was a high-charging executive with a large staff and a sixty-hour work week, studying for my MBA at Northwestern University, dating, and working out.

My life ideals had always been inner guidance, love in action, and helping people to understand themselves and their lives. I was surprised to realize that I was actually living each of these ideals more fully from my bed than I had been when I could stand.

I was learning that the truest part of me—my soul and spirit—was always able. I was learning that I could *always* live my ideals, the very most important part of my life, the part that endured. I was never limited by any circumstance.

I could always grow in my capacity to embody enduring spiritual qualities.

I was beginning to learn to move from my soul—without regard for my body—without regard for any of the limits that the physical level of life seemed to impose. I was beginning to experience that I was far more than a body, and that I—the eternal me—was not limited by that body. My creative mind and will, my soul and the infinite, ever-creating spirit that coursed through me—these were far greater than any body.

This was not failing. This was succeeding, in the biggest way possible. I could always be what I truly was. I could always be love. I could always be peace. I could always be mercy. I could always be all the beautiful qualities of God, the qualities that give life, at every moment and in every way.

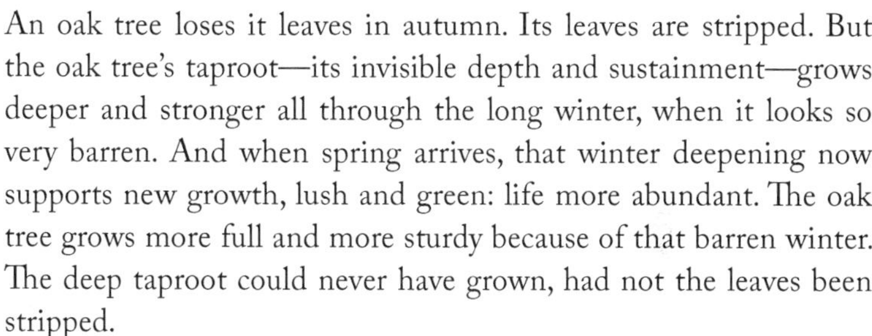

An oak tree loses it leaves in autumn. Its leaves are stripped. But the oak tree's taproot—its invisible depth and sustainment—grows deeper and stronger all through the long winter, when it looks so very barren. And when spring arrives, that winter deepening now supports new growth, lush and green: life more abundant. The oak tree grows more full and more sturdy because of that barren winter. The deep taproot could never have grown, had not the leaves been stripped.

Yes, I was stripped of all the ways I had known and cherished myself. But stripping also means to make bare, to clear. A way was being cleared.

I was living a process very important to soul growth. I realized a great truth. When we are at our very lowest, what is greatest can rise within us. Our moments of greatest pain hold the seeds of our greatest progress.

Later, I would see this process more clearly in many lives. I remember reading Tolstoy's *Confessions* in which he chronicles the story of his life. All through his life, until his early forties, he enjoyed remarkable success, with every possible privilege that fame and fortune could bestow upon him. In his world, there was no God, no room for anything but his pleasure and his will. Then he fell into a great three-year depression. Nothing in his life held meaning anymore. Waves crest, and then they crash. Tolstoy almost took his life.

But light began to open within him. Gradually, this dawning inner light led him to realize that there was a higher power. God did exist. He saw that others needed his caring. This was all that mattered anymore. He left his life of privileged wealth and status, and began living to help the peasants.

He became the Tolstoy who inspired Gandhi.

I did not realize it at the time, but I was actually beginning to learn to live in a very great surrender. It was a surrender far beyond my conscious attempts to surrender in my morning practice. It was a surrender that was simply moving through me, as the edges of my personality kept getting lopped off and polished in the tumble of my life, the way a rough, little stone is smoothed in the waves of one great ocean.

I was very gradually, day by day, learning to *be* surrender. It was such a pervasive condition that I didn't even notice. It was my only option. And I struggled against it many, many times. But there was no other choice.

I was living a very important truth that would take me years to recognize fully. Surrender was the answer to my entire life.

It was still very painful emotionally. Every day presented limit after limit, so many things I could not do that I had done so effortlessly before. Many times, I just simply despaired, tormented by yet again another setback which defied explanation. Everything I did failed, and failed, and failed again.

It felt abysmally hopeless.

Into this hopelessness, I prayed. No matter how despairing I felt, I would not give up. I could not give up. I prayed so deeply—praying, praying, praying. In my early years, I spent most of my time praying: praying constantly for help and release from this horrible situation, and once again, not really improving, praying though no one really believed I would recover, not even my medical doctor at that time.

I prayed to God, my angels, my higher self. A Protestant, I got down on my knees and prayed to beloved mother Mary. I did Catholic novenas to the saints. Constant prayers. I asked for prayer from my church and spiritual groups. Praying and praying, and then praying again. Constant prayers in a sea of despair, tossing in tumult and storm.

Gradually, the storm within me quieted. My prayers moved from active pleas to the presence of my deep spiritual heart. The words became fewer. I came to realize that the more I trusted, the less words I used in prayer. Finally, the words ceased. And I just prayed as a state of being, being in the unity and peace within my spiritual heart—a living prayer of trust.

My prayers expanded, and gradually, I began to learn to pray with my actions. Eventually, I would learn how to pray ceaselessly.

I prayed for many, many people and began to see in my prayer, the outcome to their situation. Joan, my former sister-in-law, suffered a heart attack so massive it left her in a coma; she was expected to die. Praying for her, in inner light, I saw her eyes open. I told my family the unbelievable news. Joan lived. It was a miracle.

Joe prayed so deeply for me that a new form of prayer emerged within him. Normally, when he prayed for me, he saw me as a physical form. But this time, light appeared all around him and within him, and he saw me only as white-blue light. He was no longer actor in his prayer but observer, his prayer praying him as he remained deeply absorbed in this state. A great peace came over him and with it a great knowing, and when he emerged, he knew that I would be healed.

Joe was the only one who believed that I would be healed.

Arthur Ashe, a man of great inner elegance and dignity, and one of the greatest tennis players of all time, contracted AIDS from a blood transfusion in 1983, when AIDS meant certain death. In his final book, *Days of Grace*, he describes praying with his wife. He did not pray for healing. He prayed instead for God to show him His will and to give him the strength to carry out His will.

Andrea Bocelli, the exquisitely gifted Italian tenor, was born with congenital glaucoma and knew from his earliest years that he would gradually lose his sight. By age twelve, the last light went out of his eyes, and he was blind. A few years later, a group of friends took him to Lourdes to pray and heal in the miracle waters. But Andrea did not pray for healing. He prayed instead for serenity. We hear it in his clear, uplifted voice.

Some days, I prayed so much that my days lying in bed were nothing but breath and prayer, breath and prayer.

My life had distilled down to breath and prayer, breath and prayer.

A very definition of surrender.

# 44 What Enables Healing from Such Desperate Illness?

***The question haunted me***

The answer was like some hidden key that could give me back my entire life.

I read a true story in *People* magazine about a remarkable miracle. A man whose condition was absolutely hopeless, who was days from death, walked out of the hospital a healed man.

It fascinated me. This man was older, in his fifties or sixties. He had come to the hospital to die. For years, he had fought a rare and debilitating form of cancer, and now the battle was over, mercifully. As he lay in his hospital bed one night, with death approaching, he was suddenly moved to sing a temple song from his childhood, "Hear, O Israel: the Lord our God, the Lord is one."[11] It is the prayer that Jews say at death.

As he sang, he was absorbed in warming light. The next thing he knew, he was being lifted up and out of his body. From above, he looked down upon his body, and as he did so, he understood that his body was being fully healed, made new. A few moments later, he was returned to his body. Now back inside his body, he realized that his body was fully healed. He rose from his deathbed and went home, a healed man.

How did that miracle of healing happen? Could it happen for me?

From a wise counselor came the answer: his healing came because he had surrendered. Surrender and humility heal. She advised me to surrender into the illness. I said I had already done that, and it hadn't worked. She told me to surrender into surrender itself.

And so this became the second way that I practiced surrender. I surrendered into surrender itself.

I learned a great deal through this exercise. I learned that surrender is not giving up, or giving in. Surrender is giving over.

Consider for a moment the postures of each of those expressions—giving up, giving in, and giving over.

What is the posture of giving up? For me, it looks like this: my hands go up, my head goes down, and I feel defeated. What is the posture of giving in? My head goes down, I shuffle my feet, mumble a few words, like "Oh, all right . . . ," and sort of disappear. I feel very small.

But giving over? What is that posture? I suddenly rise up along my spine, lifted into something higher. I am raised. My arms spontaneously extend gracefully from my chest, smoothly, slowly, as if they are extending something held within them. My palms are open. I raise my arms and what they hold slowly higher, until they extend out, higher than my head. I feel something reverent in this posture. In this giving over, I feel lifted up inside, into some higher grace. I am giving, and at the same time, I am made hollow for grace. And then I move higher within me. I somehow feel transcendent, sacred. I have become part of something greater.

This is the act of surrender. It is a sacred giving over into something greater. It allows us to release what was not ours, anyway. It allows what is true to flow through us, and move us into some greater action. We begin to move with some greater harmony. I feel a subtle hope and strength. I feel it will be okay.

Moments before, I was so weak. I was alone. Now I am part of something that shimmers . . . something that is Good, and right.

It is very important to stand like this with illness. We don't fight it; we surrender it to something higher. This takes it out of duality, and into unity with the great love. This alone is healing.

Now contrast this with fighting the illness. What is the posture of that? Locked in combat, anxious, adrenaline flowing. Jammed. And all jammed up. I'm afraid and tense and all wound up. There are two of us here, a duality—me, the one that could win, and me, the one that could lose.

When we "fight" against our illness, we defeat ourselves. For it is ourselves we are fighting. When we fight against an illness, we are really afraid that we won't make it. Isn't that true? Else, why would we be fighting?

So if we saw this as fighting against a part of ourselves that does not trust, then doesn't the "battle" become easier? In fact, isn't it even gone? Can you trust yourself to trust your life and where it takes you? Can you trust yourself that you are more than this body in which you see yourself failing? Can you do that? Inside you, you know that this is true. Can you be truthful with yourself, and say that no matter what happens, I'll be okay? It may not be the way I'd like it to look, but I'll be okay.

When we do that, an enormous power rushes in. A healing power. And we trust that it moves us to where we need to be this moment. This is about love. This is about healing mercy. We let the healing happen in the way the harmony unfolds it. We let ourselves be given to something greater.

We let ourselves be hollowed within, made into some sort of vessel, some holy vessel. This holy vessel allows grace to flow through us. And now our body, so sick and frail, has become a temple of the living God.

# 45 But All Was Not Lost . . . I Got the Opportunity to Study with a Great Spiritual Teacher

***From the bottom of despair, a new life forms through me***

But all was not lost. Indeed, not. I got the opportunity to study with a great spiritual teacher. The illness.

Yes, the very same illness that so tormented me. Because this torment was so relentless, so unyielding against my best effort, that I was pushed constantly deeper and deeper into my own inner resources. And I found that my inner resources grew greater with each outer restriction.

I was not going to have a life until I healed this relentless, catastrophic illness. And so, though I have portrayed the illness in all its misery, such a despairing view is only one way of telling the story.

As I lay in bed questioning what I did to get myself into this situation, I could not find anything that in combination seemed to add up to the enormity of such a horrendous illness. In fact, the only way I could answer the haunting question "why?" was that this was meant for a very deep healing.

This healing was deeper than the psychological level, where limiting personality patterns are recognized and released, and an individual successfully integrates their personality, and adjusts to their life situation.

This was soul healing. It was going to bring me into direct contact with the divine within as a living experience, a living reality. It would lead me to the Living Unity, the very life spring within my spiritual heart and soul, a living presence at once deeper, higher and bigger, purer and truer than anything else. One, without another. It would bring me a great, great gift—the way to be constantly held within the pure love and truth, the living presence of the Unity, regardless of what was going on around me.[12]

It was transforming the patterns of lifetimes held within my soul, so that I could cross to a new way of being, with expanded capacities. It would move me from personality to presence, from doing to being, from physical form to spiritual essence, from personal willing to open surrender, from inner struggle to an abiding inner harmony. It would heal my very broken heart, and with that, my very broken body.

It would totally transform my life, cleanse it, and right it on even truer foundations. It was going to root me deeper, raise me higher, and expand me into more than I had ever known.

It was that Big.

No matter how devastated my life, I would have to create a life of meaning and joy. No matter how despairing my circumstances, I would have to create with them. We always have the opportunity to create with what we are given. Nothing stops us from creating. We *must* create. It is the imperative of life.

Nature is always creating from what it is given—a dead stump, a rotten animal, a discarded plant. No matter how distasteful the waste is to our eyes, to nature, it is useful, beneficial. It is *Good.* In fact, what is least—the rotting, the aged, the discarded—is most useful, for it creates the very substance from which new life emerges: soil. Ultimately, soil sustains all life—every living being. It is the very ground of our existence. And it is formed of what appears useless.

Nature is always creating. Nothing is wasted.

When we learn to truly create, everything has value.

As we learn to work in harmony with the creative forces that give life, we find everything alive with meaning, purpose, and belonging. Everything has value to a Creator.

And so I would have to take this despairing, hopeless situation and create from it new substance for my life. A new earth. A heaven. I was beginning to learn how to create a heaven on earth, only just beginning.

I created a little saying at this time that I call "God's Arithmetic."

### *God's Arithmetic*

*+ We ask for more*
*– We are given less*
*The difference is soul growth*

In my case, I asked to heal, and I was given less. So I had to grow from my soul.

And so though these years were devastated on the physical level, on the inner level, they were extremely rich with spiritual growth and awareness. Life continued on. I was growing and progressing by leaps and bounds from my bed.

For it was not really the illness that was the great teacher. It was my soul. The soul is the great spiritual teacher. It is always teaching us how to create, no matter what our circumstances.

And the soul, like nature, will use whatever is present to teach us. In my case, it was great illness. From what appears least, and most unwanted, lifeless and useless, springs forth substance to create new life.

The soul is inner light, and as we grow spiritually, this inner light imbues our personality, guiding us to ever greater capacities for aliveness. This is what was happening to me, and later, I was to express it like this:

***The Sun that Shines Above Us Also Shines Within Us***

*There are times when our soul's light opens forth*
*and encompasses us in its golden streams,*
*and we blossom anew.*

*And there are times of dark,*
*when we must make our own light,*
*if we are to find our way.*

*This is the soul's way of guiding our conscious selves*
*so that we may grow in light.*
*It is all done in the infinite mercy of the divine,*
*as it reaches from spirit through soul to our conscious awareness.*

*And it is precisely in this dark, this silent, this still,*
*that greatest inner light is born.*

*The sun that shines above us also shines within us.*

*We must awaken to its dawn within us,*
*and travel its orb through our lives.*

*Then, we are inspired.*
*Then, we are true.*

The physical debility of the illness was accompanied by a deepening spiritual joy and wonder. I had many experiences of the subtle realms beyond everyday awareness. These sustained me.

While I know not to discuss experiences of siddhis, spiritual powers, because they distract from the core teachings and practices, I will share some experiences here because of the wonder they inspire in others, and the truths they reveal. They also make a happy counterpoint after the story of oppressive debility. It is very important to remember that as rapturous as these experiences were, a deeper grounding in practical spirituality was also forming within me, enabling me to live more and more fully from essence in my daily life. This is the true goal, not the spiritual powers.

In my early years, my life force ebbed so low that I was often much closer to the other side than I was to physical life. Many times, my conscious awareness could not go beyond the edge of my bed. My bed became an island on which I floated, and everything else disappeared.

In this state, the inner world and the other side became far more alive for me than my usual limited world of bedroom, kitchen, bath, TV, and books.

This is something that happens as we near death. Those who have sat at the bedside of a loved one as they make their transition will recognize this, for the dying person starts to recognize loved ones who have crossed over and talks with them, or reports visions from the other side.

I would hang in this state for several days, or even a week. The world beyond the physical is exquisitely beautiful. It has a rapturous quality that touches so fully and deeply within that it transforms—within moments.

In Carl Jung's autobiography, *Memories, Dreams, Reflections*, he describes his experience after a heart attack at age sixty-eight. For weeks, he floated between life and death. During this time, he had a series of visions that filled him with "a state of purest bliss" and "the highest possible feeling of happiness." He felt it was ecstasy, eternal bliss. As he recovered, he lost his visions, leaving him deeply disappointed and depressed to have to return to normal life, which now felt to him like a drab prison compared to his nights of enchanting visions. Yet the inspiration remained; he went on to do what he felt was his best work. The deeper taproot had been activated.[13]

In my case, I had many experiences of the other side as I lay on the island cloud of my bed. These were rapturous openings into a reality so exquisitely beautiful that its radiance outshines anything else.

One time, I had driven to my MD's office and was so weak I could not drive home. This was not uncommon in the first years. In those years, though I was barely able to be out of bed, if it was the least bit possible, I insisted that I drive myself to most of my MD appointments; I needed to show myself that I could at least do something. It was a huge strain on my body, and I had to sleep for several hours in an unused room at my MD's office to get enough strength to drive home.

When I did finally get home from the enormity of my trip, I was so flattened that my bed once again became an island cloud on which I floated.

This particular night, my body felt so scarily strange again that I was afraid I would die in the night. But I fell off to sleep. A few hours later, in the middle of the night, I awoke to see three beings formed of white light above my bed. They were working in beautiful rhythms of white light above my body. Their arms were like veils of light, flowing with their movements.

They were healing my body!

As they worked, they sang the most exquisite, otherworldly melody. I knew the melody was being given to me to sing during the day, to help me heal. Their song reached very deep within me. It was as if their song was part of me, being called to life through their beautiful melody.

Throughout my illness, I was given many heavenly, angelic

healing songs in the night. I was to sing these during the day. These songs were exquisitely beautiful, and transported me to a different realm. They were unlike music that we hear on earth. These melodies penetrated very deeply into my being, and had the effect of lifting me up, and out of the illness, into another realm.

These angelic beings filled me with joy and hope. I felt loved.

And that was so important in my cold and ugly, lonely illness.

I saw divine and exquisite auras, far beyond anything I have heard anyone describe. These were rapturous experiences that, once again, transported me to another realm.

As with all the other experiences, it happened without effort. It was simply there.

I wanted to go to see Betty Riley speak. Betty is a particularly gifted clairvoyant, who was lecturing on auras at Unity Church of Oak Park. Betty is particularly skilled at seeing the human energy field. But that afternoon, I was absolutely too weak, and there was no way I could go. So I asked my neighbor Lynne if she would like to go with me, and with that short notice, she graciously drove us. This took a bit of time, so we arrived late and took our place in the back row of the very large auditorium filled with several hundred people.

Betty spent her first hour telling us what the colors of the human energy field mean, assigning one quality to each color. She explained that yellow meant creativity, and green healing, and on through a basic seven-chakra-pack of Crayola crayon colors. She was simplifying for her students; aura colors are actually far more varied and exquisite.

Then it came time in the lecture for Betty to ask us to try to see auras. She placed a white background on stage and invited a few people up, one at a time, to stand in front of it while those of us in the audience studied their fields.

Pretty soon, people were calling out, "I see yellow!" "Green!"

Responding to each of these individuals, Betty requested that they interpret the meanings of the colors. The answers came back, predictably, "Creativity!" "Healing!" just as she had taught in the previous hour.

But I was having a completely different experience. I saw the auras exquisitely. I saw them in what seemed to me to be divine archetypal form, of exquisite colors in light that took on divinely articulated shapes, and I knew what they meant as I saw them. I was shy of standing out, and I thought that no one I knew was in the audience, so I felt free to speak from the back of the room. Otherwise, I would not have given voice to my experience.

So I spoke out, interpreting the colors in their diverse, specific meanings. It felt like I was bird, gliding on an effortless air current, for I had entered a different state of being, a state of perfect harmony, where things were simply made visible, their meanings clear.

The colors of the human aura are like colors of sunset—lit from within, lit with the light of God. When the person is evolved, or when the field is perceived in its divinity, the colors are clear and breathtakingly beautiful. The aura can be perceived at different levels of vibration, each holding different levels of information.

This day, what so stunned me was that I was perceiving auras at the level of divinity. I had seen them since my mid-twenties but in very rudimentary ways. Now they were vastly more. They were exquisitely articulated masterpieces in light. And they told stories.

For example, one woman stood in an arch of exquisite shape above her head. The arch was at least four feet above her, and it encompassed her. It had a very defined, articulated shape, and it was a melding of colors of exquisite light-imbued gold and peach.

It is truly impossible to describe this divine artwork. It is absolutely captivating and fills me with awe, and an overwhelming sense of beauty. When we perceive auras at this elevated vibrational level, we see that individuals are truly divine, and that we have so much divine capacity within us that it is a crime against life to besmirch that divinity with behavior that is less than harmonious and loving.

I went on to perceive several other auras at this level. I had never seen auras at this refined level before, and after it was over, I was stunned. It was a real breakthrough into a different way of knowing others and myself. It was shocking—such a breakthrough to a heightened, expanded way of seeing and being, that I began to cry from a very deep place within me.

And to my surprise, there were people I knew in the audience. They came up to me and said how surprised and amazed they were at my ability to read people's fields. They wanted to know how I did it.

I told them that believed it happened because there was very little of me left at that point. My life had distilled down to breath and prayer, which allowed something greater to express through me.

One morning, I was blessed to wake with the early dawn and hear the angels singing. They were blessing the dawn and the new day, singing a benediction. They sang, "We behold Aurora . . . ," and as they sang, the chorus rose, encompassing more voices, and still more voices, and more voices. I became aware of ranks upon ranks of angels thronging to welcome the dawn.

As they sang, I understood that the angels bless every dawning. They benedict it.

What I experienced was like the exquisitely beautiful engraving by Gustav Dore in which small gatherings of angels gracefully cascade down to earth, forming a gently spiraling path made of angels, while the spiral extends so far heavenward that it appears to ascend into infinity.

When I was forty-four, I had an experience of the ecstatic heart. I awoke on Palm Sunday in an ecstasy of the heart. I was flying through my heart. My steps had taken light, as if I were levitating slightly.

It was an experience for which I could find companionship only in Evelyn Underhill's book *Mysticism* in which she describes states of ecstasy and rapture. My acupuncturist, who read my pulses the next day, said that my heart was flying.

These events all felt so familiar that it seemed they were not new capacities so much as the deepening of abilities already held within my soul.

All through the illness, my intuitive voice always flowed, regardless of my dull left brain. That was very interesting to me because it suggested that the intuitive mind is quite definitely the "higher" mind, if it can function when the physical aspects of the brain, like those impaired by CFS, don't allow the logical mind to function accurately. It is similar to reports of near death experiences when the body and brain are dead, but the individual remains fully aware.

I lived in the deep knowing, with the capacity to utter words of such deep truth and meaning for people that it changed their lives . . . in one profound sentence. Through this extraordinary illness, I developed the capacity to touch deep within people's souls, reaching into the innermost alive part of them, bringing it up so that they could see what was truly moving their lives.

Since my early thirties, I had given readings that people found very helpful. They spoke to personality and heart. They were touching, they were meaningful. But now they moved much deeper.

Now, the ability to see deeply into souls opened, and I immediately understood what people were working on in this lifetime and in what I call their life stream, the stream of lives that is focused upon mastering a quality of being. I could see purpose and pattern in their life and help them understand how their difficulties were helping them to release into something greater.

From that leverage point, I could help them to leave behind the limitations they had adopted as their definition of self. We were not going to be bluffed by something less than who and what we truly were.

What I learned from my experience as a spiritual counselor is that when we work with someone from the level of the mind, they get insights. *Aha! I never realized that.* When we work with someone from the level of the deep heart, they are deeply touched . . . moved.

Something deep and true is struck, and becomes a reference point in their life from that point on. But when we work with someone from the level of the soul, they are moved into a different reality within themselves—a new grounding and a higher inspiration begin to move through them, and animate them. It continues to reverberate within them and reorients their entire life. And it can happen in a moment.

For only when the soul is addressed do we fully heal. It is the leverage point. All healing comes from the divine within.

Now, I was speaking with the authority of the soul. This was far beyond the guidance I had given before, where I guided people through the flowing inner voice that streamed through me. This was seeing deeper and truer. I was moving from a deeper core within the life force.

Writings and classes came through me, whole cloth. This is what happens as we live in the realm of the soul. The soul exists in the realm of what I experience as "all at once, here and now," the realm where everything exists in the invisible, waiting for the appropriate moment to birth into time and space. Poems came through me as I woke, something that had happened before, but now they were deeper and more complete. Poetry is a language of the soul; I was becoming more fluent.

After I took my first class with the remarkable energy healer Rosalyn Bruyere, I read her story of the Rainbow Warrior.[14] It is the story of a young Native American man, born into the healing lineage of his tribe. His grandfather prepares to teach him. But the young man rejects his lineage, leaves his tribe, and takes up the ways of the white man. He falls into wrong ways. His life is shattered. Only then, in his despair, does he remember that he was to learn from his grandfather the ways of the Rainbow Warrior, the one who sees the rainbow beyond the rainbow.

He returns to his people with dedication in his heart. But his grandfather is dead. So he must learn on his own. He undertakes a vision quest on Second Mesa Plateau. It is a profound initiation. In the morning, when he awakens, he too begins to see the "rainbow beyond the rainbow," the light around his people.

I was so moved by this story that when I awoke after reading it, this entire poem poured through me:

### *The Rainbow Way*

*First, you are a Teller.*
*You tell God what you want.*
*You tell other people what to do and be,*
*For you tell yourself what to do and be.*

*Then, you are a Listener.*
*You listen to what God wants of you.*
*You listen to the eyes and hearts of others,*
*For you listen to your own heart.*

*Then, you are a Pray-er.*
*You no longer pray alone, for God prays through you.*
*You no longer pray alone, for others pray through you:*
*"Tell us what you see."*
*For you see their soul.*
*For you have become a prayer, and it just streams from you,*
*With every step you take on this earth.*

*And this is the Rainbow Way:*
*When you give your heart to God,*
*You see only the Soul.*

It chronicled the journey I had walked. I had been a teller when my intuition opened so long ago, a person caught up in the world of logic and senses. Then, I became a listener, beginning to open my heart to myself and others in understanding. And now, I was beginning to perceive more deeply still, at the level of the soul.

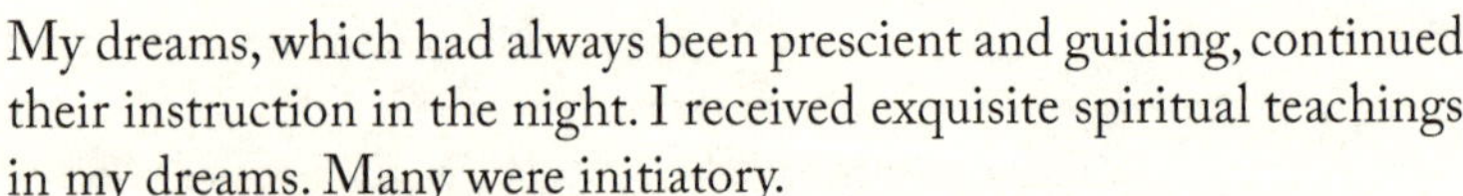

My dreams, which had always been prescient and guiding, continued their instruction in the night. I received exquisite spiritual teachings in my dreams. Many were initiatory.

Very early in the illness, I had gone to the Himalayan Institute in

Pennsylvania, advised that perhaps Swami Rama, its founder, might be able to help with my healing. Though I could barely make the trip, I got myself out there, but had to remain in bed for most of my stay.

No advances in healing came from my trip, but I did get to attend some lectures with Swami Rama. I remember one night doing my bhakti yoga service of washing a mountain of dishes in the kitchen while I wished that I could be with everyone in the woods, as they received an after-dinner teaching from Swami Rama.

Months later, when I returned home, I finally found a copy of the *Bhagavad Gita* that was translated in a way that revealed its true essence. I had been looking for quite a while. I finally found what I was looking for in a translation by Eknath Easwaran. I brought the book home that evening, and placed it on my coffee table to look at later. I never really looked at the cover closely.

Later that night, I had a dream.

In the dream, I was once again at the Himalayan Institute, washing dishes in their big kitchen. Out the window, I could see people walking to the woods for tonight's after-dinner teaching from Swami Rama. I wanted to go! But I couldn't because I had to complete a mountain of dishes.

As I stood there washing the dishes, I realized that I could hear the talk through my heart. As I washed dishes, I listened to the teaching through my heart, and heard every word perfectly.

But I wanted to hear Swami Rama. So as soon as I finished the dishes, I began walking to the woods to catch the last of the lecture. But just as soon as I began to walk toward Swami Rama, the inner teaching in my heart stopped.

I understood that the teacher was inside my heart, not outside. As soon as I sought a teaching outside, the inner wisdom stopped flowing.

My dream then spoke these words: "Let God play through your heart like a flute."

It carried the understanding that our bodies are flutes, and the flute's keyhole openings that allow the song to flow through are the spiritual centers. We allow God to play our body like a flute. This then, is the Song of God, played through us.

On waking, I realized that "Song of God" is the translation of the words "*Bhagavad Gita*."

I went downstairs eagerly to open the book, and when I looked at the cover, I discovered that it featured a beautiful sculpting of Krishna with his flute!

I was learning to let God play through my heart like a flute. All the guidance I needed was within my own heart, flowing through me constantly.

I was integrating at a much deeper level, embodying my soul much more fully, and I was now moving from my soul's guidance into action, without hesitation. It was like a song, a beautiful song of harmony with life, one flow of loving melody that moved through me in grace.

I was entering the deep current of harmony in which my life flowed.

# 46 And Slowly, Ever So Slowly, My Health Improved . . .

***Until I could live a half-life***

My progress was very limited and jagged and not linear at all, until I met a wise and caring medical doctor who was expert in anthroposophic medicine, an integrative medical approach that combines conventional medicine with spiritual science. Then I began to progress on the physical level.

I had spent about seven years in the care of holistic medical doctors, who, it turned out, knew very little about how to heal chronic fatigue syndrome. It's a large part of what made the illness so relentlessly defeating.

Yet I believe that there is usually a way to heal, and we must pursue every lead until we find it. It is very important for those with severe illness to hear this. When medical doctors tell patients that their situation is hopeless or that they are terminal, it can actually be more of a statement about the medical doctor than the patient. In other words, a truer statement is for the medical doctor to say "I do not know how to cure your illness." There is a great deal of hope in this, for an answer might be found elsewhere.

I kept pursuing healing, and when I got more of my mental function back and could think somewhat more clearly, I changed doctors. It took me seven doctors and as many years to locate the wonderful physician who finally helped me to heal.

Anthroposophy is the medical system developed by Rudolf Steiner (1861–1925), the spiritual genius who gave the world entire systems of spiritual understanding, such as Waldorf education and biodynamic agriculture. His system of anthroposophic medicine seeks to bring mind, body, and spirit into balance.

Anthroposophic medicines are spiritually-imbued homeopathics that are made in reverent, caring ways that capture rhythm and warmth. They are subtle substances, and not well understood in our physically-focused culture. They brought warmth, light, and life to me.

My medical doctor worked with Rudolf Steiner's anthroposophic medicine to bring my soul forces into my life and my body. The anthroposophical medicines she prescribed I soon began calling "love in a bottle," because they felt loving, nurturing, and supporting to me compared to anything else I had taken. Drugs felt harsh, herbs felt earthy and less harsh, and homeopathics felt soft to me. But this was love, a gentle essence of love that I was taking into my body. How could it not be healing?

One of the first medicines she prescribed brought warmth into me. It warmed my body, and it warmed my heart. I had been so very ill, with so little capacity, that, just like a sick animal, I retreated into aloneness. I did not want to be with people, I did not have enough energy. And so I felt cold, and lonely, and deeply sad.

But after I took this medicine, my heart opened in warmth. I felt like Scrooge when he woke up on Christmas morning, a changed person. For the first time since I had been ill, I felt the warmth of wanting to have people in my home. A sense of warming, gracious connectedness flooded my heart.

After this, she gave me a medicine that finally brought some strength into my muscles. Up until this time, I still could not reliably walk to the end of my block. I remember the thrill I felt when I could walk along Lake Geneva for about a mile. It had been at least seven years since I could walk a mile, and it was fabulous. The negative ions coming off such a big lake gave my energy a boost, and the medicine allowed me to keep on walking. I could physically feel my muscles strengthening. It was so exciting after years of confinement.

Progress is rarely linear after such long and severe illness. My health weaved back and forth, but now, I had a slow and general progression upward.

Now, I had hope.

I began to teach intuition again and greatly enjoyed being with the people who came to my classes. I felt loved and appreciated by them as they hugged me for what had opened within them.

I was opening to the world again. I was able to function a bit in the physical world.

And then, I took another leap. I fell deeply in love.

# 47 And Then I Took a Great Step

***I wanted to give myself fully to a great love***

All the time I had been ill, I had love relationships. First with Joe, and then with Adrian, an English gentleman, both very exceptional men. They were actually both quite extraordinary men—loving and kind, spiritually developed and growing, highly intelligent, cultured, and very accomplished in business and other significant areas, like art collecting and the intuitive and healing arts. But marriage did not feel right to me. I had promised myself I would not remarry until I was well. I knew that when I was ill, I would not make the same decisions that I would make when I was healthy.

But something else was also at issue. I could not find "the one," the man that felt right. Looking a little deeper at my dilemma, what was happening was that my heart was closed to love with a man, and I did not even know it. In truth, I was so very afraid to try again that I hid from love. The only thing I was in touch with was that I was not able to find someone to whom I could say "yes." A clever defense, allowing me to be in relationship with a man, without having to risk the deep pain I had felt before. I was simply afraid to trust a man again.

Yet at an even deeper and truer level, I wanted to share a deeply loving and committed relationship with a man. When I had asked in meditation what I could do to experience this, and move beyond my love for my former husband, I was told that I must give my heart fully to someone.

At that point, life cooperated. Unbidden, a man friend of eighteen years stepped forward, and told me that he wanted to marry me. He'd been making advances for quite a few years. I had never taken it seriously; in fact, I'd never paid it the least attention. It was always a platonic relationship for me. We were friends. But this day, when he arrived for lunch, I had just ended my five-year relationship with Adrian.

I was still working through my big emotions, so I told him that I *had* to go to the beach in Wilmette to let it all go in the waves and the wind. So we went to the beach and talked through my just-ended relationship.

We came home holding hands. Somehow, it just felt right.

It still didn't make sense to my mind because he'd always been only a friend. But my heart was saying yes. I felt deeply comfortable with him. Over time, the conflict resolved as I absorbed what was happening, and it began to make sense. All our years of friendship seemed a perfect plan by which we grew in trust and safety, until our relationship ripened into partnership.

This was so safe. I could trust again. I had known him forever as a good friend, and now, he told me he wanted to marry me, promising everything that I longed for at that time—marriage, Colorado, and grandchildren. After years of pain and illness, and nothing that had worked, here at last, was something that I could trust.

My heart flung wide open. I wanted to love with abandon! It was a new way for me to feel in love. It felt so free. I gave him my whole heart, the fullness of my body. I was giving everything, holding back nothing, as I had so long ago with my husband. I was so happy! My heart opened wide, and I gave and gave and gave.

But he did not fulfill his promise to me. It was not as I had thought. After three months, it became apparent to me that he really could not find his way to marry me. He never confessed this to me; I had to drag it out of him, angrily, after I realized I was being used sexually.

How foolish of me to believe him when he said he would marry me. After all, he was a salesman, and knew how to close the deal. And I was emotionally vulnerable after years of suffering. I was still very weak physically. I likely would have behaved differently, had I been well. He had promised me everything I wanted—marriage, Colorado, and grandchildren. And I fell into the trap. What a salesman.

Another betrayal from someone I deeply trusted.

Why bother anymore?

But there was a gift here. My heart had opened wide enough to want to love with abandon. My heart was saying it was ready to give fully to a man once again. And deeper still, in a way I did not even consciously recognize, my heart was saying that it wanted to give itself fully to a great love.

I never realized it at the time, but I was surrendering in yet another way, a greater way. My capacity for surrender had been growing, ever so quietly.

This was when I walked into my first Sufi classroom.

# 48 I Meet the Pure Love

***You're the One I've been waiting for!***

There is a saying in the Sufi world: "No one comes to the Sufi path except through a broken heart." That was certainly true in my case. When I walked into the room, it was clear to me that I was going to take some time off from men. It clearly was not working.

A lady friend came with me that first Friday evening, a free event that I could afford. At dinner before the two-hour talk, I told her that I felt I was dying. I had begun to get weak again, colossally weak. I had felt my body dying for months now. I had told my primary MD almost a year ago that my body was dying, and I had been working with her and other medical people to find the cause. But none could be found, and I continued on, getting weaker and weaker. Five months earlier, after I came home from celebrating Christmas at my sister's, I had written farewell letters, and had begun to organize my affairs.

In truth, my body *was* dying. We just had not discovered the cancer yet. And so this is also how I came to the Sufis—in a dying body.

And I came to the Sufis with a great longing deep within me, unformed and full, a profound longing to surrender everything into a great love. It was so profound that I did not even fully recognize it.

My body was dying. My heart was broken. And my soul was longing deeply to surrender into a great love. I was ripe.

I really knew nothing of the Sufi path when I walked into the seminar. The only thing I knew was literally the one sentence I had read somewhere in a book. It said that Sufis practice repeating the name of God. I remember thinking how boring that must be.

But tonight was to be a revelatory experience.

The evening's talk was about healing, and about love. It was about our spiritual heart center, and the deep, pure love that is the Unity that we call God.[15] The instructor told a story about how he had healed himself rapidly. Having been home sick now for ten years, this was intriguing to me. I wanted to know more. So from within the audience of over one hundred people, I asked the instructor how he had been able to heal so rapidly.

I thought it would be just a simple response, that he would communicate some facts to me. Instead he spoke directly to my heart, and in the few words it took him to answer, deep tears rolled down my face. He had touched something that needed to be touched.

Needless to say, I returned for the three-day seminar, a huge stretch for me financially. There was no way I could stay away from this.

That Saturday morning as I readied for the seminar, a song from *Joseph and the Amazing Technicolor Dreamcoat* played through me. It was "Any Dream Will Do", which tells the story of Joseph's dream of his prowess. I knew it meant something good for the day.

In the Saturday morning session, we learned Remembrance. Remembrance is the foundation practice of the Sufis. It is a profound prayer of the spiritual heart.[16] It embodies what the deep heart is always praying, which is communion with the divine. For the deep spiritual heart, at its very core, always abides in communion with God. And the Remembrance returns us to this place of union with the divine, right at the core of our spiritual heart. In so doing, we return to the pure love. We find ourselves held within the pure love, ever abiding and eternal.[17]

This love is not a personal love, it is impersonal. It is not a sentiment or an emotion, it is a force within the universe. It is the love that sustains us, that ever abides within us, the love that breathes us, warms us, moves us, guides us, and lights our way. It is absolute love, beyond the idea of "unconditional love". It is the love that loves us always, regardless of who we think we are, and how we feel about ourselves. Its presence abides within us, regardless of what we think or say or do. It remains pure and ever full, regardless of what we experience of it, or know of it. It loves us for what we are, which is what it is: pure love. A unity.

This pure love is a living force in the universe, so great and so vast that it is beyond our comprehension. It is the foundation of life, the living substrate of the universe, the Creator of All. It is the abiding harmony within which this vast universe and this immediate moment are constantly being created anew.

The practice of Remembrance invokes the Unity within us through words of light, sacred words that are the names of God. When intoned rhythmically within our spiritual heart, these sacred words spontaneously evoke the presence of divinity within. We remember who we really are. We come home to our deepest truth. What is less falls away.

And so the Remembrance becomes a prayer of living Unity, where one moves into the state of Unity, and separation ceases. Simple and deeply profound, Remembrance enables a direct and immediate experience of the living reality we call God. It is profoundly life-changing.

Having experienced this extraordinary state, we then went on to another prayer. This was a heart-prayer of forgiveness for something within our hearts that we wanted to release. Beginning, "My Beloved Lord, my Beloved God, please forgive me. Please accept me. Forgive me, Oh Lord Most High," we prayed the Sufi prayer of forgiveness through our hearts.

The prayer went on and on, as the forty people in the room repeated and repeated it from their spiritual hearts. After the prayer had gone on for some time, the instructor asked everyone how they felt. The room soon filled with comments like, "It feels lighter in my heart," and "I'm feeling better."

But that was not my experience. Not at all. For every time I repeated the heart prayer, my heart dropped deeper and deeper into pain. The pain grew bigger and bigger. It was so painful, in fact, that I put my hand up in the air, insisting on help from the instructor because I had been in a great deal of pain since we began the prayer.

He explained to me that I was going into a very deep surrender. Then he asked me to come up in front of the group, on the stage. Once I stood there, I closed my eyes, so that I saw no one in the room. I didn't want to be so intimately exposed in front of other people.

He asked me to make the posture that my heart was making. Immediately I knelt down, stretched out and fully prostrated myself on the floor, my face touching the floor. I had never done anything like this before in my entire life. But my heart compelled me. It was the movement that was flowing through my heart. I was surrendering myself to God. I did not know it at the time, but Sufis prostrate themselves like this.

After I stood up, he said that he would walk me through my heart, guiding me through the stations in my heart. The Sufi way has twenty-eight stations of the heart, each a further step into the Unity. They are grouped into four realms of seven stations each. The first realm is that of the outer world, of the senses and logical mind. This is the station of the "nafs." "Naf" is an ancient word that refers to the unrefined self, the lower, unillumined self. Most people on earth are living in this realm, and most of them are in the early stations. The next realm is the heart realm; it encompasses the pure love. The third realm is the soul, loving consciousness, with its qualities of God, the prophets, and eternal truth. The fourth realm is the most subtle; it is the Unity itself, where separation ceases. It is the state where our entire being, personality, heart, and soul, disappear into the Unity. In Rumi's words, "If you are fire, I am wood."[18]

As he guided me, I dropped down into my heart, and passed the first station of total darkness, and then the second station of still questioning. I kept moving deeper and deeper within my heart, through the third station of faith and trustfulness, then the fourth station of security, and the fifth station of no longer obeying the misguidance of the lower self, the nafs. Continuing deeper and deeper within my heart, I moved through the sixth station of accepting without asking and, finally, the seventh station of the perfection of the nafs, the perfection of the lower self.

When I came to the first station of the realm of the heart, my heart rested. This was what the Unity wanted me to study.

The instructor said he had never seen anyone move through the heart stations so rapidly. He stated that my heart had been open only a tiny slit, but that by my surrender I had been able to move deeply through the first seven stations. I did not realize it yet, but that was a remarkable feat for many of the people in the audience. Most of them had been working to move themselves into the second and third stations of their hearts through several years of practices and study.

He said that this was an example of what the Guide Sidi

al-Jamal[19] speaks about. In one moment, we can come home fully to the Unity. It all depends on our willingness to surrender.

I did not know what any of this meant at the time. I simply returned to my seat, quietly knowing that I had found the deep surrender for which my heart had been longing. I knew that something formless and full within me, waiting to flow out, had finally found a vessel with which to express.

It was only later at lunch, as I sat quietly, absorbing all that had happened within me, that I understood what had happened for some of the others. A lady Sufi student, who had been attending classes for several years, turned to me at the table and said rather caustically, "You'll slide back right into station two again next week." I felt her wanting to take away my experience. That was when I knew that what had occurred up there had been remarkable to many who watched.

Later that day, we had a dhikr, the Sufi way of community worship of the divine. We formed a great circle, holding hands, and moved through spiritual practices that bring the presence of God deep within us, traveling the realms within our hearts.

The third prayer is "La ilaha illallah," which means "There is no God but God" or "There is only love." I noticed that my heart had become warm like kindling, big and so open . . . lighter than it had been in years. I was filled with joy, the sheer joy and ecstasy of the divine, of the pure love . . . the ecstatic drunkenness of which Rumi speaks. My heart was overflowing with bounty, a fountain of pure love.

I was *so* happy! I had found where I belonged, after so many, many years of feeling so alone. I had come home to the pure love within my deep heart. I had found the heaven in my heart. It had been there all along, a hidden secret, hiding right inside me.

I was beginning the journey of the deep heart, endless in its capacity to be the pure love, ever growing, ever abiding. This love was always within me, secure and safe within the eternal me. I could abide in this place through all that happened to me, for I was now living within the pure love itself. Even death could not deny it.

Nothing could take this from me, no difficulty, no person . . . this place "most high" within me was the living reality from which I now could live.

I had found all that I needed.

I had stepped consciously into the harmony that I experienced once before, so long ago, the day I stepped out onto the Chicago street, when everything unfolded before me in exquisite harmony. Then, it happened through grace. It was something I slipped into—a spontaneous, wondrous occurrence. Now, I could travel through my heart to a state of *conscious* harmony, and learn to abide there always.

Then, it encompassed me in an unfolding harmony and grace. Now, it was healing the pain and hurt of my personal life and transforming them into grace.

What I had experienced so long ago, the absorbing, enrapturing experience of being fully immersed in harmony, was like a great masterpiece in oil. Now, I was learning one very important brushstroke of those required to render the magnificence of that immense canvas.

And over time I began to experience something wonderful. As I practiced this inner harmony, the world around me began to unfold in harmony. Over time, rough places were made smooth. And even with the rough places, it did not matter what happened "outside" anymore. Because inside was a place of purity and peace, and pure love. I had found where I belonged, forever and ever. I had found the One I was looking for.

The next morning when I awoke, my heart felt huge. My heart was filled with immense gratitude for all the pain and suffering I had experienced with men. It overflowed with thanks for the suffering. For had I not had the pain, had my heart not closed so severely, it could never have opened this big into pure joy.

When I awoke Sunday morning, I was amazed with what had happened to my heart in the last two nights. I had traveled so profoundly into my deep heart through the night. Some enormous fire, some cavern of greatest depth, some deepest knowing like embers of a soft-glowing radiance had been lit within me, and it just kept growing and growing of its own. Surely, this was the light of the Unity moving through me.

Something so huge and deep was growing through my heart, glowing through my being. I was filled with an impelling to give and give and give. It wasn't an action; it just flowed out of me. And along with this inner fountain, a graceful path of humility, of service and deepest love had opened before me.

All this came to me through surrender.

All this . . . through surrender to the Unity.

I had finally understood what surrender truly means. Surrender is bowing in our hearts to the pure love at the core of our being. Surrender is letting go of everything that is not the pure, true love. Surrender leaves only the pure love, turning and burning through us, glowing and guiding our way.

I was home, forever and ever!

# 49 The Golden Radiance of God Pours Its Splendor Through My Soul . . .

### *It filled me to overflowing with joy*

For the next three weeks, I was so wild with the ecstasy of this path. I jokingly called it "Sufi madness,", because so much light had opened within me. My heart was flying.[20]

And the most wonderful thing happened—above my head appeared in subtle light, a mass of gold, a huge mother lode of spiritual light that was penetrating into my outer consciousness and body. It was really the light of God pouring through my soul, reaching to my conscious awareness.

I am clairvoyant, so I see the aura around people, the human energy field, the lightwork of color and form that moves and pulses as people live their lives. For many, this light is not a reality because they have not experienced it. But this wondrous light does exist around us, and all of life. It's inspiring to know that we live as more than a physical body—we also live as beings of light.

It is a deeper expression of who we are than our physical bodies could ever communicate. It is who we are, written in light. Clairvoyants, those who see in light, can read a person's field and see what is coming into their experience, what they are going through now, and what they have gone through in the past, including their distant past. They can see what faces and confronts people. They can see people's bodies in light, and understand where physical problems are coming from, by reading the pathways of this light. The light is of many colors, form, and movement.

To relate this to what I was seeing above my head, when someone is about to receive inspiration, I perceive this clairvoyantly as little flashes of light, like gems going off above their head. This means that they are about to receive inspiration and understanding. And the ideas will come into their conscious awareness over the next few weeks and months; I understand the time it will take as soon as I perceive the little stars of light. Normally I only see a few flashes of light like this over someone's head.

With that as a reference point, what I saw above my head was a gold light, of rich, deep golden hue, at least four feet wide and three feet high above my head. It does not even feel right to put it in a quantitative sense because it has no relationship to the world of quantity. It is something from a completely different realm.

This was an enormously huge mass of golden light. It was something I had never seen above a normal person's head before.[21]

In my case, this light was the golden radiance of God outpouring through my soul, filling me, and coming into deeper embodiment within me. It would bring an enormously inspired book through me.

I was ecstatic, in bliss. I had found where I belonged. I had found home, right in the depths of my own spiritual heart.

# 50 I Surrender to the Pure Love, and Come Home to the Heaven in My Heart . . .

### *The pain of so many years begins to wash away*

I came home from the Sufi seminar a new person. My life had changed entirely. I *had* died, and been reborn.

I began my days with Remembrance. It was such a powerful experience for me that I would call the name of God only once into the depths of my spiritual heart and let it rest in my heart, penetrating deeply. It was so profound. The light of God penetrated deeper and deeper, traveling through my entire being.

When I had absorbed that experience, I would slowly sound the Name once again. The Remembrance was transforming me.

During those first mornings, in those first weeks with Remembrance, so much guilt and pain washed away from my heart. All the pain I felt from not being able to say yes washed away. And the deep pain and grief in my life, the sadness and sorrow caused by so many people and events, began to release.

Along with this, the deep, pure, and true inspiration of a book began flowing through me.

And a new man entered my life with the Sufi teachings. His name was Jules. He was the first teacher, and then the first master teacher that Sidi appointed in Chicago. I found him a superb communicator and exemplar of the Unity. When he would sing "La ilaha illallah," a chant that I could not yet quite repeat myself, the room would fill with a golden dome of light above us. La ilaha illallah, there is only God, there is only love. Golden Joy.

We soon began teaching together, sharing the Remembrance and healing practices with others.

And we began to share inspirations for the book that was forming through me. Jules' phrases and insights were brilliant, they carried so much light. A wind was carrying the book through us. It was great fun.

And Jules was to be a teacher and guide to me. Jules has a poet's gift for penetrating the heart of Sufi teachings in a few stunning words. He taught me, in his own words, that "Our truest relationship is with love itself" and that "Surrender is letting go of everything that is not love." These two phrases embody the essence of the Sufi path.

He would give me a living experience of the Sufi way of Unity. Through him, I would have to confront my personality nafs and experience how the deep love truly worked. My study and the practices had given me the precepts, and now, we were actually integrating them into my life.

Jules would wrest out my resistance with men, and help me to recognize it for what it was—a choice to stay separate from the love. He would stay with me through my recovery from cancer. And having done that, he would leave my life. Or so it seemed, until more than a year later.

# 51 I Am Inspired to Write a Sacred Story of What Love Can Truly Be . . . in a Place called Balasera

***I wept as I wrote passages . . . the story was washing my heart, opening it to trust again***

One night, after teaching an intuition class, I went to coffee with Jules, came home, and to my surprise, a book was pouring through my hands. Normally, I would be in bed almost immediately after the class for my health. But that night, I went to my laptop and typed the story that was simply there.

It was the story of a woman in Argentina who wakes one morning with golden sun streaming over her, and the inspiration to begin braiding. The story continued on—she met a man, Ramon, and soon they began slipping into an ancient time and place called Balasera. Yet Balasera still remains. And in Balasera, people live and love in a way that is true and pure, in a way we can only dream of. Three pages flew through my hands as if I was recognizing something that existed within me, something I had never touched until now.

I told Jules about it the next morning, and he wrote an email back that contained an exquisite paragraph that continued the story. I exclaimed in delight, "Jules, you're writing a book!" He was surprised; he didn't think he was writing a book.

Then I began waking up with phrases flowing through my mind, exquisite renderings of a sacred love. And it was then that I realized that *I* was writing a book!

The book kept flowing through me in a series of images, awarenesses, and words that were riveting, almost spellbinding. An exquisite and captivating love story unfolded, about what a shared love can truly be. It began with all the struggle and difficulty of people who have been deeply hurt in love. It was the story of how to take the struggle and turn it to grace, together.

As I wrote, during certain scenes, I just cried . . . the story was washing my heart of all that had gone before. Through the inspired flow of the pages, a new way to relate in love was emerging within me.

The story kept pouring through me. It was one expression of the golden radiance of God that I had seen above my head. Each scene was like the square of a patchwork quilt, complete in itself. I had to sew the scenes together, filling in all the missing pieces.

But all this came intuitively, too. Every question I had about how to place the characters, how to develop their personal stories, was answered effortlessly, intuitively. For example, Ramon lives in Argentina, and because of his nature, he cannot work in high tech. He has to be in something "high touch," working with something living. It was obvious that he could work in the cattle industry, so prominent in South America, but that didn't fit at all.

So where should Ramon work? Wine came to me; Ramon should work with wine. But was there even a wine industry in Argentina? A little research in the library brought back the emphatic answer that not only was there a wine industry in Argentina, Argentina is the *capital* of South America's wine industry.

It went on like this for every question that came up as I wrote the book. The answer was given intuitively, and when I researched it, sure enough, each answer was perfect.

Readers of the book have found it deeply inspiring. I have a friend, married with two children, who read it in the family SUV on her way to Disney World. She told me that she wept all the way from Chicago to Florida and insisted that if this book was sleeping, she wanted to wake it up. The book was opening her heart to her deepest longing, moving her to a new reality in love.

Another friend read the prologue, which occurs at dawn. She was so inspired by it that she began to wake with the dawn and become absorbed in its mystery and love, just as the lead character does.

My gentleman friend Adrian, who was been raised in a spiritual household in England, where spiritual greats like Alice Bailey and others were regular guests, told me that it was remarkably inspired writing, breaking with the past.

So I am very excited about it. I am hopeful that it will inspire others as it inspired me. The book is called *The Desert Wind: A Sacred Love Story.*

## 52 I Teach the Deep, Pure Love . . . and am Stunned at the Results

***People experience the living presence of God***

Along the way, I was made a master teacher of the Sufi path by the beloved Sufi Guide Sidi al-Jamal. This designation connotes that the teacher's heart is the earth on which other beloveds can walk on their journey into the Unity.

And so I began to teach. One of the very first classes that I taught was an afternoon program for the Unity Church to which I belonged. It was attended by about twenty people. In that class, I taught two very profound foundations of Sufi practice.

The first practice was Remembrance. This ancient practice offers a remarkably direct, immediate, and profound experience of God. The second practice enables us to travel down deep within our spiritual heart, experiencing its four realms. It offers a very profound experience of deepening into the pure love that exists at our very core.

Both these practices enable us to experience being held in the deep, pure love that is in the core of our spiritual hearts, a love that is always abiding, always guiding.

Very, very few people have ever experienced these states of being. They are beyond words, and must be experienced to truly understand what they open within us. It is a very sacred, deeply holy experience.

Because these experiences enable us to touch the living reality of pure love, they are immediately healing. We return to pure love. What is not love is released. It is deeply profound and moving. Simply touching into these levels is transformative. Over time, the experience deepens into an abiding, pure love that is constant.

Each individual enters this inner presence as deeply as they can allow. It is possible, with surrender, to travel into the Unity immediately. Yet most people find that it is a journey, taking time. In truth, it does not take time, it takes only surrender. We trust that the place people reach in their heart is the place that is appropriate for them in the moment.

The results of this simple class stunned me.

One of the attendees, a woman who had been a psychological counselor for thirty years, began sobbing as she broke through to the living reality of the deep, pure love within herself. She sobbed, "I've been trying to get here my entire life!"

Another woman had an equally profound experience. In her sixties and on kidney dialysis, she passed away just two weeks after the class. But before her death, she told two church teachers that the Remembrance class had given her an experience of the living presence of God. She said she had seen God and had known God through these practices. We were all so glad. It was a miracle.

And so we give all praise to God, the Living Unity.

This is an example of how deeply profound these practices are. It is impossible to describe in words where they carry us. I can only say that the Sufi practices transform us, moving us deeper and deeper into absolute love. They enable us to clear away all that is not love. And what is left is blessing upon blessing, grace upon grace.

For this is what is truly Real. This is how we are meant to live.

# 53 But I Wasn't Done Yet . . .

### *My body was truly dying*

But I was not to be well yet. There was a great deal ahead of me.

After a decade of illness, I had improved to being able to live a half-life. But then gradually I became weak again, until once again, I was horribly weak, at times unable to stand. Though my heart and soul were healing in the golden light of the Unity, my body continued to die. Visits with eight medical doctors and practitioners could not locate the problem.

Over a year earlier, I had been in a car accident, hit by a woman driving a big Town and Country van. As she exited a suburban shopping mall, she had accelerated sharply, not looking for oncoming traffic on the street to her left. It was an amazing oversight. I had three feet and three seconds to avoid the oncoming crash. It wasn't enough. She smashed right into me.

The accident caused severe damage to my neck. Less noticeable was the pelvic pain. Months later, an ultrasound revealed that my IUD had been pushed into my cervix. That fall, I had the IUD removed surgically. But I never saw the operating report; I didn't even know that such reports existed. I have no record of ever having been told by the doctor that I had cervical dysplasia, which can lead to cancer if not treated.

A year rolled by. I was in so much pain from the damage to my neck, and so frail, that my focus was mainly on my neck, and just getting through the day. Somehow, in the mass of medical appointments needed to avoid neck surgery and keep my body going, I forgot my pap smear that year. It was the only time in my entire life that I had forgotten it.

I grew progressively weaker, to the point where once again I could do very little.

But I was a different person now. Where before the debility was crushing and I lived in anguish, now my life was not dependent on my body. I had learned to live beyond the confines of my body. I had learned to live from my soul.

All the intense difficulties during the past years of debility had enabled me to progressively cultivate inner resources of greatest ability.

Great physical debility enables great spiritual ability. We can birth spiritual treasure from the physical devastation of our lives. This is "God's Arithmetic," the formula for soul growth.

All the experiences through which I learned had now merged into one greater way of being. I was living in a much wider expanse of myself. A gracious and spacious inner presence had opened within me. I had grown to live in the warming light of my soul. It was so much bigger than my physical body. The physical limits had lost their power, much as if a snake had shed its skin to reveal a glowing inner light. There were no more games with myself, no more belief in debility. I knew who I was. I knew what coursed through me.

The next summer, as I lay on the couch, I was so weak, once again, that I could barely stand. I barely had the strength to make pasta. I waited until I finally gathered enough strength to get up and put the pasta in the pan, and then hurried back to the couch to rest. But when the timer went off eight minutes later, I no longer had the strength to get up to take out the pasta. It had to cook away until I could get up again.

But this time, there were no tears. For I had learned an entirely different way to be. I had learned to live from my soul, and the enduring qualities within the soul that call forth life.

I had grown past allowing debility to limit my experience.

For though my body was severely weak on the couch, a beautiful book was flowing through me, and I was happy and enthralled as I wrote about a wine harvest. I was in Mendoza at a wonderful, warming family harvest, with loving generations of a wine family gathered together on a beautiful night under the stars in Argentina. It filled my heart with a family love I had not known in decades.

I had mastered a great lesson: I was as limitless as my heart, as free as my soul, no matter what the limits of my physical circumstances. I was far more than my limited physical body. I was soul. I was spirit, enduring and eternal. I was living in the warming expanse of my spiritual self. I was happy and fulfilled. I had become so much greater than the person who struggled and anguished, fighting to get well.

I had become complete, no matter where I was.

# 54 I Surrender into My Death . . .

***And heal from the power and the presence of my soul***

And all that summer, I kept hearing the words "September 18" in my mind. I knew it meant that something important would happen on that day.

Early that fall, I was too weak to attend an all-night prayer retreat with the Guide, Sidi al-Jamal. Instead, I sent a request through Jules, asking if Sidi could pray for me.

Sidi did, and I am ever so grateful. For within twenty-four hours of his prayers, I rushed to the hospital, gushing blood from the hemorrhaging tumor that I did not know was in my cervix, hoping to make it while I was still conscious. Luckily, I made it, while bleeding profusely.

I still remember the stark, cold outlines of that night in the emergency room, the cold, gray, deathly feeling of it all—lying on the cold gurney in the cold air, staring into the harshly bright fluorescent lights overhead at 2:00 a.m. while a gynecologist examined me, my sister at my side.

The noises he made said enough, and then he added words, "Oh my, necrotic tissue . . . oh this is bad, very bad, but I can't say yet that it is cancer until the tests come back . . ." Unstated, but understood, it felt like a death sentence. He seemed to be amazed at the condition of my body.

Weak from the loss of blood, weak from over a decade of CFS, and weak from the cancer, I immediately turned to my sister and said, "That's okay. I never found anyone, anyway, and I have suffered so much for so many years. It's okay, people are more souls to me than bodies and personalities, anyway. It's okay."

I surrendered immediately into my death. I accepted "what is" without argument. Of course, I would have preferred to live. But I was living from a deeper place now, a place beyond the physical. I was okay, whether I was in my body or not. I was not afraid of physical death.

It showed how very far I had grown with surrender. I was now able to accept a surprising and sudden verdict of death with grace. And yet I was able to keep working fully for life.

I had learned to live my life like the aikido artist who absorbs the thrust of his opponent's oncoming blow. He allows his body to move back in harmony with that oncoming thrust, letting it express fully, following the motion until it is exhausted. Then the rhythm powers forward once again, and now the power of the opponent's thrust fuels the aikido artist's own thrust into his opponent. The aikido artist's thrust is made more powerful by what once opposed him.

I was now used to yielding to the wisdom of what is. I no longer fought. I moved from a deep inner power that was beyond that duality. And just like the aikido artist, I was taking "what is" back within me, and then coming forward from the deep center that coursed through my soul. I flowed with the river of what is, using it to power the loving life force within me into action.

It was a mastery of surrender.

That night in the hospital, I barely slept. I was sure the test results would show cancer; it was the perfect explanation of everything I had experienced during the past year. I had been so ill, I had never seen it.

I called my primary doctor immediately the next morning and talked with her. As we discussed my weakened body and the difficulty it would pose for recovery from cancer, I told her, "I'll have to heal from the vibrancy of my soul." It was all I had. I didn't have much left in my body with which to heal.

Around the time that I spoke with her, I saw an image within of the CFS swirling down in a vortex, being washed down the drain. It meant to me that the CFS debility would wash away.

The next morning, I met with the doctors at my bedside, surrounded by Jules and my family. The oncologists were concerned that I might not be able to withstand the treatment due to my weakened condition and the CFS. They described the protocol they would use on the plum-sized tumor—radiation supported by chemotherapy, but no surgery. Due to the blood loss, I could not comprehend what they were saying about why they could not perform surgery. It had to be repeated again and again: it's progressed too far. They scheduled radiation for the first date available; it was the only way they could stop the bleeding. Radiation was to begin September 18th.

The doctors were concerned that I might not make it.

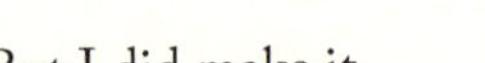

But I did make it.

I was healed of cancer by November 7th. Thanks to all our combined efforts, I recovered fully from the cancer within seven weeks of treatment. For me, recovery from cancer was extremely easy compared to the CFS with which I constantly lived.

And when I recovered partial strength after the radiation and chemo, though I still did not have nearly normal health, I had the best health I had known in over a decade. Something, indeed, had washed away. I felt very encouraged and hopeful.

Yet there was more for my body to endure. There was the serious injury to my neck. After several years of differing medical opinions and interventions to avoid spinal surgery, I had an appointment with a new medical doctor—the founder of Chicago's leading neurosurgery center. As he reviewed my films, he tapped the table nervously with his fingers, bounced his knee under the table, and told me in no uncertain terms, "You get in here right now for spinal surgery."

So no sooner had I gotten a bit stronger after the cancer treatment than I was to have major spinal surgery, replacing half the vertebrae in my neck. I signed the papers required due to risk of death or impairment and went under the anesthesia. Three vertebrae in my neck were removed and replaced, and a three-inch titanium plate inserted. The operation was a success.

I was moved to my hospital room and fell into a deep sleep. When I awoke the next morning, I received an understanding. This was the last of my long suffering in my physical body.

It was all over.

My years of severe illness and debility were done.

It had been fourteen years.

It was over!

I felt an amazing feeling of freedom and release from a horrible life of constant crises and setbacks with my body.

It would take me many, many years after this to regain relatively normal health.[22] But the most severe traumas were over. My years of crawling through the twilight of a half-life were done.

A whole new dawn lay ahead of me.

# 55 I Walk into My Book . . . David and I Recognize Each Other Immediately

### *And I move to Balasera*

To help my recovery from the surgery, I spent my time writing the inspired story that flowed through me.

As I wrote certain passages, I wept and wept. All my pain poured out, as I relived a different way to be through the pages I wrote. The deep pain, the years of sadness and grief, were washing from my heart. And with that, the painful limits were released. My heart was being cleansed. I was getting ready to love a man again.

Through my writing I lived what a shared love can be. Rhapsodic scenes flowed through me, and I wrote the story of how Estra and Aliman recognize each other immediately in Balasera, because they see each other's light.

During this time, I walked and walked in nature because it was healing my body. I'd spend hours in the forest, winding through hidden deer trails, gathering blackberries in the rays of the early morning sun. I'd hide in the secret places made by tree boughs and brambles. And I dreamt of living in the woods, living a life of simplicity. And it grew into a dream of living in the woods with a man.

And then I got on the plane to Hawaii. And so it was that David and I recognized each other immediately, just as Estra and Aliman did.

I had walked into my book.

I had fallen into the arms of love—first the deep, pure love of the Unity that we call God, held within my spiritual heart, and then the arms of my beloved husband David and Hawaii. I had learned how to enter the heaven in my heart. I had learned how to give up anything that was less than pure love. And then it outpictured as a heaven on earth.

And so David and I began as beloveds from our first days together. And David brought me home to his little island home in the great big woods. And here we live together in simplicity, growing in love each day.

# PART SIX

# LIVING IN THE HEAVEN IN MY HEART

*At the center of our heart is a point that belongs only to God,*
*a point of emptiness and deepest surrender,*
*of purest communion with a love so all-embracing*
*that it sweeps away all else.*

The practice of Remembrance

# 56 I Had Learned What Surrender Truly Is

***Surrender is letting go of everything that is not pure love***

My years of deep illness had been a journey of surrender.

I had tried to surrender one way, and then another. I began in a clumsy way, with what I knew, learning through my own halting, slowly growing experience. My greatest strides in recovery began when I finally learned what surrender truly is.

Long, long before the illness, decades before, I would often pray to God, "Use me as thou seest fit." It was a simple prayer of surrender. I truly meant it. But I couldn't do it fully. Through the illness, I learned to live that prayer much more fully.

At first, I thought surrender meant giving up everything I had, everything I was. And so I surrendered my body, my home, my money, and all my possessions. I surrendered all my relationships, all I loved, my hopes and dreams, my world views, all my attachments, even who I thought I was. I surrendered everything I had.

I was surrendering from my conscious self and my personality, what my mind thought surrender looked like. And though I did it fervently, with all my heart, it was not complete surrender.

I thought surrender meant giving up everything I was. In reality, surrender meant giving up everything I truly was not.

Surrender is more about giving up false identity than giving up possessions. It is about using everything in our life—our body and possessions, our heart and mind, and our soul—as an expression of loving consciousness. It is allowing ourselves to be used as an open flow of loving consciousness, rather than as a block to that flow. We are meant to be a flowing river of vibrant waters that opens onto an ever-wider ocean, rather than a small little self-contained pool.

Even though I didn't understand fully yet, this was progress. I was learning to consciously let go of my personality, with its endless babbling needs and misunderstandings of how life truly worked. In its place grew a firm footing in what is true and enduring. I began to live far more fully from the soul, actively choosing and living the essence qualities that call forth life. I began to live within a larger experience of myself, with deepened experiences of the subtle realm of soul, and remarkable capacities within the soul realm.

I now understood that surrender held the key to my entire life.

Yet I was tormented by my lack of recovery. I wanted my life back. It appeared that I had no power to heal myself. I kept asking two hauntingly unanswered questions: "*What makes a miracle healing? What enables healing from such desperate illness?*"

Finally, I received an answer: humility and surrender. I was told to surrender into the illness, and to surrender into surrender itself.

And so this became another way I consciously surrendered—deepening my practice, yielding into an illness that had destroyed my life.

But I was not giving the illness power in doing this. I was truly not surrendering into the illness. We only surrender to God, the Living Unity. I was accepting the illness completely, while surrendering into the Unity, allowing its greater power to move through me. In doing this, I was allowing my body to be hallowed, filled with something greater.

Through this, I stopped fighting the illness, and stood within a greater identity. I stopped the duality and moved into unity, unity with my true self.

This practice of deeper surrender opened up a place of peace inside me, a gentle yielding into what was. It was effortless. When I hung on the torment of what I couldn't do, and what I couldn't be in the world, then it was jagged inside. That struggle actually thwarted healing. For when I resisted the illness, I closed down the life force that could flow through me, restricting and limiting it. This gentle yielding is part of what healed me.

I had surrendered into surrender, deepest surrender, with no personal volition save this. Breath and prayer, breath and prayer. Nothing of my personal will, and everything of a greater will. I had learned how to bow in my deep heart to the Unity, the Great Harmony we call God.

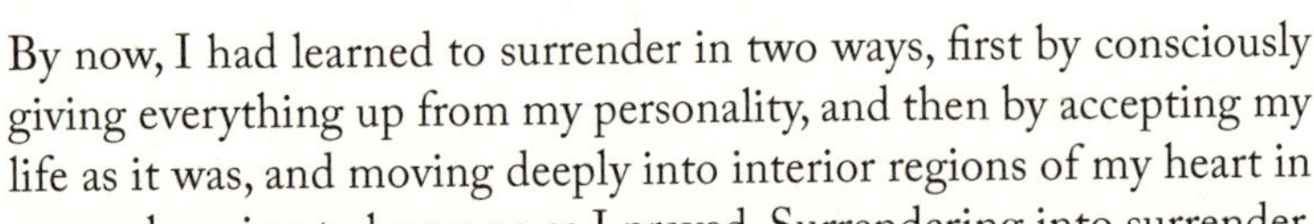

By now, I had learned to surrender in two ways, first by consciously giving everything up from my personality, and then by accepting my life as it was, and moving deeply into interior regions of my heart in prayer, learning to be peace as I prayed. Surrendering into surrender.

And beyond this, all the while, a deeper force was moving through me, one that was quietly, imperceptibly making me soft and yielding, pliable in some greater hands, amenable to some greater will, some greater good.

I was learning to be opened, and vulnerable. When we allow ourselves to be vulnerable, our hearts open. As soon as our hearts open, we connect—with God and with others. Only when we open our heart can we receive.

I was learning to be empty. Only when we are empty can we be filled.

I was learning to be humble. Only when we are humble can we know the magnificence of the soul's light.

I was learning to surrender my own volition, and to follow without hesitation the unerring guidance of divine breath.

I began to see a mysterious goodness winding its way through the world's evil.

Just as soil gives life, and is made of what is rotting, aged, and discarded, so I saw how the rotting, the aged, the discarded parts of humanity—the greed, the hate, the fear—were being used by a loving wisdom, woven back into a soil that could nourish humanity and sustain greater life, life more abundant.

I saw how conflict leads to harmony, when met with loving consciousness. And I saw how conflict forces the growth of that loving consciousness. A Great War in Europe, 1914–1945, fought in hatred and greed and fear, ultimately enabled cooperation between the very nations who had fought each other. It expelled the poisons, and allowed people to see what had always been there, underneath. World Wars I and II eventually transformed Europe into an Economic Union, and the world into a United Nations.

I saw how an entire people who were allowed nothing gave their nation something of inestimable value. Afro-Americans, black in a world of white, first enslaved and then freed into an existence of life-numbing discrimination, led their oppressors into a greater way, a way of love. Afro-Americans delivered their fellow white Americans to a way of life freed from enslavement to bigotry and injustice. When blacks walked free, whites were freed also.

I saw how people's petty greed and shallow self-interest were inevitably woven back into a greater power for everyone, creating a common good, and a common wealth. All through history, the cruel domination and greed of kings and dictators paved the way to eras of shared power. The ruling class of France—King Louis XVI, the nobility, and the clergy—refused to give any power to commoners, which led directly to their undoing. Ultimately, commoners received power. The road wasn't smooth, but it led surely in one direction.

The power of Unity kept moving like a slow river through the desert wastelands of humanity's separation. Like a loving gardener, the Oneness moved to make those deserts bloom. Nothing was wasted. Every bit of greed, every scrap of hate, was ultimately turned to good, to something that could sustain and grow a greater cooperation, a greater caring, a greater harmony.

I was learning that there was a much wiser hand in all of life. I began to see how God uses very imperfect vehicles to do His perfect work. How people throughout history, pursuing their own crude greed and gain, ended up delivering the world to a better place, without even realizing how the goodness of life was using them.

China tried to eradicate Tibetan Buddhism, and instead spread it around the world. They killed its physical form—its monks and nuns, its monasteries, its culture, even its natural resources—but its spirit only increased on earth. Physical death amplifies spiritual presence.

I began to live in a very deep trust of life. I saw that what was happening now was necessary, and part of a larger canvas.

In all the ruins and destruction caused by humanity, I saw love.

I saw wisdom. I saw a creative force, winding its way through the rubble, bringing humanity home to a place long forgotten, in the very depths of their hearts.

I was surrendering from a deeper place now, because my heart had grown deeper. Our spiritual hearts are always growing—deeper, wider, higher—just as our capacity for love is always growing—deeper, wider, and higher. Eventually our spiritual hearts grow so great that they have no boundary, and so they appear to be nothing. And everything.

As a clairvoyant, I perceive people's subtle spiritual hearts. When people are Great Ones, their hearts do not appear to exist to me. They are so subtle and so vast that they disappear. And so I see that Gandhi's heart was so vast that it held all of his countrymen. He loved them all. What a Great Heart. And I see that selfish people's hearts are dark and solid, like a black fist in the middle of their chest. When you hug them, it is cold and empty.

By now, I had moved beyond a great deal of my personality conditioning and limits. And I began to experience at times, something most wonderful—a current of harmony within life that I could ride, just as a bird rides an air current, gliding. I discovered that the hidden passageway to this secret harmony was a surrendered heart. The world began to feel joyful. There was a harmony in life that was singing, and now I knew how to join it. Even though my body was still not fully able, I was fully able.

I was ready to let go, to be free of the boundaries, the limits I had placed on my heart. I asked within how to move past my former husband, and was told that I must give my heart fully to someone. And so I surrendered into love with a man, a joyful and wild love, a love I trusted. It felt so safe that I wanted to love with abandon.

But it didn't last. And I felt used and betrayed. Ah, but the Oneness of Life would use this seeming loss to weave wondrous good into my life, regardless of how I interpreted it at the time. For a greater, truer, and ever-lasting love was waiting for me, right within my own heart.

By now, the capacity to surrender had grown so great within me that I could surrender from my soul. This allowed me to go deeply and immediately into deepest surrender to the Unity, or God. There was so little left of me that the great presence we call God could pour through me. Only an empty vessel can be filled.

And that is when I learned the Remembrance. And when my heart opened to the deep, true love that was within it all along, waiting there like a hidden secret.

And the radiance of spirit poured through my soul, through my heart, and into my life. It rooted me deeper, raised me higher, and expanded me into more than I had ever known.

I was freed of all my ideas that love should come to me from someone else. The source of love was flowing right within me. And when I learned how to reach it through Remembrance, my mind's idea that love was outside me just evaporated. I had become full. I had become the fountain.

What occurred without could no longer harm me. Oh yes, it might hurt at first, but I could very rapidly let it become love through my heart. I could see what the wise and loving hand of God was making here, through the flowing wisdom of my heart.

I went through cancer, I went through major spinal surgery, and I was okay. For I was living in that "secret place of the most High . . ." where "it shall not come nigh thee," as the 91st Psalm proclaims.

I no longer needed a man in my life. I still loved the idea of a partner, but I was fine on my own.

I was living in conscious harmony, moving on heart streams of love, a momentum of love that carried me within it. I was accomplishing things through that stream of harmony that ran like a song through my life.

It doesn't mean that suddenly everything was just the way I would have liked it. No, not at all. It meant that I could enter the difficulties of life through the pure love now. For example, I had tremendous physical pain in my spine; nerve pain is excruciating. But I was given a song to sing in meditation that helped reduce the pain. The first lines began, "Life is music, all my life is music, when I know the notes to follow." I had learned the notes to follow.

I grew terribly weak, so weak I could not get the pasta out of the pot. But I was happy. No longer did the debilitation of the illness stop me. I was living fully, in my debilitated body.

When I was diagnosed with cervical cancer, the examining gynecologist made noises and comments that pretty well said I would die. I was all right with that. I yielded to it immediately. I was living from a deeper place now, a place beyond the physical. I was just fine, whether I was in my body or not.

I had come home. I had found where I belonged, forever and ever and ever. Nothing could touch me now.

Surrender is the perfection of the personality. It is giving up everything that is not what we truly are.

For when we surrender fully, we discover that we are only pure love.

# 57 I Learned How to Transform Tragedy into Grace

***By living in what is real and enduring, moment by moment***

In a subtle, slow way, I had learned how to transform the pain and illness of my life into grace. It was a way that wasn't easy to find in our culture.

In our culture, we like stories of recovery that are heroic. Big and bold, dramatic and stunning, back in the race before you know it. Like Lance Armstrong's story, where he was given up for gone at the early peak of his young career when he was diagnosed with testicular cancer that had spread life-threateningly to his abdomen, lungs, and brain. Given only a 40 percent chance, he made a miraculous recovery in just four months and shot back into racing, rising to new heights and ultimate stardom, winning his first Tour de France in 1999, following up with six more stunning victories in each following year.

But my story isn't like that. It is a hero's journey of a different kind, and one we can all accomplish. It is consistently, persistently, choosing, moment by moment, the most life-giving quality we can imbue in the situation that currently confronts us. It is the slow, consciously thoughtful, artful work of creating a life.

No matter how horrible, how ugly, or how tragic our situation, we can call life from it. We can bring ourselves to greater life through it. This is our work as creators, co-creators with the Unity that we call God.

This is how I transformed tragedy, moment by moment, and how I created the beautiful life that I now live every day. This is how I walked out of the quicksand of the illness, one step, one breath, one prayer at a time.

In the early years, since I had extremely limited physical capacity, I could not be effective on the physical level. But I knew, ever since that night I realized that I was actually living my ideals more fully from my sickbed, that I could still be very effective on the spiritual level.

Why not use my capacity most wisely, by growing what endures within me? That way, I would be accomplishing the most important part of my life, anyway. That way, regardless of what I could or couldn't do in the physical world, the important things would get done.

So I began to practice doing my activities through spiritual qualities. In other words, I focused on the spiritual quality I wanted to call forth within me as I went through the motions of my life. It began with a choice of the spiritual quality I wanted to experience and build within myself. This is how I learned to pray with my actions.

For example, for years, my inner meditation had counseled me to "Be at peace." So I would write an essay from bed while I practiced being peace. I found that within the debilitating, distressing weakness, I could still practice peace. I could still *be* peace, as soon as I let any lesser identity go. And so I practiced peace as I lay on my bed, weak and writing. I began by practicing peace within the torment. And gradually, choice by choice, my life became more of peace. Little by little, what was not peace in my life got refined away. Because gradually, choice by choice, what was not peace within me got refined away. I became more of peace.

Eventually, this simple choice to live through spiritual qualities, moment by moment, was to lift me from my sickbed, and build the beautiful life that I live today.

Today, I write in Hawaii, within deepest nature—in a lush green valley, within a beautiful forest, surrounded by fields of flowers. It is so peaceful here; I could not have a more ideal place for writing. I am writing from peace all the time here, because there is an abiding peace within me. And I no longer write from my bed; I am much better. And I am writing to help others learn what I learned.

And all this is because I gradually became more of peace, moment by moment, choice by choice.

I was learning to live consciously in what is real and enduring.

In this time of dark, I was consciously making my own light, to find my way. This was my soul's way of guiding my conscious personality self to become more of light, more of my soul's gracious beauty. The sun that shines above us also shines within us. I was traveling its orb through my life.

I was beginning to learn to live through my soul ever more fully, moving from essence as I moved through the motions of my daily life. By holding a meditative heart-presence of the spiritual qualities that give life, I was activating them in my experience and the world around me. I would fill my spiritual heart with them, and they would abide within me, enlivening all I touched, all I thought, all I was, as

I moved throughout my day.

The soul is peace. The soul is love. The soul is grace. The soul comes alive within us as we live through its qualities that give life. These are qualities like love and mercy . . . peace and patience . . . humility and surrender . . . devotion and discipline . . . integrity with truth . . . will to good . . . harmlessness . . . grace and beauty . . . freedom and justice. We might call these essence qualities. They are qualities of God, qualities of the creative force that brings life.

When we live through essence qualities, we are living by what endures, not by what transits. Then no matter where we are, what we are doing, or who we are with, our life has value, purpose, and meaning. Then, we are living our life purpose most truly.

Essence qualities transform everything we do, even the most common of tasks, like washing the dishes. It is remarkable how many spiritual adepts have discovered essence qualities in the dishes. Teresa of Avila (1515–1582), the great Spanish saint and reformer, said, "Be ardent in your work, and you will find God in your cooking pots."[23]

Brother Lawrence (1614–1691), the gentle Carmelite monk who practiced the presence of God, famously used his kitchen noise and clatter to practice living as if there were no one but God and him in the world. In the clatter of his kitchen, he attained a state of tranquility. And Thich Nhat Hanh practices mindfulness as he washes dishes, aware of his breath, his presence, his thoughts, and his actions.

Imagine what we might build within us and our world, as we simply wash the dishes.

When we wash dishes, or do anything through essence qualities, it is elevated. Then, no matter what we are doing, it will not matter how it turns out on the physical level. For we will have transmuted fleeting physical experience into enduring spiritual essence. We will have grown greater within ourselves. This is what endures.

How many everyday motions in our lives could come alive, and become purposeful and eternal through essence qualities?

Essence qualities are our essential nature, our deepest, truest self. For in our deepest, truest self, we are peace. We are love. We are grace.

Ah, but how many of us know ourselves in this exalted way? And so it is our purpose on earth to refine ourselves until we come to know ourselves as peace, as love, and grace, and all the other beautiful essence qualities. We do this through gradual and persistent spiritual practice.

Through spiritual practice, we grow until we actually embody essence qualities. They become us; we become them—a living unity.

There are so many ways to practice living from essence qualities. We can live them in very simple, moment by moment ways. Through this steady, simple method, they gracefully transform our lives.

In fact, simple acts, done in love and mercy, humility and kindness, create a life of grace. These become the way we move through life. The capacity to live through essence qualities ranges all the way from that of the novice stage of deciding to think more positively, to the masterful stage of becoming a channel through which miracles can flow this very moment.

We might recognize essence qualities in others and appreciate them for it. For example, when we are doing a transaction with a cashier in a store or a phone representative, we can thank them for an essence quality, like their patience, graciousness, or kindness. It takes them by surprise. They smile inside. As we recognize the qualities in them, they grow within us. And they grow within them. Life is a unity. We grow together.

Practicing humility can be offering to let another go first in a busy shopping aisle. As we offer kindness, we experience the world as a kinder place. Life is a unity. What is within is without.

A practice of kindness might be two spouses thanking each other as they do the simple, repetitive tasks that make up each day: "Thank you for washing the dishes . . . Thank you for taking out the garbage . . . Thank you for driving us home . . . Thank you for paying the bills." The thankless tasks suddenly take on new life. It feels good to be appreciated for doing them.

Loving kindness might be choosing to make a supportive statement to everyone we encounter this day. And then watching them light up as we surprise them by understanding them; so few people are authentically recognized by others. Recognition is a great gift.

It might be choosing what is most life-giving, by watching how we are affected by movies. How did you feel afterwards? What grew within you? Did you feel more for it? Or less? Did you feel like something grew greater within you? Or did you feel like taking a shower? Our responses can guide us to what is most life-giving.

Mercy might be being angry with someone, but catching yourself before you criticize them in your mind and start to judge them. Judgment and labels are like a box, fixed and solid—and just as restricting to everyone. Mercy might be, instead, staying in your fluid feelings, which allow adaptability and ease. So that "He's such a jerk" becomes, instead, "I'm so angry." It's much more honest.

Mercy might also be remembering that they are still growing, just as we are, and extending a little prayer that they will grow their next step. And that we will, too. Life is a unity. We grow great together.

Peace might be simply accepting that someone did something to you that was deliberately hurtful, instead of fighting with it inside yourself. Peace might grow into forgiving those who have betrayed you. Peace might be realizing that what we don't forgive, we continue to live.

Harmlessness might be rendering that person's behavior harmless in your life. When we do this, we cease harming ourselves with its memory. Life is a unity.

Hope might be being hope for those who have little. Loving wisdom might be praying for everyone you meet, that they will remember who and what they truly are.

Surrendering what is false within us might be realizing that defending our personality is a lot of unnecessary work . . . and that what is true within us needs no defending, no presenting, no promoting . . . and that it is so much easier and more graceful this way, too.

It is in the little things, done persistently and consistently through essence qualities, that a life of value and grace is built. We do this moment by moment, choice by choice. And gradually, choice by choice, we find ourselves living in a heaven.

We can only experience heaven on earth after we discover the heaven in our hearts. Once we begin, it grows in blessing and grace, until we realize that it is endless. For our hearts are endless in what they can be, as endless as this ever-expanding universe.

This is how we transform tragedy into grace.

This is how I created the beautiful life that I have today: no great goal, no affirmations or visualizations. I didn't do it through my personality or desire. I did it by surrendering to something greater, right in the depths of my spiritual heart, and through living in love and peace and humility. And loving what was natural for me to love. This is far more graceful than "making it happen." How beautifully simple. And how powerfully effective.

This is our part. This is all we have to do. The Great Harmony does the rest.

Along the way of living essence qualities, I created a practice that filled my heart. I called it "Taking a Heartful Walk." When I was terribly ill, it took a great deal just to take a little walk. I felt so very frail and weak, and I walked so very slowly, my body bent down and curved around my stomach, as old people walk. I was also depressed and grieving. And this is how I would start out on my walk. Then, I would begin my practice. It went like this:

**Taking a Heartful Walk:**

1. Notice what you are most attracted to, what is most life-giving, in what you see ahead of you.

2. What is the quality within that?

3. Now, notice what is growing within your spiritual heart because of what you have experienced.

4. Then choose the next scene that feels most life-giving . . .

It was very simple. And profoundly effective. I began in frailty and sadness. Yet when I came home, fifteen minutes later, my heart was full.

As I walked in the autumn, for example, I might notice a patch of golden aspen trees quaking in the wind ahead of me. What is the quality in that? Joyful radiance. Then I would notice what was growing within my heart because I experienced this. Of course, I felt joy. Next, I might notice birds at a water fountain. Playfulness. And a sense of play increased in my heart. And so on. By the time I arrived home, my heart was brimming. And I had more energy.

I had taken on more life force, simply by walking with essence qualities. I didn't relate to the frailty and sadness. I related to what was most life-giving, right in front of me. I consciously felt those qualities, like joy and playfulness, growing within my heart. The physical illness and the emotional pain had less and less power, the more I lived from essence qualities.

In all the examples above, we can see that each person, each experience, came more alive because the actions were done through essence qualities.

As we live through essence, we bring ourselves and all of life much more alive. We literally quicken these qualities within us and all around us. We transform ourselves and our world.

How does this work? Essence qualities, like love and wisdom, do not belong to us. They are a force outside us, which we open to within ourselves. We allow them to flow through us. So we don't contain love, we allow the pure love to flow through us. Essence qualities are not a personal power; they are a power beyond us.

And essence qualities, like love and wisdom, are alive. They are always growing. They grow by being expressed by each of us. You've heard the expression "Love grows by being given away." The more love we express, the more love we experience. It grows and radiates out all around us. It brings everything more alive—our plants grow bigger and healthier, animals come closer, people brighten, their hearts warm, and they blossom into what they might be, families become harmonious, and cultures thrive with well-being and creativity. Humanity evolves yet another step.

Within ourselves, when we activate love, we experience a harmony in our world. The puzzle pieces of life suddenly fit together, things flow and are easier, and we discover ourselves moving with a harmony that powers us on to greater things. All, because we activated more love.

And so it is with every essence quality. Each brings more glow and radiance, more joy and more life . . . more capacity to *be.*

As we grow in our capacity to live from essence, we discover many remarkable truths. One facet of these remarkable truths is that by living through essence qualities, we transcend form.

For example, the more we live from the essence qualities of the soul, the less we are limited. We can take the limited physical forms of our life, and experience through them unlimited spiritual qualities. The sage arrives without leaving.

Imagine, for a moment, being homeless, not a penny to your name, not even knowing where your next meal will come from. Your only possessions are the lightweight clothes on your back. You are confined to living out of doors and bedding down wherever you find yourself, with no food or shelter, until some kind soul gives them to you. How destitute. How horrible!

And yet this is Peace Pilgrim. Peace began walking for peace at age forty-four in 1953. She carried only a pen, a toothbrush, and a comb. For twenty-eight years, she walked and talked peace, being peace with everyone she met. She lived in radiant happiness and increasingly good health. Peace didn't see homelessness and lack of possessions. Peace saw joy and freedom and truth—the fulfillment of her life.

Now imagine growing up, sleeping on the floor of a big, drafty room in cold, cold winters, with mice running over your bed. Such poverty. Such misery!

And yet this is the Dalai Lama. This is how he grew up as a boy in the Potola Palace. The Dalai Lama didn't see vermin—he saw friends. He played with the mice and found companionship with them.

Now imagine stinking heaps of coconuts, garbage rotting in the heat of the Calcutta sun. What a stench. How unhealthy! But now imagine instead, seeing jobs in those stinking heaps—using those same coconuts to create jobs for those who had none. And imagine that, nearby, you see a man dying in the streets, his body being eaten by maggots. How repulsive. How abhorrent!

And yet Mother Teresa didn't see disgust. She saw love . . . in the face of a desperate and dying man. And she brought him home and loved him. She didn't see poverty or slums or untouchables . . . she saw love creating, as it flowed through her heart, into what was right in front of her.

Just as Peace Pilgrim, the Dalai Lama, and Mother Teresa have demonstrated, our peace and freedom, and the love we can experience are available to us right now, right here, from an endless and ever-increasing source: our own hearts. Our experience of peace and freedom and love do not depend upon our surroundings. They depend upon what is within us.

The more we live from essence qualities, the less we are limited.

The physical forms in which we find ourselves hold no power when we truly know how to create. When we animate them with essence qualities, we literally transform the physical forms of our lives, and they take on new life. They become filled with qualities that give life.

Mother Teresa lived her life on vows of poverty . . . and yet fed thousands daily.

Thomas Merton did not speak. As a Trappist monk, he lived on vows of silence . . . yet his written words inspired the world.

Gandhi was a toothless little man in a loincloth . . . and yet he led India to independence from its well-dressed British governors.

By moving through the actions of our day with essence qualities, we determine the qualities by which we live, regardless of our circumstance.

I was in the high mountains of Colorado one summer, where over the course of time, I met several Tibetan Buddhists who had escaped when the Chinese occupied their country. I found in all of them a heartfulness and peace, a gentle love and contentment radiating quietly through their conversations with me. These are people who have lost all they love to the destruction of the Chinese. They have lost their loved ones, their homes, their country, their entire way of life. Yet they are full.

One peaceful young man, handsome and strong, had a Tibetan tattoo on his arm. It looked like a small, very ornamented, and beautiful barbell. I was attracted to it and asked, "What is that symbol?" He explained, "It is the vajra. It means indestructible truth. It is a symbol of strength. It covers where I was tortured." When he looked at his arm, he wasn't looking at torture. He was looking at indestructible truth and strength.

When we live from essence, we are not defined by the circumstances in which we find ourselves, we are made greater by the spirit flowing through us.

We must not confuse the forms of our life with the meaning and merit of our life.

Ultimately, we are able to take the most difficult of circumstances and call forth this life force. When we live through essence qualities, we can take any situation we are in, even situations we dislike intensely or feel are meaningless, and transform them into something of great and enduring value within us. For anything done through essence qualities is ennobled. It is lit with inner light, and elevated.

Prison is an extremely confining, depressing state. Its purpose is to punish and limit, and perhaps destroy. It is the exact opposite of freedom. Yet lest we think we cannot be free in prison, let us remember Gandhi.

Gandhi spent so much time in prison that he often gave the Yeravda Prison as his mailing address. For him, it was no different than home; life continued on. He even named his prison home Yeravda Mandir, meaning "Yeravda temple." There, he conducted life as usual—meditating and praying, carrying on his extensive correspondence, caring for both his friends and self-designated enemies, and converting fellow inmates to nonviolence, simply by his gentle, loving example.[24]

Gandhi did not see confinement, or repression, or reduced capacity. He saw, instead, Satyagraha, "Truth Force," growing through everything. One of Gandhi's greatest secrets is that he saw everything through essence qualities, not through physical form.

A concentration camp is a horrible place, just a few steps from death. It is a torturous road of despair and suffering and constant want, struggling through slow starvation, cold, denigration, filth, disease, and torture before you arrive at your destination—an intentionally cruel and unjust death. It is an extreme example of cruelty and hate. How could anyone take a situation like this, and call forth life from it?

Well, someone did. Lest we think we cannot love within cruel hate, let us remember Wild Bill Cody. His story is told by George Ritchie in *Return from Tomorrow*.

As WWII ended in May 1945, George Ritchie, then a U.S. soldier, was dispatched to a concentration camp near Wuppertal, Germany, with a team designated to provide medical assistance for the newly liberated prisoners.[25]

Many prisoners were beyond help. But within the desperate horror of the camp, he found Wild Bill Cody. Wild Bill was Polish, with a seven-syllable name so difficult to pronounce that he was named for his moustache. Wild Bill had obviously arrived at the camp recently—his eyes were still bright, his energy still indefatigable, even though he often worked up to sixteen-hour days with remarkable strength and endurance.

Because Wild Bill spoke five languages fluently, he often served as an invaluable translator between his fellow prisoners. Ritchie noticed that Wild Bill actually glowed with compassion for his fellow prisoners as he helped them. And Wild Bill helped all of them, regardless of their nationality. This was almost unheard of, because most prisoners hated those of different nationalities.

Yet as Ritchie examined the prisoners' records, he was stunned to discover that Wild Bill had actually been in the camp since 1939. He had lived through the same disease and starvation that had debilitated and killed the other prisoners. Yet amazingly, Wild Bill showed no signs of deterioration, either physically or mentally.

Wild Bill was looked on as a friend by all, and when fighting broke out between prisoners of different nationalities, he was the one they came to for arbitration.

Wild Bill advocated forgiveness.

Ritchie heard him suggesting forgiveness, and commented to him that it was understandably hard for the prisoners to forgive, since they had all lost family members to the enemy. At that point, Wild Bill spoke to Ritchie about himself for the first time.

In 1939, Wild Bill had watched as the Germans entered the Warsaw ghetto and lined everyone up against a wall. His entire family was against the wall—his wife, his two daughters, and his three small boys. He had begged to be able to die with them, but the Germans would not allow it because he spoke German and could be used for work. In the next minutes, the Germans shot his entire family with machine guns, right in front of him.

In one moment, all those he loved most dearly were gone.

It was devastating. But on that horrific day, he made a decision. He decided not to hate.

It was an easy decision. As a lawyer, he had seen what hate did to people. And he had just seen what hate had done to his family. He decided at that moment that he would love. He would love every person that he encountered, for as long as he lived, be it days or years.

That choice changed his life. With the physical deaths of his family, a new spirit was born within him. That spirit of love enlivened his body and his life . . . and kept him alive and safe through the worst horrors of war.

Wild Bill Cody's story gives us an inspiring, unforgettable

experience of what living through essence qualities can do. And the greatest of these is love.[26]

And so we see the transformative power of living through essence qualities. Gentle, slow, and quiet, they transform our lives into peace and love and grace. Though at first living through essence qualities appears to move slowly, the qualities acquire a vast, all-powerful momentum. Choice by choice, moment by moment, they gradually move mountains.

This is how we create heaven on earth. We all have that power now.

# 58 It Is Through Our Spiritual Hearts That We Join Heaven and Earth

***The more empty and pure we are, the more we allow the pure love to create through us***

The most important concept I am trying to convey in all this has nothing to do with the pleasing physical appearances or forms of my life. That is not the point. The physical circumstances of our lives will always change and cycle, as all physical forms do. The most important understanding is that the inner qualities of my life—the joy, the beauty, and the love—have come alive within my experience because I have consciously united with these essence qualities within my deep heart. We experience what we hold within our hearts. Our experience of essence is independent of the physical forms of our lives.

Another important key is surrendering my will into a greater will . . . and yet following the soul-inspired longing within my heart to love, to write, and to share. I don't worry about the forms in which that will happen. I know that the Unity is always allowing this to be expressed in the way that is most harmonious with what is happening this moment. My concern is with expressing the essence qualities of soul within this moment, and refining away anything less.

So the method I offer by which to create heaven on earth, and heaven in our lives, is with the two practices that have been described in the two prior chapters—surrendering what is not real within ourselves, and living from essence qualities. These actually are two facets of the same movement in consciousness. For as we surrender what is not real within ourselves, we find ourselves living in what is real and true, the essence qualities of soul and spirit. The relationship is direct. The more we surrender what is not real within us, the more we experience the beautiful essence qualities. Essence qualities have the power to create, they are creative forces. Eventually, they create us in their image. We become those qualities. This vastly changes everything. We become soul. We become grace. We become creators.

So to continue my story . . . As I practiced "doing" the actions of my life while "being" the essence qualities of the soul, my experience deepened into a more profound rapport with my soul. I began to experience that I was not choosing essence qualities, like love and peace, so much as that they were already streaming through my heart. This was new. I hadn't felt this when I began choosing essence qualities through which to live. But a deeper merging had occurred between soul and personality, and now soul essence qualities were pouring through my spiritual heart, like a flowing river, substantive streams that were almost palpable.

So I wasn't really "creating" with essence qualities at all—I was *joining* them as they poured through my spiritual heart. As my personality became more of soul, this became so obvious that I could physically sense it in my spiritual heart.

As our personality integrates more deeply with soul, the soul overlights the personality. As this happens, the soul streams its lovely qualities through us, filling us with their grace. These streaming soul qualities are true and pure, life-giving and good. These soul streams create. They are alive, and hold vast creative power.

When we have grown to the point of being able to receive essence qualities like love and peace streaming through our heart, and we are conscious of them, this immediately empowers these qualities in our lives. Our consciousness activates the qualities. Without consciousness, they remain mere potential. Once we consciously unite with essence qualities, we open to their vast power to create and transform through us.

Then a far greater power than we have ever known moves through us. We are no longer doer. We are vessel, purified vessel, pouring out in service to all. We are being moved by a higher force that creates through us, bringing to this moment exactly what is needed. This only happens when we surrender our personality to what is true, what is essence, what is real. This practice of surrender purifies our personality—our body, emotions, thoughts, and personal will.

It is through our spiritual hearts that we join heaven with earth. This is how spirit enters form.

This is how miracles occur. Miracles occur through a purified heart and mind. So we do not create miracles, we *allow* them through our purified self. What seems a miracle is only the natural harmony and goodness of the universe being allowed free expression. Only a purified heart can transmit the life force to earth, the life force that creates and transforms. Only a purified heart can unite heaven with earth.

My experience of the process is that as the heart becomes pure, it expands into the mind, purifying perception, until the mind is no longer restricted by illusion. Heart and mind now experience what is true and real. They are free. There is no more personality conditioning, only Truth. When the spiritual heart and spiritual mind join, we experience the soul. This is the realm of presence. The process spirals deeper and deeper, higher and higher, clearer and clearer, freer and freer.

This method of creating will not even be apparent, or make sense, or even be possible to do until the personality, spiritual heart, spiritual mind, and soul are integrated. Then the great powers of life and harmony are released. Then we recognize that we are not the "doer," but instead, the qualities of life that flow through us are the "doer."

Most people do not even realize that this river streams through their heart. It is something that is activated as we go deeper and deeper into our spiritual selves.[27] Because this experience is well beyond what most people have experienced, I will attempt to convey it with an example. And though the experience of heart presence cannot be fully captured in words, I believe you can begin to sense it through the following example.

The best way I can share this is by describing an exercise I call "Blessing Water."

Before I begin, please note that this exercise is distinctly different from Masuru Emoto's work with water crystals. His experiments use active volition and directed thought.[28] This exercise works through presence alone, without active volition or directed thought. It works from a deeper aspect of our being that is created when spiritual heart and spiritual mind merge into a wordless, volitionless pure love. It is done through the power of pure love.

In classes that I teach about the deep, pure love, we do an exercise called "Blessing Water." We pour common, chlorinated, unpleasant-tasting tap water into a glass. Then we hold the tap water in the presence of our spiritual hearts, gazing at it before us. Then we drink it. This exercise only works when one has mastered the skills of the deep heart, and can enter the deep core of the spiritual heart and abide in the pure love there.

This exercise is done through spiritual presence, not through the mind or the will. We are not asking or praying through words. We are not affirming or visualizing or intending anything. In fact, we are not thinking at all. There are no words. We are simply *being* the pure love, holding the presence of pure love within us. And we are radiating that love within our hearts to the glass of tap water in front of us.

The results are quite remarkable.

Every time, the water changes. It becomes something of much finer and higher quality than the tap water. For everyone in the room, it no longer tastes like tap water.[29]

And even more delightful, it becomes exactly what that person needs at the time. For one, it becomes sweet. For another, energizing. And for yet another, thirst-quenching. Interestingly, the water changes to become just what each person needs at that moment.

This exercise demonstrates how we enable the creative forces to create through our heart and soul. A pure heart allows the pure love to flow.

It also reveals a great secret of life. When we unite with the deep, pure love, the loving force that powers life, then that love will create exactly what is needed now. The pure love creates exactly what is needed now when it has a pure heart through which to express and anchor on earth.

And notice another great secret: we did nothing. We took no action. We formed no thought. We merely remained in the pure love. The pure love did the work. This is what we want to embody—being so clear that the pure love can move through us to do its work. Action which is actionless.

This is how miracles are created. Miracles are created by a mind that knows the truth: that what is true, and real, and enduring is love, is peace, is beauty, and all the other essence qualities of God, and nothing less. Miracles are allowed expression by a heart and soul that embody that truth.

Gandhi expressed this very well. Gandhi had the power to melt his enemies into compatriots and champions in the cause for India's equality and independence, which he led. He appeared all-powerful as the momentum of the Satyagraha movement swept away Britain's rule in India. When asked how he had acquired such power, Gandhi answered, "There comes a time when an individual becomes irresistible and his action all-pervasive in its effect. This comes when he reduces himself to zero."[30]

Gandhi was speaking about complete surrender of the personality to divinity, to essence.

Gandhi spent every day of his life meditating on the *Bhagavad Gita's* "Way of Love," the way of grace: "He is dear to me who runs not after the pleasant or away from the painful, grieves not, lusts not, but lets things come and go as they happen. That devotee who looks upon friend and foe with equal regard, who is not buoyed up by praise, nor cast down by blame, alike in heat and cold, pleasure and pain, free from selfish attachments, the same in honor and dishonor, quiet, ever full, in harmony everywhere, firm in faith—such a one is dear to me."[31]

The *Bhagavad Gita* is the Song of God. We let ourselves be used as the flute that the Song of God can play through. "Let God play through your heart like a flute."

God only sings of heaven, the inherent harmony and oneness within all life. And heaven is right within our own heart, when we surrender all that is not true. As we join that harmony, we bring it alive in the world around us. The more we surrender all that is not true within us, the more the harmony of life plays through us.

*This is the prayer of Love.*
*This is Love praying through us.*
*This is Love praying us, like a flute of God.*

We bow in our heart, surrendering to the Love, letting ourselves be used by Love, until we become the Love. And so we pray the melody, the prayer our deep heart is always praying: "Let this become Love." We pray this in every circumstance, facing what is right in front of us, just as the students did with the glass of water.

And so we pray:

*Let this become Love.*
*Let me become Love.*
*Let us become Love.*
*Let this become Love . . .*

And every time we pray this, heaven grows.

# PART SEVEN

# SETTLING INTO MY NEW LIFE

*It took me a long time to "get" living on an island . . .*
*But that all changed when I met a marimba band from Puna*

Osha Breez, of the Musasa Marimba Ensemble

# 59 Something for Me . . . The Story of My Wedding Dress

***Though I cannot begin to afford it, I allow myself to try on this one most beautiful dress***

We waited to marry so that our families and friends could get to know us as a couple. Then after a year, it was time to marry.

Since funds were limited, I had set a target wedding cost of between two and three thousand dollars. And from this sum, I planned to spend $200–$300 for a wedding dress.

What a surprise when I looked at wedding dresses online! The dresses that I liked cost as much as I had planned to spend for the entire wedding. What I had budgeted would not even buy a simple chemise, something that looked like a slip of silk. The dresses I liked cost ten times what I had hoped to pay, $3,000 and higher.

I looked at hundreds of dresses online. One particular dress caught my eye as soon as I saw it. It was perfect. No matter how many other dresses I looked at, I kept coming back to it. It was a Da Vinci dress. And I loved it. It was exactly what I was looking for . . . softly feminine with a flowing skirt, tiny waist, and lovely sweetheart bodice. It was exquisite. And it cost $3,500.

There's something very special about a wedding dress. When you see the one that is meant to be yours, you know it. Sort of like husbands. And this one felt like mine.

I called a local wedding dress shop to see if they carried it. They explained to me that it was no longer on their line, it had been discontinued. I called all the other local wedding dress shops . . . same story. So I called the Da Vinci wedding dress company in New York City to see who might still be selling it, and they explained that they no longer offered that particular style. Oh well. I'd have to find another dress in the retail stores.

And so we began the wedding dress shopping expedition. My sister and nieces headed out with me for the grand adventure. We stopped at David's Bridal first, and as we went in, I breezed by several lovely dresses, each breathtakingly priced at around three to five thousand dollars. Whew! The price I could afford to pay certainly did not fit this store. Yet I tried on about four obligatory dresses. I didn't really like any of them. They clearly were not my dress.

Next stop, House of Brides. This store also featured very lovely and expensive wedding dresses, in this case, a virtual warehouse of them. When we entered the store, there were rows upon rows of white and ivory gowns, hung up high, stretching all the way back for what seemed to be tens of yards. There were so many wedding dresses that the store took on a fluffy cloudlike appearance, as if we were in some sort of wedding dress heaven.

But the prices were not heavenly. Once again, the price tags were staggering. But I noticed a new section this time—the discard area, where damaged wedding dresses were marked down. The dresses were thrown in a bin, rumpled, and not even placed on hangers. The bin was filled with sadly stained satins, disheartening ripped lace, and unfortunate torn zippers.

My dress would have to come from here. How sad, for such a special moment. But this was nothing new. Having been so ill for so long, I was used to going without, living like a little mouse.

During my many years of illness, I had crimped and limped along with extremely limited funds every month, always living with the gnawing anxiety that I might not be able to keep my home. Many severely ill people live this way.

For years I constantly had to say no, no, no to any discretionary purchase or to anything fun. I often had to choose between what I called to myself "your money or your life," because I regularly had to balance financial decisions between securing adequate healthcare and keeping my home.

And now here I was again, having to say no to a wedding dress that I would be happy and proud to wear on my wedding day. With that, I began to rummage through the damaged dresses in the discard bin.

But this was my wedding! I would have hoped for something special. With a touch of sadness and wistful regret, I gathered about four dresses to try on, making the best of it.

But how wonderful to have a beautiful dress! Suddenly, I was inspired with a thought—why not just try on one of the really beautiful gowns?

I knew that there was no way I could afford a beautiful dress, and that I would be buying my wedding dress from the damaged bin. But this was my *wedding,* after all. Just this once, I wanted to give myself the experience of putting on a really beautiful wedding gown. Just this once, I wanted to see what it would feel like to try on a really beautiful dress from the good racks. Something for me.

Something for me. It was rather a rare concept for me. For all of my life, I had seldom taken anything for myself. I was always so focused on giving, and making things special for other people that I rarely thought about something for me. Giving to others came easily to me; taking something for myself did not come very easily at all.

I walked down an aisle in the wedding dress heaven section, and looked up at about three dresses, the first ones I came to. After all, it didn't really matter what I picked, this was just for fun. In moments, I reached up and took out a wedding dress that appealed to me. It was in section 241, as I recall. No gowns in the store were identified by manufacturer, they were all identified only by numbered rows.

Into the fitting room I went. Out I came in the dress with the torn zipper. No, definitely not. Back in I went, and out I came in a second damaged dress, this time with stained satin. No, still not my dress.

Then, for a break before the last of the sad dresses, I decided to try on the dress from section 241. It was lovely. I slipped it on, and it fit me beautifully, its shaped bodice flowing into my tiny waist and then out again in a full skirt that was exquisitely beaded and laced. I loved it. It felt like the one. How beautiful!

It was so lovely that I wanted to see it in the large viewing area. And so we all traipsed out to the fitting platform, every bride's "Queen for a Day" moment. I stood on a little podium surrounded by a circle of mirrors. I loved the dress; it was a delight. I circled happily around. My sister, observing, said emphatically, "That's it." It was that obvious.

I looked at the dress more carefully. It was indeed lovely. I noticed that the tag said that it was a Da Vinci, and it cost about three thousand dollars.

I looked at the style number on the tag. It seemed familiar. That did seem to be the number of the style that I had seen on the internet, the one that I had chosen as my dress. As this remarkable coincidence sank in, a sales associate appeared to begin pinning the dress.

As she worked, I told her that I thought that this was exactly the dress that I had loved on the internet. And I mentioned that everyone had said that it was unavailable because it was discontinued. With that, she looked at the tag on the dress. "Let me take a look, honey," she said as she turned the tag over. "Oh my. This is from our Michigan Avenue store. You're right. It's discontinued. It should have been marked down before it was shipped to us. Just a minute. While you step out of the dress, I'll check to see what price it should have been marked."

And so I stepped out of this one most beautiful wedding dress while she went to the front to research the correct price. When I arrived at her front desk, I could not believe what she told me: "I've taken the adjustments on that dress. There were several. The total should be $298.00." A mere tenth of the price.

I had tears in my eyes. I could barely believe my good fortune. I could have this one most beautiful dress! I could look beautiful on my wedding day.

How artful, how amazing, that I should go to the exact store that had the discontinued dress, even though they had told me they no longer carried it, pull it out of a rack of thousands of white fluffy dresses, the only good dress I chose, try it on even though it was almost ten times what I could afford . . . only to be told by the sales associate that it actually was exactly the price I could pay. And it was in my size, size 8.

It certainly was my wedding dress!

# 60 Putting It Together Again

***Going back and forth, navigating the waves of two different realities***

"It gets into your soul," David told me the night we met. "The islands change you. You're never the same after." Even going home that night on the plane, I knew what he meant. I was still experiencing the waves, just absorbing them, as if they were still all around me. The experience had been that big.

"But it will take some time," he said, "I had to go back and forth many times to realize what I had here. You will need that."

And so like the waves, I went back and forth, back and forth, mainland to Hawaii, mainland to Hawaii . . . then Hawaii to the mainland. In my first years in Hawaii, I was on the mainland twice as much. At first, being in Hawaii felt like I was missing something. I'd have to run back to see what was happening, as if I were missing out on life. After all, it's all happening back on the mainland, right?

Then, we would return to Hawaii. The soft island breezes would catch us in the open airport, caressing us with aloha. The softness, the gentleness, the love would begin to fill us, and tears would come into our eyes. Home. This precious place.

On our land, it would take a moment, a few days, to sink into the silence again, the richly comforting depth of nature. It was all-encompassing. And I would begin waking up filled with joy for the day, the golden warm sun streaming through the windows, the green gold of our land beckoning. I'd have to go outside first thing, to walk barefoot in the glistening morning dew, to simply be with the joy and beauty of this day. Sometimes I woke up before dawn, and took one pure moment outside to watch the last of the stars and moon, breathe the flowered, fragrant, pure cool air of dawn, and listen to the birds begin to sing with the rising light. What more could I want? It filled me.

Then, back to the mainland. Seeing the hard faces, the hurrying, the lack of personal connectedness . . . the struggle. Visiting with dear friends and family, feeling the warmth and good-heartedness, traveling the old, well-worn and loved pathways. Appreciating the intelligence and well-informedness of friends, the savvy and top expertise, the intellectual stimulation, the speed with which things get done, the courtesy and service of sales associates, relishing the books at the library, getting high-quality medical attention, enjoying our favorite eateries, entertainments, and amenities.

Then, back to the islands. And each time, appreciating more, belonging more, my heart settling deeper and deeper into this island home. David says it goes deeper and deeper into your heart, each time you return.

It is a transformation as gentle as the ocean's lullaby, this drifting into a new way to live, the waves of two different realities, ebbing and flowing through a life . . .

# 61 And Then There Was the Island Girl on the Plane . . .

***Showing me a different way to be female***

I was moving between the waves of two different realities, happy in both places. Chicago and the Big Island were so very different, I couldn't compare them. And I couldn't keep both places in my head at the same time. When I was in Geneva, I was "all" in Geneva. When I was in Hawaii, I was "all" in Hawaii. They were too different to keep in my head at the same time, in the early years.

One time, as I was going back and forth between Chicago and the Big Island, settling into my new reality, I sat next to a softly beautiful Hawaiian girl on a flight to Kona. Obviously part Asian, she smilingly told me she was an "island girl," raised on Oahu. (Oahu is our "city island," usually called "L.A. on an island.")

She was lithe, with long brown hair and dreamy, soft brown eyes . . . delicate and gracefully petite. Her clothes were soft and fluid, and her hair streamed down her back. She flowed. Even the way she sat in her seat, pulling her legs up cozily under her as she read, showed that she was very comfortable in her body, very relaxed with herself. She had a captivating quality to her—island ease with sparkling eyes. When she spoke, her voice was lilting, teasing. Playful.

But she was no lightweight. She was coming back from New York. Late thirty-something, she'd been educated in New York, in something forensic, and of course she had her obligatory Honolulu realtor's license on the side. She was married with two bubbly young girls who would meet her at the baggage carousel.

We spoke of island chant. I told her I was interested in ancient Hawaiian chant, and she commented that she would never consider chanting. It would take years of study with a kumu, a master, until she would feel safe chanting the sacred words. She did not want to offend or anger the gods.

Interesting. An educated woman, careful to not incur the wrath of the Hawaiian gods.

And also thought-provoking. This was a different way to be female. It was gentle and soft, at ease, natural, and very feminine. Easy. What you might call "yin"—deep, receptive, flowing, relaxed.

I was used to hard-driving Chicago women, women going places, with objectives and assertiveness. Very "yang." Conversations with women in Chicago were so often driven by goals—what I'm doing about my goals, how I am addressing my issues, what I'm asserting here. What I'm working on, what I want to get, problems to solve. Conversations were filled with career, activities, opinions, personality—getting there, asserting self in the world. Stout, assertive women with short hair in statement-making, presentation clothing. Yes!

This was so very different.

# 62 Chicago Was Now No Longer "Chicago" but the "Mainland"

***And it was becoming even more distant in lifestyle***

Chicago was now no longer "Chicago" but the "mainland," and when we visited Chicago, we were "off island." Here, we would travel to "Hilo town" or "Kona town" and "talk story" with friends.

My possessions made the transition too. My busy little leather appointment book became a simple one-page monthly island calendar. My fine-quality watch was damaged by the moisture, and became a ten dollar Walmart special, which I replaced as needed. My purse became a fanny pack. I stopped wearing any jewelry except for my wedding ring. My leather shoes were all damaged and changed to island "slippahs" and quality Keen hiking sandals. The casually dressy Chico's and Coldwater Creek clothing that I brought with me barely ever came off the hanger—I was living in shorts and Capri pants, never even a long skirt. I barely wore makeup, could not find a capable hair stylist, and on the very rare occasions when I needed dry cleaning, had to wait two weeks for delivery from the only drycleaner I could find on the entire island.

My laptop was learning a new language too. So many words used to describe Hawaii are not in my Word program and had to be added . . . delicious fruits like rambuton, jaboticaba, longan . . . beautiful places like Kilauea, Ka'u, Mauna Loa . . . flowing Hawaiian words like lani, lanai, ali'i, mana . . . hundreds in all. My Word program now speaks Hawaiian. And it's even bilingual in pidgin . . . howzat sistah?

I began to relax deeply.

One of the first things David had said to me when he met me was "I want you to be deeply rested." "Deeply rested!" The phrase was totally new to me—I had never even *thought* of being deeply rested my entire life. It was a new concept. I had always thought about pushing my limits—doing more, being more productive, how far I could get on my mountainous "to do" list. City girl.

But "deeply rested" was an enticing idea. And a healthy one. I had been sleeping, at most, about five hours a night. As I gently transformed into Hawaii's way, I began to sleep sometimes as much as eight hours a night, a major accomplishment. I hadn't done that in over twenty-five years. And my sleep was deeply nurturing. Being encompassed in nature, in its silence and total dark, away from people's activity and thought, all enabled me to get a very rich, deep sleep.

I hadn't realized it before, but in my townhome on the mainland, there was a constant "buzz" that kept me going till about eleven o'clock every night. Simply living in my much higher density townhome subdivision, watching TV late at night, being on my laptop or with people—all these contributed to my sleeping just a few hours every night. Even subtler things, like the "buzz" of electromagnetic fields or the constant lights of a suburban neighborhood, have an effect that isn't normally noticed, until you get away from it. And if you are sensitive enough, as I am, even a neighbor's thoughts or strong emotions will affect you.

Being so removed brought me back to the time of my grandmother's childhood, when the world became fully dark at night and the only sounds were those of people, wind and rain, and animals. There is a rightness to that, a harmony with life in that. A comfort.

I began to learn to slow down.

And I had to learn to slow down; it didn't come immediately. But the island is a good teacher. I learned, one experience at a time.

One time after racing to make my acupuncture appointment on time—and missing—I discovered that my acupuncturist considered arriving fifteen minutes late "on time." In Chicago, I would have missed my entire appointment.

Another afternoon, after grocery shopping, David and I went for a little adventure to an island inside the town of Hilo, where there is a waterfall that looks like a miniature Niagara Falls. On the island is a famous historic home, built by an early merchant, now restored as a bed and breakfast. Curious, we drove up to it, just to see its magnificent Victorian turrets, porch, and curved-glass windows a bit closer. The owner came to the door, thinking we were his next guests. When we explained we were interested in the home, he promptly invited us in. We discovered he had been busy stringing up Christmas garlands all afternoon. Yet island style, he took us on a tour of the elegant home. We spent over half an hour touring with him on the spur of the moment. That would rarely, if ever, happen in Chicago . . . and then by appointment only.

People have time here. Or as we say on the island, "Relax. You're on island time." We can arrive unannounced at a friend's home in the valley, calling, "Aloha!" as we walk across their open fields under the trees, and then sit and talk for an hour . . . the casualness is remarkable. No appointments. No date books.

Here on island time, people move slower. I watched the locals walk to the store and post office in the little town outside our valley. Their speed was about one third that of mine, and that was before they stopped to talk with their friends along the way. That taught me to slow down in town so I didn't stand out.

I found myself in a new world of almost no calls, no distractions, no interruptions. Pure silence.

A helicopter flying overhead is an event here; David and I go outside to see who it is. It happens about four times a year. One time, a few months after I arrived, David said one Sunday afternoon, "There they go again!" I asked, "What do you mean?" David explained, "The motorcycle club. They ride through the valley on Sundays every once in a while." I hadn't heard them at all because I still had "city ears"—I didn't hear car noise. But then, I too grew to hear vehicle noises in the valley, and began to say, "There they go again!" on Sunday afternoons.

And then there was the overwhelming gentleness of the island. It lulled me into its ease. Riding with David up to Kona with the balmy ocean breezes flowing over us in the car would put me to sleep—my tired, tense, exhausted body was not used to such ease.

And sitting on the beach, I would drift effortlessly into the mindless now of wind, waves, and sun. For me, the beach is where time dissolves into an endless infinity of now. Rather like the turquoise ocean dissolving into the infinity of the blue sky. Beach therapy. As good as any massage.

I kept remembering the island girl I met on the plane. She was beginning to represent something to me that I was to see more and more of here—people at ease and happy, enjoying at a relaxed pace. People here smile a lot. They're having fun. Their faces are relaxed and soft, not tense and hard.

They have time to talk with one another, and they speak slowly. I am still surprised at how much they laugh together. In a bank teller line, women are laughing; at a checkout counter, people joke. It even happens in doctors' waiting rooms, of all places. I have seen grown women, age fifty-something, collapse into giggles all through their conversation at Starbucks. It is the way of this island culture. Strangers smile at you; their faces are open, innocent. I find myself smiling back. Island aloha.

A wise woman told me long ago that Chicago is a place of struggle. It didn't make sense to me at the time. Struggle? In Chicago? But now that I have been on the island for a while, I have a different vantage point, and I understand exactly what she was describing.

Here, there is so much less struggle. David has even told me that you cannot press and rush on the island; it will work against you. Many people experience this. The rush and crush is gone, replaced by an island breeze.

You can't push on the island. Life slows down to the speed of trust here.

Islands teach a way of trust, not push. Of slow, not rush. No worries. Hang loose! You don't see wrinkled foreheads on the island. You see smiles and surfboards . . . or maybe just long hair, fluid clothing, and easy walking paces . . . but at least a lot less push. People live a lot longer here, too. Hawaii has highest life expectancy of any state in the United States.

I went to an appointment with a board-certified MD who breezily arrived at his practice in Hawaiian shirt and shorts. (Where was the thousand-dollar suit under the white jacket?) And he was sporting a pair of Crocs, not wing tips. What else would you wear with your professional MD shorts? Wing tips just don't cut it here!

Another lady MD wore a patchwork denim skirt that had campus-casual, fringed edges under her white doctor's jacket. Easy. Breezy. So very different.

Our tax accountant told us that his CPA boss didn't wear shoes to the office. What did that mean, I wondered—does he come in barefoot? No, the accountant explained, he wears island "slippahs," plastic thongs. Our accountant himself was wearing what he considered "shoes"—regular sandals.

I learned to "talk story" before doing business and to always joke. In my years in business, rarely anyone but salespeople joked. You cannot do business here any other way. Sometimes, with a local, I would "talk story" for fifty-five minutes of an hour, and then do business in the remaining five. Just the opposite of how I had been raised. I had been raised to place a premium on people's time, to take as little of it as possible, to move immediately into the business at hand, and then to thank them for their time. Such extreme time consciousness. I never noticed it because I had no basis of comparison. My corporate experience only cemented this. But here it was reversed. It is more about enjoying than about time, more about relating together than pushing to stay on schedule.

I remember listening to Kenneth Pelletier, PhD, MD, a pioneer in holistic health, speak decades ago. He described his trip to the South Pacific, where islanders would come up to him and laugh at him, shouting, "Time is money! Time is money!" They laughed at Ben Franklin's famous phrase. It made no sense to them.

In an island culture, neither time nor money holds the value it does in Western cultures. Islands grew up as barter cultures, where money and ownership did not exist. Time was not about money. Time was about the sun, the moon, and the tides, and how crops grew and fish swam in rhythm with them. Time was a cycle of life being lived, not a clock or a concept. Time was simply living, in tune with natural rhythms. And money was about the vegetables, pigs, and fish that islanders could trade within their family or tribe. Nothing needed to be stored for a rainy day because land and sea provided all everyone needed, every new day.

In fact, I noticed that even today, the general relationship to money here was very different. One event brought this home in stark contrast to me. I'd been on the island long enough to experience that people just don't talk about money here. We talk about other things. Then I returned to Geneva, Illinois, a lovely, affluent, and homey suburb of Chicago, and went out to Egg Harbor for breakfast.

At the table next to us, a woman was showing off her gorgeous new turquoise purse to her lady friends: "Two hundred dollars—and I got it for only $55 online." "Really?" A few tables away, a table of men huddled around their goal: "Yeah, so when we flip it, we'll clear $50,000." And then, nearby, a young man, opining to his wife, "It'll return 20 percent easy—in fact, with the iPhone, they'll create a whole new franchise. It's a buy, we gotta do it."

I was surprised to realize how many conversations in Chicago were made of quantities and of money. When I lived in Chicago, I thought nothing of it. I was used to it. But now, it stood out in stark contrast.

I remember that back in Chicago, Thanksgiving dinner in my family had often included a volley across the table of tech stock candidates to ride into the coming first quarter price surge. My first Thanksgiving with the neighbors here covered topics such as how to track bear, how to locate water on a long mountain trek, and the issues involved in planting purple potatoes. So very different.

Somehow, life was simpler here.

That simplicity showed up in so many ways. Where before I drove twenty minutes to take water aerobics in a big state-of-the art wellness center attached to a prominent hospital in suburban Chicago—in drab, gray water in a drab, gray pool room—here I splashed around outside on a sunny, blue day in a warm outdoor pool edged with bright magenta bougainvillea under the warming, golden sun. And the classes were free. So simple, so open, so free.

Yet with all the simplicity and seclusion here, at first when I arrived, I thought I would go brain-dead on the island. There was so little outer stimulation. I missed the intellectual stimulation of Chicago, with its high activity level. I was used to talking with people who had high levels of expertise, used to having a depth of resources and resource people available, no matter what the need. There's just something about the intellectual and cultural life of a city; it's brisk and moving. There's always a new exhibit at the Art Institute, a new performance by Cirque du Soleil, or new book on the well-stocked library shelves . . . a fascinating speaker, a fun community play, or a dinner picnic at an outdoor concert in the summer . . . and simply, all the fun events that come with belonging to family, church, neighborhood, and community.

I missed that.

But gradually, with every passing day, I found solutions. It was a bit like survival training, where you learn that you can actually feed yourself on the desert—you just need to develop a different way of perceiving—and different food preferences.

Luckily for me, there was the internet, with its vast array of possibilities, and Amazon, where an entire library can be purchased from the "Used—Like New" category for a mere fraction of what it cost before. Books replaced the heartwarming conversations I had enjoyed with friends, and my books became even better friends than before. They also helped make up for the community I missed with my spiritual circles in Chicago.

With less distractions and far purer concentration here, I could make much deeper studies of subjects, things for which I would never have had time on the mainland. As the years progressed, I began to look toward Henry David Thoreau and Helen and Scott Nearing, who chose to live away from the city and its dictates, devoting themselves to the single-minded, upright, lean, and sturdy integrity of their lives.

After a while, I ended up actually better informed than I had been in Chicago. It reminded me of my dear friends who live back in the ski mountains of Colorado, the Palmateers, tucked away near the mountains of Vail, far, far away from the world. I was always amazed and delighted to discover them far better informed on events and trends than me or my friends.

So Hawaii ended up being just as mentally stimulating as Chicago but from my self-directed efforts, rather than from joining in with what was already happening all around me.

After a while, I moved a step further in my viewpoint. I began to realize that so much of what I had considered stimulating about city life was not really stimulation, but *over*stimulation. We call it "overstim" on the island. Here, the level of "stim" felt just right. But then, I never know what I am missing on the mainland.

And nature became a much bigger part of my world.

I began to live in rhythm with the sun and the moon. Their movements became so much more obvious on the island.

When I first came, I went outside at 2:00 a.m. and was captivated by the magnificent glow of the moon. (Remember, this is when all we had was the outdoor bathhouse!) The moon was stunningly brilliant, almost as bright as day. I could see everything. It was so bright it even cast shadows, like the sun. I just had to sit under the stars, within their spell, and watch them, brilliant and sparkling, in the crisp, clear, dark night sky. I had never lived with this. And the pure, fragrant night air was intoxicating.

Living with the big open sky, it was easy to become keenly aware of the moon. It was always obvious in the sky, and I watched its shape change as it moved throughout its cycle, appearing in different places in the night sky. I began to trace its cycle, watching what happened at new moon, full moon, and quarter moons. Pink justicia flowers opened at the new moon, and guests always showed up unexpectedly at the full moon. New projects, and renewed energy generally began with the new moon, and big inner awarenesses occurred like clockwork at the full moon.

I had worked with all this before from the pages of my calendar and ephemeris. Only here, it wasn't coming from the pages of a book—it was coming from my life with the night sky. I began to pattern my life in even more harmony with moon cycles, guiding my spiritual development in soul growth cycles that unfolded with each moon cycle, for the moon's rhythm is a natural cycle of growth and unfoldment.

I realized, for the first time, that stars move through the night. Embarrassing to say, but true. I simply had not had a chance to really observe stars for hours at night before. Now in the valley, we watched the heavens turn, stars traversing their silent, wide arcs at night as we and friends warmed ourselves over bonfires, watching the brilliant moon as it set over the rim of the pali cliffs.

The sun, too, began to govern the rhythm of my daily activities. The sun was just a more obvious part of my life. I began to actually live the cadence of the sun's energy as it shifted throughout the day, and naturally, of my own accord, found myself choosing certain times for prayer and spiritual practice during the day. I was beginning to experience the natural, living rhythm of prayer and spiritual practice as it breathed throughout the day. Prayer times were no longer an idea set on paper—they were a living, breathing rhythm during the day. I began to understand why Saint Benedict and the Desert Fathers before him had prayed with the sun's turnings throughout the day.

As time passed, I settled in more and more. I no longer felt crazy, being on an island, all alone in the Pacific. I felt happy, and deeply fulfilled. Content. And it was deepening with every day.

I remembered a phrase from Thoreau that I had loved since I was sixteen: "A man is rich in proportion to what he can do without." It appears in *Walden*, in his chapter titled "Economy," in which he describes how simply he lived.

I had learned a different way to be. This was full, and balanced. In rhythm with nature, sustained by the substance of the earth. This for me was true wealth—the ability to choose how I spent my time, and to live within the wealth and endless beauty of the earth's garden and the abundant food it provided.

I finally had ground under my feet. This was a deeply stable root from which to grow my life. And to bloom.

# 63 From City Girl to Island Girl

### *Everything I needed to know I learned from a marimba band*

It took me a long time to "get" what living on an island is about. What finally did it for me was a marimba group from Puna.

They played at a concert in Hilo. We'd all been warmed up by a good hour of drumming, pulsing to the hypnotic beat of drums from around the world. The beat built slowly, starting with the quiet, hypnotic thump . . . thump . . . thump of a Hawaiian gourd, pounded on the ground to the rhythm of an ancient chant and hula. Then it moved on into meditative Korean drumming. It cut loose with sexy samba beats and hot flamenco, dove right into intense, strident martial Japanese taiko drumming, then drove on through the night with Caribbean, Cuban, African, and Conga drums . . . the beat, beat, beat surging on, on, on . . . building into the warm island night.

Then onto the stage stepped the Musasa Marimba Ensemble. Six marimbas of all sizes appeared with their players. Soon, their dulcet tones, softly muted, chimed out together in a tantalizing harmony that teased out into the night air . . . unwrapping tensions, soothing . . . easing and unwinding . . . sheer pleasure.

On stage, a graceful blond slip of a woman with long hair played her marimba. She got out of her head as the music started and let go into an ecstatic trance, giving her entire body over to the rhythms, letting the music fill her, play through her. Dancing behind her marimba, her head and long blond hair bobbing and swaying with the island music, she blissed out and wove back and forth as some beat within her hit the keys with her mallet, moving with the music's spell. Ecstatic. Natural marimba!

Sweet marimba sounds flowed out, their bubbling bliss winding into places that eased, then yielded. Their undulating, sensuous rhythm opened bodies . . . and spirits began to rise.

Marimba unwraps your worry, and it begins to soothe. It winds its way into your hips, and they begin to move, it gets into your heart and it begins to groove, and suddenly, you've moved into a much bigger groove . . . your spirit is free and overflowing, and you're gliding on joy!

People began moving with the music, spilling out into the aisles, dancing, hips jiving, arms swaying . . . carried by the music . . . joining the trance . . . smiling, laughing. More and more dancers filled the aisles, marimba ecstasy filled the air . . . bigger, bigger, bigger . . . the tantalizing beat, beat, beat, surging on, on, on—until the night, the theater, the dancers, the music—all came alive in one great pulse, one unity of hearts and bodies . . . one great explosion of happiness!

After that, I understood what it was to live on an island.

# 64 Our Little Cottage in the Woods . . . Or, How Simply Two Can Live

***Happy campers, once again . . . and once again, only cold water . . . but this time, not even a bathroom!***

When we come to the mainland, we live in a tiny little cottage in a great big woods in Geneva, Illinois.

It is a tiny little home of three small rooms, dwarfed under giant oak trees. The oaks are a century old and tower above, magnificently massive and protecting. They shelter a dancing stream that sparkles over rocks as it winds its way down to the Fox River. There are deer so gentle here that they watch us bring in our groceries from twenty feet away. Red foxes leap away in the fields as we come in at night, and "Mr. Lumpy," our resident groundhog, lumbers away as fast as he can—which is not very fast—when he sees our headlights. When we settle into the cottage at night, we hear the deep hoot of the great horned owl echoing through the great forest. This is the forest primeval!

When we sleep, we hear acorns hitting our roof, only ten feet above us. They fall from the giant oak that overarches our home. When it rains gently, it is the most beautiful, soft feeling because it is raining just over our heads. And when it rages with violent claps of lightning and whipping rains, we feel we are part of the storm. And we are. We are part of nature here, living just a wall and window away in our tiny home.

This little cottage in the woods is our joy. It is remarkable how we found such a precious place to live.

But once again, finding that gem didn't begin as a joy. It began one very hot summer in 2007, when David and I were both frazzled and weary from the intensity of our early lives together—so much to integrate and align together, constantly moving between mainland

and Hawaii, and constantly on the run to get things done—and now struggling with how to handle the logistics of our plan to travel and live yearly in the Chicago area for half the year. I felt very torn apart by it all.

Since we planned to be in Chicago half of every year for the indefinite future, we needed to find a place that we could stay. Ideally, it would be a place we could return to each year and, even more ideally, a place where we could keep our Chicago household so that we didn't have to schlepp it into, and out of, a new apartment every year. And even more ideally yet, it would cost almost nothing, because that's the budget we had to work with. We really didn't have budget to rent even the least expensive apartment. It was an impossible mission.

I even insisted, on top of all this, that it have a dishwasher, because I had grown tired of having to take time to wash dishes by hand in Hawaii.

Yet despite all these impossibilities, I felt driven, even desperate, to find a place to live, a place that was comfortable and that could remain ours throughout the year. Chicago at that time was still my "roots," and I needed a place to call home there. We were living in Lake Geneva, Wisconsin, that first summer, and I remember commuting to Chicagoland in July's intense heat, scouting budget apartments in the western suburbs. Everything I found was unappealing to me, unfriendly, and congested. And too expensive. And it was so hot and dry that summer, that it was like a tinderbox, an unforgiving, blistering tinderbox. It made the search feel even more barren.

After searching for several days in the wearying heat, I presented the most viable apartment complex to David, one just off a major street. To my chagrin, David responded to my efforts by saying, "Actually, I want to live some place where there are woods." Aargh! How impossible is that? I told him that a place like that in the western suburbs was a house, and it would cost at least $500,000. A bit beyond our means. It was already an impossible mission, and now, this made it doubly so. How frustrating.

I remember feeling very desperate that summer, all torn up from too much moving around the past two years and pressured by many issues. This home search was just one more struggle. And so I meditated on what to do about a Chicago home. My inner voice told me in meditation, "You will be given a home, a perfect home." My inner voice, as always, soothed me and gave me peace. Yet it seemed impossible to find a "perfect home." The message certainly didn't fit the data, but then I always respect what I am told within. When that happens, I just "put it on the shelf" and wait for more information to arrive.

Days passed, and no leads appeared. Then, one Friday evening, David and I were down in Illinois, readying to head back to Wisconsin, when we decided spontaneously to pay a visit to my friend Jeanette since we were in her neighborhood. It was a fun idea, something I rarely did—a spur of the moment breeze-by. Jeanette told me that her friends Joanie and Dennis would be coming over later after a movie, too.

So within an hour, all five of us were sitting together around the patio table. While we were talking, I received a sense that I should ask Joanie about our search. It felt like she was the next step. Did she know of any possible living situation with trees and woods?[32]

And remarkably, Joanie answered, "Yes, actually, I do." Remarkable. "Cindy, a friend of mine, has just decided to sell her little cottage in Geneva by the river. It is exactly what you are describing—a huge beautiful woods with a little cabin. She's been thinking of selling it for several years but has never been able to let it go until now."

Oh my gosh. It sounded wonderful. The next day, David and I looked at the cottage online. We got so excited! We discovered the cottage was part of a little village of tiny Swedish homes, gnome homes, we called them, in a beautiful forest of sixty-six acres adjoining the Fox River. They were enchanting. So tiny and cute!

The next day, we were on the phone with Cindy. Her asking price was $6,500. I thought I heard wrong. She did mean $65,000, didn't she? But no, she said it again, "$6,500." I could not believe my ears. $6,500 for a darling little cabin in the woods. That was less than most real estate taxes in the county.

We bought it on the spot.

And once again, we began with only cold water. And this time, not only was there no dishwasher, there was no bathroom!

It has become home to us.

We named our country home in the English country manor tradition. It's called "Falling Acorns." Not quite as dignified as Apsley House, Balmoral Castle, or Chatsworth . . . or even as graceful as Falling Waters for that matter, but it fits perfectly. Our private name for it is "Squirrelville" (definitely lower on the blueblood scale), inspired one fall day watching squirrels romping and undulating over the grass, digging and burying their acorns for winter.

It is a wonderful place. Here, we can walk in deep quiet woods and be surrounded only by a circle of ancient trees and the wisdom they hold. We can hear a great horned owl hooting in the full moon. We have happened upon a baby fawn, nesting in dried leaves by the bridge over the river, and have stared at it as it returned our gaze, sharing a moment of reverent and tender awe together. Berries line the shrubs and fill our summer with delicious, pure delight. Exotic mushrooms grow here—big as our hands, red and spotted, and plainly weird looking . . . perhaps, home for a gnome or nature spirit. When we rest on our bed, we look up at towering, graceful oaks, fluttering in the wind, and an expanse of blue sky.

Often, we are all alone in the park. At home cozily in the silence, we love the serenity, the deep nature. And all this, only one mile from the historic heart of a very charming, little river town, commutable from Chicago. How ironic, to be so far away from it all, when so close. And yet how delightful. The park is a hidden secret that many people in the town do not even know exists.

Our tiny little cottage is only 350 square feet, sans bath. There is a community bath house across the grass, down the steps, across the bridge over the river, and up the stone-lined footpath. A quarter-mile round trip in all. Difficult with diarrhea! And watch out for mosquitoes! But then, what a unique experience—after all, how many people can meet a friend on the way to their morning shower? And for another happy camper special, try being in the shower, a quarter-mile trip away from home, and realizing that you forgot your towel! Thank heavens for paper towels. A little ingenuity, a little playfulness, and all the problems dissolve—that's the Happy Camper motto.

A lot of people would not put up with this. It is deluxe camping to be sure. We love it. But then, we are Happy Campers. I cook on a Coleman camp stove (only the best—two burners, not one) and toast in a toaster oven. Thanksgiving turkeys are out of the question.

We have only three rooms—a kitchen/dining room, a living room, and a bedroom. Each is only about eleven feet by eleven feet. There is a little loft over the living room. It is a gnome home, to be sure.

This tiny 350-square-foot cabin teaches us how easy it is to live simply. And how little we need. For we must throw away anything that is not essential. There is simply no space to entertain thoughts of saving or collecting. It reminds me of Thoreau and his cabin at Walden Pond. He readily fit his entire life into a cabin of only ten by fifteen feet, which he built himself in 1845 for the sum of $28.125. He built his cabin free and clear, for a cost equivalent to one year's rent. He described it to a neighbor as light, tight, and clean. This left him free to live life deliberately, not beholden to, nor burdened by his possessions and debtors. It was a remarkable experiment.

We are extremely happy here . . . it feels light and free and easy. It is something I really can't put into words. The feeling of lightness is so rare in today's world. And then, it is charming because it is something so tiny, so creative, so made by hand. Its handmade imperfections invite creativity. It just feels good and fun to be in.

It reminds me of Rudolf Steiner's thoughts on children's toys. He recommended dolls with no faces, so that children could create their own stories, and develop their imaginations, rather than have the doll's story presented to them, as with Barbie dolls or *Little Mermaid* dolls.

Having very little is very freeing, almost in direct relationship. Simple. Light. Closer to essence. There is a great joy and relief in releasing possessions. We do not realize how much they burden us until we experience the lift of living without them. And the lack of cost to live here makes it effortless.

Guests are delighted when they cross the threshold and enter our home. It is like entering a different world. They become playful. Their faces light in fascination, as if they had entered a life-size doll house in which they can play. This little cabin invites creativity and happiness within people.

If only all could live as happily and freely and lightly!

# 65 We Buy a "Beach House" on the Ocean . . . Or, How Little We Really Need

***One deluxe Walmart tent, a camping permit, and we're sleeping next to ocean waves, held in warm breezes, watching the stars travel through the night sky***

One time, we got "caught" in Kona . . . too tired and too late to travel all the way home, not wanting to invest in a Kona hotel experience. What to do? Answer: sleep on the beach!

A quick trip to Walmart, our island's everything emporium, and we were set. We found a tent as big as a room in our cottage in Geneva—twelve by ten feet with a spacious eight-foot-tall ceiling. David could even stand up in it. Some flannel cloth sleeping bags (no need for a -35° rating here), a couple cheap pillows, a blowup mattress, a flashlight, and we were on our way. We had purchased and completely furnished our beach house in less than one hour.

David drove us to a fine little beach, Spencer Beach, up north. On the spur of the moment, we got in for the $12 permit fee. Try that in California, where you pay hotel room prices and have to make reservations up to one year in advance.

Not only that, but we found a spot right next to the ocean, where we could hear the ocean waves lapping all night long. We set our tent up in the dark, blew up our air mattress, and we were home. Happy campers, once again.

How easy is that?

The top of the tent was open, with just netting over it, and we got to watch the stars sparkle their way across the sky during the night. (That's when I first noticed that they move through the night.) Sleeping right next to the lullaby of the water was so relaxing, like being a baby in a womb. And we woke up feeling far more renewed and healthy than we would have had we slept in a hotel room.

Through the night, I was fascinated with how simple all this was. How lightweight, in a world burdened with complexity and redundancy. Where the choice for simple organic food, the way nature intended it, must be obstacle-coursed through GMOs and growth hormones . . . where homes are purchased at closings with monstrous levels of paperwork, inspections, and legalese . . . where weddings have become spectacular productions employing all kinds of consultants . . . and investing in stocks has become trading, then speculating, all at real-time speed.

So much of the Big Island teaches simplicity.

How much do we really need?

# PART EIGHT

# LIVING ISLAND STYLE

*Having entirely too much fun!*

Island abundance, so freely given

# 66 Trying to Capture How It Feels to Live Here . . . Easy, Full, and Rich . . . and Ever So Natural

***A night in the valley, a night at the Hilo Palace***

I'm trying to capture how it feels to live on the island, and it always manages to elude me in words . . . but maybe that's what islands are all about . . .

But just to give a feel for the island last evening, David came home from a long day in Kona, and he brought the most beautiful flowers that he had cut alongside the road. They were gorgeously, effusively, elegantly, beautifully—flowers—long, gorgeous plumes of soft magenta purple with stems of luscious chartreusey leaves—and they filled my arms. *Beautiful.*

How perfect for tonight's dinner with friends. As I arranged them into bouquets, I reflected: plenty. Plenty for us, plenty for them. That's the way it always feels in Hawaii—we take fruits back and forth to each other's homes, and flowers, and potted plants. The women in our valley are always sharing flower cuttings with one another; it's one way we express friendship here. *Plentiful.*

David and I talked about going and getting cuttings of the bouquet beauties on our next trip to Kona and then planting them in our garden. It's that easy to start a garden here. You just take cuttings, come home, and stick them in the ground. Voilà! Le jardin. *Easy, even effortless, because the aina, the earth, just gives and gives.*

Then we went over to our neighbors' for dinner. Their home, built out of glowing red and golden koa wood on the inside, was softly lit with candles all around on this beautiful valley evening. The home is stunning, with a distinctive architectural design created by the owner. It is elegant, with a massive koa ceiling and beautifully carved, gigantic braces at the sides of the walls. Truly unique, as so many homes are here. *Glowing warmth.*

The night was filled with stars, and we sat out on the open lanai around a dinner table filled with twinkling candles, glowing brighter as the deepening Prussian blue of evening settled around us. We looked out in the dark over the very large and long, long lawn rimmed by tall cypress, and island palms growing up to one hundred feet on all sides. *Elegant.* It could be an estate, it could be a formal garden, a privileged reception area, but it's simply the valley, and so it has no such pretense, only a relaxed enjoyment and beauty. The valley night air was so sweet, so balmy, so silent as it enveloped us. *Rich and leisurely, flowing and so well cared for . . .*

Dinner is simple . . . and artful. The wife is an artist, through and through. Sushi made with smoked salmon is followed by an island delicacy—ahi belly, the belly of the yellowfin tuna. Delicious simply grilled, it joins the table with a salad artfully colored in slices of orange carrot, red cherry tomato, and fresh spinach from the farmer's market at the plantation town down the road, a simplicity of beauty. Dessert is a first try, and it is a fabulous panna cotta. We figure out how to unmold it from its little bowls in the kitchen (a bowl of hot water does the trick) and then cover it with her delicious raspberry coulis, a sauce she strained very carefully through a sieve (how long did *that* take?). Topped with blueberries and perfect raspberries. "How did you get such perfect raspberries on our island?" I ask. "Oh, I just handpicked them from the frozen ones." *A labor of love, delicious, and unforgettable for its love and beauty.*

And the next day, we traveled to Hilo for a tango concert. We saw some of the world's best, a troupe of top Argentinean tango dancers. They danced at the Palace Theatre, which is an ancient theater in Hilo, grand for its day, but in a bit of genteel poverty today. And every time I'm in it, I so appreciate being on the Big Island. It's so different from the polished theater districts of Manhattan and Chicago that I had known before. It is not slick—we sit there in a non-air-conditioned theater with the paper fans they offer, fanning ourselves. Even so, it's wonderful, and this afternoon, we can hear the island rain pouring down outside, because the open door is right near us.

It's all so informal that it's delicious. The island is so small that everyone in the theater feels a bit like our neighbor, whether we know them or not. There's a closeness, a lack of distance. The emcees for the evening are always very plainspoken people, someone like your next door neighbor, just some kind person who got up, took courage, and introduced tonight's entertainment to the six hundred people who fill the theater.

A technician or two might walk out on the stage during intermission or before the performance, something we'd never see in Chicago or New York's theater district, where everything is so professionally perfect. Just like the casual steps that lead up to the stage on either side, noticeably marked with white tape so no one trips. Something you'd never see in a big-city theater! The band is just to the right of the stage, sitting in the audience. It's all so informal and easygoing. Friendly. Human. Community. Like you are part of something, something you can participate in and create.

The tango dancers are fabulous, and our audience grows warmer and warmer in their applause. The aloha keeps growing bigger and bigger until, at the end, as our emcee gives each performer a Hawaiian lei and a kiss, there is a palpable, close-to-tearful sense of how beautiful this has all been. I think we surprised the tango group with our outpouring of warmth and love. It's something true Hawaiians are known for: big aloha, big mana. The concert itself was called "Aloha for Japan," a benefit for the Japanese after their quake and tsunami.

I guess what I'm trying to put into words is that it's not air-conditionedly perfect. It's not polished, sanitized, and slick. It's real—comfortable, natural, sweaty, something you can relax into and feel part of. You're never an observer on the island. It's so small and friendly here, so unstructured, that you are always part of what is being created. Island life is always alive and growing, waiting for the next creative impulse.

And I still can't quite capture it in words.

# 67 A Group of Seniors Dancing the Night Away Under the Stars . . .

***In a hidden valley, on a speck of island somewhere in the Pacific, on this spinning globe***

Nothing much happens in the valley. But one night, a happy senior resident turned sixty. And he threw a party.

He brought in his favorite live band from Alaska and rolled out a wheelbarrow overflowing with limes (from his own trees) for the margaritas.

Everybody from all around came, which is to say we had a bunch of seniors. Farm and work clothes were shed, and neighbors appeared as we'd never seen each other—dressed up, made up, and looking downright pretty and handsome—looking as we'd never looked to each other across our fences, with the coffee farms and mac nut orchards in the background. We all looked "Wonderful Tonight."

As dinner moved through dessert, dusk grew to nightfall, encompassing us all in the total darkness of the valley—no street lights, no house lights, just the wild that is the valley. People warmed themselves by open fires that flamed gold and orange in the "Deep Purple" night.

And then the band began to play. We danced to the tunes of the sixties and seventies like it was only "Yesterday." People who I'd only seen behaving like sedate seniors now danced together like the wild things they were in their secret hearts. "Crazy." One new lady resident asked every single man to dance; she was the "Dancing Queen." "Get Down Tonight."

Normally, the valley is filled with the "Sounds of Silence," but tonight, strains of "(I Can't Get No) Satisfaction" and the Beatles' "Ticket to Ride" joined the crickets, and floated out into the fragrant night air. Almost the entire valley had "Come Together" under the stars and the tall palms in this "Blue Velvet" of a night.

And above it all, the moon and stars silently arced their way above, over all the merrymakers, a group of seniors dancing the night away in this hidden valley, on a speck of a remote island somewhere in the Pacific, on this spinning globe . . .

"Still Crazy After All these Years."

# 68 "Lani" Means "Heaven"

***And never will you hear the phrase used more often***

In no language have I heard the word "heaven" used so often. It is everywhere in Hawaii—in people's names, place names, resort names, even things as mundane as street names. It is part of everyday life. And it is understandable, for nowhere is there so much beauty.

Just recently, when we were celebrating our anniversary in Kona, we had a lovely island girl for our dinner waitress. She was born and raised on the small island of Lanai. Her name was Mahealani, and she carried the beauty of the islands. And like the islands, her manner was gentle and unassuming, graceful and flowing.

With her quiet, subtle grace, Mahealani moved like the gentle, soft rays of moonlight. We were charmed by her softly delicate manner as she told us of how she grew up on Lanai, where she could see all the islands circling round her. Lanai keeps to the older Hawaiian ways, and she lived with these customs during her childhood there.

Mahealani is named for Mahea, the full moon on its third night when it just begins to lose its roundness and is hazy. Her name means "heavenly moonlight." She embodies her name. How lovely.

It was not always that babies could be named "lani." In the old days, that distinction was reserved for the high-born girls of the ali'i, the kings and queens. In those times, every Hawaiian was given a name unique to them. And each name flowed like poetry.

Listen to a few of their high-born names . . . Keopuolani, the "gathering of the clouds of heaven" . . . Kapiolani, "the heavenly arch, the rainbow" . . . and Ka'iulani, the "the highest point of heaven." Each one is touching and graceful, and each of these women brought blessing to their kingdoms.

Keopuolani was the most sacred of the great King Kamehameha's wives, with rank so high, in fact, that Hawaiian commoners, the makainana, had to bow in her presence, their faces touching the ground.

This queen did something quite courageous and revolutionary in 1819. She ate with the men. Not only that, but she also ate banana and coconut. Both these acts were forbidden, punishable by death, because they could incur the gods' wrath, causing disastrous quakes and poor harvests. But lo and behold, no vengeance was wreaked upon her by a Hawaiian god. This was news. It changed their way of life. In this way, she did an enormous amount to release the Hawaiian kingdom from its harshly punitive, superstitious kapu (taboo) system.

After her came Chiefess Kapiolani, who also lived during the time of the earliest missionaries. She too, helped move Hawaii from superstition—but at very high risk. She challenged one of the most powerful gods in all Hawaii, the goddess Pele, ruler of the great volcano at Kilauea. In 1824, she walked across the lava fields to the great volcano. There, she defiantly broke a custom that could mean death at the wrathful hands of the goddess Pele—she ate sacred ohelo berries without first offering them to Pele. Then she went further and prayed a Christian prayer, the first ever uttered by a Hawaiian to Pele. To Hawaiians, this meant imminent death.

Going even further, she boldly stepped down five hundred feet into the main vent of the volcano. Yet she remained unscathed, to the amazement of her fellow Hawaiians. Her heroics were immortalized by Alfred Lord Tennyson in his poetic tribute to her, "Kapiolani"[33]:

*Great and greater, and greatest of women,*
*island heroine, Kapiolani*
*Clomb the mountain, and flung the berries, and dared the*
*Goddess, and freed the people*
*Of Hawa-i-ee!*

Princess Ka'iulani, a beautifully graceful, regal, and intelligent young woman, was educated abroad to prepare her to lead her Hawaiian kingdom. Yet she suffered the heartbreaking experience of watching as her kingdom was lost to the interests of American businessmen. She died at only twenty-four, in 1899, after the loss of her kingdom. A recent movie of the same name tells her story.

Today, "Lani" is a favored girl's name, and so you will hear names like Leilani, "heavenly wreath of flowers," and Pualani, "heavenly flower." Many names celebrate Hawaii's natural beauty, such as Kailani, "heaven and sea," Kalani, "sky," Nalani, "the heavens," and Noelani, "mist of heaven."

We have place names like Wailani, "heaven of water," and Aolani, "cloudy heaven."

The streets are filled with lani names. In just a few short blocks in downtown Hilo, our major eastside city, we pass Lanikaula Street, "heavenly prophet" . . . Leilani Street, "heavenly lei" . . . and Kawailani Avenue, "heavenly water." Honolulu has an Ala Lani Street, meaning "road to heaven."

Even resorts are called lani, like the Mauna Lani, "heavenly mountain."

And so it goes, the word "lani" being used everywhere. But it's understandable—Hawaii is about as pililani, as "close to heaven," as it gets!

# 69 As Free As an Aloha Breeze

***Free to be who you are, naturally . . . as free as the wind blows***

Free spirits!

One of the things that struck me early on about the island is that people are free to be who they are here. And they express themselves as they are. There is no sense of "being careful to fit in" or of being judged as more or less. People are free to be their own, very unique selves. Probably, a lot of this is because there is no homogenous culture within which to fit.

I remember a man who called himself a "minimalist," meaning he had no possessions, and was content to live that way. He was a classically trained cellist who made CDs and sold them on the beach. He'd maybe make $50 a day—on a good day. Island style. No car, no home, just vagabonding it around the island, finding shelter wherever people would take him in.

Islands have probably always been this way, free as the wind.

One thing that helps the Big Island be so free is that there is no dominant culture. The island is home to more ethnic groups than any other place in the U.S. And it fairly well reverses the ratios of the mainland. Here, Caucasians are the definite minority, only about one third. Asians make up about one third, and by far the biggest group is mixed ethnicities, or what the U.S. Census calls "mixed race."

Our island is a brew of so many ethnicities that there's no dominant way to do anything. We have Hawaiian and part-Hawaiian, Caucasian mainlanders, mixed-ethnicity locals, and Japanese, Filipino, Chinese, Korean, Thai, Afro-American, Samoan, Tongan, and Marshallese. We can celebrate New Year's three ways here, and on three different dates—Chinese New Year, Tibetan New Year, and of course, mainland New Year, the only one I knew before.

We can eat breakfast many ways—Japanese miso soup, Portuguese sausage, or a loco moco, a local favorite of rice topped with hamburger patty, fried egg, and brown gravy. McDonald's serves not just burgers but also teri-burgers for Asians and taro burgers for locals.

People build incredibly eclectic homes here—say, an exotic pod home over a lagoon or a treehouse, high enough up that it's far from the eyes of the building inspector.

A surprising number of people live very lightly here, people who are happy with almost nothing. There are kids who live at the beach in their tent or converted van, selling cane juice to tourists or weaving hats. Some adults have lived this way for years. Others live in buses or greenhouses or yurts. One woman even lives in a lava cave.

And there are kids who trade garden and farm work for housing. These aren't islanders, they're often college-educated, mainland kids. In fact, there's a formal program for this—you just become a WOOFER. What's a WOOFER, you might ask? Well, a woofer is a member of Worldwide Opportunities on Organic Farms, someone who has contracted with a farm to trade work for housing.

As you might guess, there is no dress code here. How could there be with all this diversity?

In Hilo, we see kids from Puna, our southeast hippie area, with their dreadlocks and body piercings, wearing soft droopy clothes and artful tattoos . . . and possibly rainbow hair. They're called "Punatics." They stand out. When you see a Punatic, you'll know it.

Delicate, little Japanese ladies wear tiny-patterned, careful dresses as they shop in our fine Japanese fabric store in Hilo.

Native Hawaiians and locals often dress in T-shirts and jeans, their strong, sturdy bodies and massive shoulders carrying a lot of weight. Their stunningly strong tattoos speak of ancient tradition, with triangles that display their generations of "bloodline," their Hawaiian blood.

And just as we have many different ways to dress, we have lifestyles to match, all over the map.

There's a woman who's devoted her life to saving bees from their current scourges. She came to our home to remove more bees in the wall, and happily sang to them as she gently coaxed them out of the wall. She wore no protection at all, only her song. A guidance dream of bees led her to the island and to her work.

A rebellious old local named Abe owned up an entire surf beach, squatting there for decades, claiming royal blood. For years, he played the role of gatekeeper at Kawa Beach, determining who got to come and play and stay at "his" beach. For years, he defied realtors and government officials, until one fateful day government helicopters came in and closed him down.

Where else could you find a retired gentleman who makes his living by painting gourds, which he sells for thousands of dollars? Or people working in wild pig control? Or coqui frog control?

And so it goes, in the breezy flow of the island. Free to be as you want to be, as free as an island breeze.

# 70 "Aina" Means "Earth"

***This island is a living, breathing being, bursting with life***

Living on the island, we become part of the land.

To touch the earth here is to be immediately filled with its presence, and to become part of its mana, its spiritual presence. It is a sacred and reverent experience. This is the way it was held by the native Hawaiians.

Everywhere around, we can feel plants breathing with the wind, growing voluptuously in the soil's rich nurture. Everywhere we step, the earth is pulsing with abundant life. Every breath we take is filled with sky and sweeping wind, the perfume of island flowers, the spray of ocean mist. The life force here is astounding.

It is so relaxing, so opening, so loving . . . so giving. In Hawaii, the earth is called the "aina," which means, beautifully, "that which feeds." All of nature around us is abundantly nurturing, feeding our bodies and all our senses. Land gives life. It breathes life into us.

We cannot help but be aware of the aina all around on the Big Island . . . it is so encompassing in its power, so sweeping in its majesty. Its powerful life force is everywhere . . . in the breathtaking power of Akaka Falls, which sweep all the way down a huge tropical cliff in misty feathers of cascading water . . . in the soothing lullaby of ocean surf with softest, clearest warm blue waters and caressing white sands that hold us in a place of timeless ease . . . in the vibrant display of countless brilliant shimmering fish and coral under the water . . . in the sheer power of the life force here, where plants can grow many inches, even feet, after the gentle nurture of an island rain.

The mana of the aina is everywhere. The elements here are overwhelming. That is why it is easy to see how the ancient Hawaiians brought the powers of the land to life in the forms of gods and goddesses. For example, Pele is the goddess of the volcano and makes her home in Kilauea, while Laieikawai is the goddess of rainbows and lives beyond the clouds. Lono is the God of abundance and fertility, ruling rain, peace, and music. Kanaloa rules the sea and the waters and all their life forms, as well as healing. And Kane is the greatest God of all. Kane is the creator.

The aina was always sacred to Hawaiians. They valued the earth and the sea greatly, as do all native peoples, even to the point of feeling kinship with the plants. They considered the taro plant, a diet staple, their elder brother.

That tradition of reverence continues. Even today, someone who is "pono," right and true with Hawaiian sacred tradition, always asks permission of the spirits before entering a sacred site, whether it be a historic Hawaiian site or any natural enclave like forest or seaside, or even another island in the Hawaiian chain.

This reverence is expressed with an offering of flowers, plants, or food. Then, permission is asked to enter. Only then is it pono, right and in balance.

And always, heartfelt thanks are offered for the blessing of being part of this wonder.

# PART NINE

# DEEPENING IN THE PURE LOVE TOGETHER

*What we are really doing is learning to remain in the deep love within our hearts as we relate to each other.*

As we extend this deep love to each other,
we walk to God through each other's hearts.

# 71 A Sacred Wedding

***I promise to be a real beloved for you . . . the beloved Guide Sidi marries us in a circle of angels***

Many months before we were married in a traditional Protestant ceremony, we had a spiritual marriage with Sidi. This was deeply spiritual, and far more powerful than our traditional ceremony. In fact, it was far more powerful than any wedding I have ever experienced.

Long before, we called Sidi in Jerusalem to ask him if he would marry us when he came to the United States. Sidi goes to God and asks for permission in everything he does. No sooner had I asked the question than he replied in his powerful, deep voice, "When I come, I make it."

Sidi is a man of very few, very powerful words. Beloveds, those who have taken the promise with him, phone him, he answers, they ask their question, and he replies in one powerful sentence, and hangs up. He doesn't speak fluent English, so his brief words, combined with the power of his presence resounding through his strong voice, resonate like a pebble through the pool of a longing heart, penetrating out in waves that grow deeper and deeper, wider and wider, within the listener.

One phrase from Sidi can change your life. This has been my experience more than a few times.

Permission to be married by Sidi is not always given. For another Sufi, a woman who asked if he would marry her and her beloved, Sidi said, "Be patient, beloved." Every time she called, this was his answer. He never gave permission for them to marry.

To understand this and not feel that Sidi is taking unwarranted license with people's lives, you must understand that Sidi carries great wisdom. Many consider him a perfected being, the divine within human form, almost all-seeing and all-knowing. His presence alone can return people to the Unity, God. And this is sufficient to know. Not everyone sees who Sidi is, however. In fact, most people don't see Sidi at all.

And so many people like the assurance of examples. So I will tell you one simple story from the many, many stories of his miraculous healings and his remarkable seeing. One morning, from his home in Jerusalem, he called a Sufi leader on the east coast to wish her a happy birthday. She was delighted that he knew that this was her birthday. I don't believe that she had ever told him. But whether she had or not, she also noticed something very special—Sidi had called her at the exact minute of her birth. When she mentioned this to him, he said simply, "All praise be to God, beloved." He tells us that he has known our souls since before we were born, and with examples like this, it is easy to believe.

Sidi never takes anything to himself—no praise or thanks, no money, no comfort. It is all for Allah, the One, the great Unity. He wears a robe, one of about three that constitute his entire wardrobe. He travels with a suitcase, but it is empty. He raises millions for charity and sleeps on the floor. He is a holy man.

Once, when he was teaching the Sufi teachers, there were about twenty-five of us gathered around him. He was speaking of service, giving his life in service. Suddenly, I was drawn into his heart. In one moment, I felt my energy field far bigger than I have ever known—way above me, and way below me, through the floor. And my field was shaking. In the same instant, I felt collapsed into nothing. And at the same time, I was filled with something I cannot even describe. I was taken into an instant experience where I was filled with a capacity, a presence, a commitment for service far greater than any I had ever known before. Bigger than I had ever felt, smaller than I had ever felt, consumed by service. All, in one instant.

The experience was shattering. I ended up sobbing, just to integrate the shock of it.

These are examples of the profound presence of the Guide Sidi al-Jamal. He would surely say "All praise be to God, beloved" rather than have me talk about him. So it is really grace that he is imparting when he gives his blessing for marriage or withholds it. It is all in the mercy.

Sidi married us in June.

David and I had just flown in from a whirlwind of busyness in Hawaii and had just barely gotten there, arriving in California late the night before. We were coming to attend several days of Sidi's teachings, knowing that on one of those days, he would perform the weddings.

That first morning, we dressed quickly, just grabbing any nice-looking clothes from our suitcases, and rushed out to drive through the lovely rolling wine country of Napa, California, and on into Pope Valley for Sidi's teachings. The day was crisp and sunny, gorgeously blue—a perfect day for a wedding.

We arrived a bit late, took a place on the floor, and listened to Sidi's teachings. Then, suddenly, at the end of the morning teachings, Sidi said he would perform the marriages.

It was not at all as you would expect a wedding to be—no fluttering arrangements, no pomp, no flowers, no dress . . . no physical preparation on our part at all. The emphasis was entirely spiritual, just the reverse of most weddings.

Sidi was teaching on a low platform, and David and I sat just in front of him, facing each other. We held both hands together, looking into each other's eyes. Another Sufi couple also being married sat immediately behind us. And all the other Sufis present surrounded those being married in a loving, tenderly admiring circle. A hush fell over the room.

Then the wedding begins. Sidi approaches the throne of God, and asks permission to marry us. When permission is given, angels come and encircle Sidi and both wedding couples. Within the angels' grace, Sidi then spiritually weaves together our bodies—our physical bodies, our minds, our hearts, our souls, and our spirits—so that they are entwined in a unity.

He then intones the vows, slowly, one at a time, as we repeat them. These are very deep promises to God, the One, the Unity:

> I promise to be a real beloved for you.
> I promise to be all for you, and only for you.
> I promise to give you everything.
> I promise to give you my body, my mind, my heart,
> my soul, my secret.
> I promise to always be honest.

I promise never to break your heart.
I promise to always take care of you.
I promise to always stay with you.
I promise to love you
All my life.

As we are repeating our vows, Sidi works to clear our karma. He may ask one of the people being married to repeat a special vow, based on their own personal karma, for instance, emphasizing that they will remain in the marriage.

And then at the end, Sidi intones, "God is the witness." And we repeat, "God is the witness."

And then, we kiss.

It is all over in a matter of moments.

It is about as simple as a wedding can be. And it is as profound as a wedding has ever been.

# 72 Writing Our Own Sacred Love Story . . . Together

***Learning to be the complete love for each other***

Once, I wrote a sacred love story about all that love could be. It was a story that flowed through me, heart and soul, pouring out in images that appeared as I woke, images that spilled into words on paper.

It was a story of difficulty and struggle in love, lyrically counterpointed with an enchanting story of all that love could truly be. Most important, it was the story of how to take the struggle and transform it into the grace of pure love. It was what I had lived with my own life, and now, it was writing itself through me as a shared life.

It was a story of living together in the deep love.

I walked into that story when I met David at the airport.

And now, we write our own sacred love story together. What was once a story on paper now has come to life as we weave it through the fabric of our daily lives. The deep love has given us so much. Through that love, we have healed a great deal of what is not love, which allows us to travel deeper and deeper into the pure love together.

For we are learning to be the complete love for each other. We are learning to relate to each other, not as "you and me" or even "us" but as people who live and move in relationship to the deep, pure love that abides within our spiritual hearts.

For our truest relationship is with love itself. This is the sacred love story.

And as we learn to see each other through this love, we make our marriage sacred.

When we see each other through this love, we enter the place where we are One. Two people, in one unity. This is the true definition of spiritual relationship: learning to live in the pure love within ourselves, and learning to walk to God, the great Beloved, through each other's hearts.

We begin to see each other as carrying qualities of God. This is the way we see the Face of God in our partner's eyes, and in our partner's essence. We have Sufi names, given by Sidi in his loving wisdom, to remind us of the qualities of God that we carry. The names quicken those qualities within us.

This sounds very idealistic to many, I am sure. But it is true and real, and here is how you can begin to realize that this just might be possible: somewhere in your heart right now, you were touched by this. You either wanted to move closer or to pull away, but either way, you were touched.

If you find that true, I would ask you to stay with that feeling of being touched until you become more aware of it. Let it deepen.

Now, drop just a little deeper in your spiritual heart, and see if you can touch the longing that lies there. Just sit with this for a few moments. See if you can allow that longing to express itself to you. How does it feel? What is its physical sensation? Its emotion? How does it move? What color is it? What does it look like? Does it have a sound?

After you have explored this, then see if that longing can express itself to you in words.

You are beginning to touch the place in you that is only love. It feels like longing, because you do not know it. But oh, you remember it! Stay here a moment.

Let this longing lead you deeper still, to the very core of your spiritual heart. This is the place where you are always loved, just as you are, this moment. Let yourself feel this. Let yourself touch what it feels like to know that this pure love is always loving you, no matter what you think or what you do, no matter if you are feeling loved or unloved, worthy or unworthy. This place is the point of God in you. It is the communion point where you partake of God. It is God in you. This place, this state of being, is always loving you, just as you are this moment.

As you abide in this place in your heart and stay true to it, it will open a loving world to you.

This is the pure love, the divine love. As we grow, we allow ourselves to disappear in this love. We move beyond the world of senses, through the subtle world of the heart, to the subtler world of the soul, and finally, we disappear in the Unity of God.

It is always a journey, this deep love . . . always a deepening, a growing into more. It is a process of letting go, again and again, of what separates us from the pure love. Along the way are many veils that we let go, as we travel to the purity within our hearts.

Marriage provides us with many opportunities to release the veils and travel deeper into this love. For the way we experience each other reflects to us where we are within our own heart. Are we living in a world of pure love together, or something less? If it is something less, then we look within ourselves to learn what God is asking us to see. What do we need to release?

We can make of this shared moment a heaven, or something less. It's not as hard as it might seem. It just requires giving up what is not love in ourselves.

So David and I have a different way of dealing with conflict than most people. Basically, we don't believe it. We believe the love. And we allow the conflict to become love as soon as possible.

This makes things very artful. We didn't begin this way. We began with some very rough edges. But we *learned* this way. We grew and refined ourselves so that we can return to love quite gracefully now.

We call the light of God into the heart of every difficulty.

When we have a conflict—a misunderstanding, an argument—we work with it together through our spiritual hearts. We pray the Remembrance together, entering holy space within our hearts, saying the name of God over and over, bringing the light of God deep into our hearts, until our hearts themselves become light. And the separation is washed from our hearts, dissolved. A lot of the time, that's all it takes. Remembering.

Or we pray the Sufi prayer of forgiveness, until the hard, defended places in our hearts soften. It begins with David and me each praying separately on the couch, again and again bringing the words of light into our hearts. The light moves deeper, washing away what is not love. After a little while, we open our eyes and look at each other as we continue praying. A hand reaches out. Eyes begin to sparkle, we smile, and it is over. We apologize. I am so sorry. I understand you now. We melt into the love that we truly are.

Without effort, what began as a separate, individual prayer becomes joined. Without effort, what was argument becomes understanding. The light of God does that. We have moved through our deep hearts to our souls, the place where we are one.

When we enter the deep love together, we become peace together.

Before, we were locked in relating, personality to personality. Now we are essence to essence. It is so easy to expand our compassion when we relate this way. It is so easy to grow in love together this way. It is so easy for personality defenses to melt into something greater, together.

This is the joy and thrilling capacity we are discovering in our marriage. This is the sacred love story we write together.

And so we pray, "Our Beloved Lord, Our Beloved God, help us to be the complete love for each other." God willing, may it go deeper. May this be true for every one of us.

# 73 Healing What Separates Us from Love

### *A beloved relationship begins as a healing relationship*

The way to this deep shared love is always through healing. This is actually what marriage is about after we commit to each other. For within the hope and safety of a shared love, many aspects of ourselves that are less than loving will rise up. They rise up so that they can be healed—recognized, and transformed into love.

And so a beloved relationship begins as a healing relationship. Being committed to each other means being committed to healing together. This is very important to realize, because our cultural stories do not prepare us for this. Cinderella ran off to "happily ever after" with her prince, not to a healing relationship!

And so it all goes much more smoothly if we remember several principles. I will share several of these here and, hopefully, more later in another book about sacred relationship.

The first principle is *Only love is real.* Love is the only reality. That's all that is here.

Just thinking this feels good. It is whole. And it is a unity. But this view seems incorrect and unbelievable because, clearly, there is a lot of non-love all around. Why, just today, we all experienced unloving behaviors in our world, our nation, our work life, our family, and maybe even ourselves.

So how do we resolve this apparent discrepancy?

One way we can resolve it is to look at the world on two levels—what is real, and what is temporary. Our test for reality is that it endures, is changeless, and is ever true. Like the sun.

When we reflect on what is real and enduring, and what is transitory, we realize that only love is true. Our definition of love is the love that moves the stars, that sustains the universe. This is not our personal love, or even the love we share together, but the great love in which we are all held.

So it follows then that, ultimately, anything less than love is illusion, and must eventually pass away. All unloving behaviors are temporary and changing. Just like clouds over the sun. We can let ourselves be blinded and deceived into believing that the sun is not there, yet it remains all the while, shining, warming, and nurturing us.

Another way we can resolve this apparent discrepancy is with the test of our own heart: we are only at peace when we are loving. Anytime we experience less than love, our heart is restless until we return to the love. Our hearts tell us what is true.

So when we look out on the world, we can believe either the pure love or the illusion, the sun or the clouds. But only one choice leads to peace and happiness. Only one choice enables a foundation from which we can create.

The second principle is *Our truest relationship is with love itself.*

At the deepest level of understanding, we are only in relationship with the pure love, because that is all that is truly here. The pure love is true, real, and enduring. Another way to say this is that we are only in relationship with God. Everything is an expression of the pure, true love, just as everything is an aspect of God. We learn to see everything as the Face of God; we learn to see God in every face.

The third principle is *The source of this pure, true love is within us, not in our partner.*

How clarifying this is, for now we can seek the source directly, within our own hearts.

When we are in the love, the only thing we can do is give that love. This is the true nature of love. If we are seeking something from our beloved, then we are actually not within the love ourselves. Instead, we are looking for the love. The true, pure love flows freely, like a river, giving to all.

Love does not seek for itself, it is full. Love only knows how to give.

The fourth principle is *When we experience something that feels unloving, we look within ourselves to see where we are separate from the deep love.*

We don't blame someone or something outside us. We accept that everything that happens to us happens for a purpose. We look to see what God is making here. We use skills of the deep heart to clarify this purpose.

So our job is not to be deceived when something less than loving rises up, in ourselves or our partner, but to realize that it is a part of us that has lost its way and is seeking to come home.

Our biggest responsibility in relationship is staying within the love ourselves through all of this.

This means we keep clearing away the illusions until we learn that only love is true. So we keep bowing to the love in our deep hearts through healing practices. As we gracefully work with ourselves in this way, we become more and more loving. This spontaneously enables our partner to become more loving, without effort on their part or ours, because we have opened a gracious space that invites them to join us in the deep love. It is simply easier to join the deep love than to resist it.

It takes practice until this becomes a living reality in our life, going back and forth between the deep love, and the unloving experiences the deep love brings up. But after a while, we begin to realize that indeed, only love is true. Only love remains.

When we reach this point, it becomes easy to wash away the personality clouds because we begin to readily understand that it was only illusion anyway. We may still have habitual patterns that separate us from the love, but they progressively lose their power, and one day they will be gone entirely. For they no longer serve a necessary purpose; no defense is necessary in the sun of this pure love.

When we reach this point, only the love remains, shining from our eyes, and our partner's eyes.

For we are traveling within our own hearts to the divine . . . and through this, we are seeing within the light of our partner's eyes, the love and light of God.

This process of washing away personality illusions, and realizing again and again that truly, only love is here, leads us to all we can be together.

For we are not always going to be each other's dreams. It is not always going to be the way we had hoped it would be. But we can promise ourselves, in commitment to ourselves, that in the hard places, we will be the deep love. We will be the compassion that radiates a love that transforms. We will be mercy and forgiveness. We can do that. We all have that power now.

That's all we have to do. The God presence does the rest, and it does it beautifully.

And gradually, we will find ourselves less limited and more able, less frail and more strong, less conflicted and more at peace, less trying and more true, less suffering and more graced.

It is all so simple. All it takes is wanting the pure, true love more than anything less. All it takes is letting go of our illusions that there was ever anything less than pure love here.

And this brings a reality far greater than any dream we could ever dream: that we could be loved for who we are, exactly as we are, and in that love, be transformed to all we truly are. Together.

# 74 Two Joined in One Harmony

***Two handles of one great vase, which filled to overflowing, pours out in blessing to all***

Our love has given us the fulfillment of our lives. Through our marriage, we have each been able to be and express so much more than we could have been and done alone. We are truly living the deepest joy and the truest meaning of our lives . . . together.

We share a remarkable harmony together. We flow together. This happens any time two people meet each other in the deep love. In our case, we know this "flowing together" in many ways. It extends from physical, emotional, and mental levels to the realm of our spiritual heart and soul.

On the physical level, we move in the same rhythm, join at the same moments. We can both be working in different areas, unaware of each other, David outside, me in my study, and yet David completes his task outside at exactly the same time I complete mine inside, and we meet in the kitchen without even trying.

We really function as one person, in many ways, while at the same time, keeping our independent personal identities. It is a flowing affinity, two streams coursing down the river of life to the same great ocean together. We share the same response to life. We have an affinity of values and tastes, so that our response to the events of our personal lives, or the events of the world, expresses different facets of the same perceptions and values. We are two containers for the same water.

Our individual yet shared impulse to live in deep nature, to eschew the material focus of our culture, to live quietly and in peace . . . the remarkably similar path we traveled separately through family for decades before meeting . . . the constant kindness and caring . . . these all speak of the same flowing impulse, coursing through us, reaching from body to soul.

It is a shared simpatico. My mood shifts in the car while David is driving; I had just begun thinking of a concern unrelated to him. There are no visual clues. And yet he immediately asks, "Is everything okay?" There he is, instantaneously aware of me.

One time when we were still so very new to each other, when David had just arrived at my townhome, I was sleeping on my couch downstairs, he upstairs in the bed. My neck was still adjusting to the major spinal surgery I had undergone. To my shocked surprise, I woke up choking. I could not get my breath. It was 2:00 a.m. David was sound asleep upstairs, and I was downstairs panicking, unable to breathe as desperate seconds ticked by. I stomped on the floor to get his attention, and instantly, there he was. He literally woke out of a deep sleep, flew down the steps, and put his hands on my chest over my lungs in seconds. The tension and congestion in my throat gave way. I could breath. After so long without breath. How did he know?

When he's coming home with the mail, I sense the news before he's inside the house, because his heart is my heart, and I just tune in. I can feel his brightness or displeasure long before he is visible to me.

Since we're in tune emotionally, we're pretty much in tune with our thoughts, also. Talk about transparency!

All this can happen when people live in harmony together. We reach a higher state of being together. In the physical world, we could compare this to a system that begins to function at a higher state of organization, or coherence. For example, a distance runner starts out running really well. Then somewhere along the way, he becomes winded, feels quite fatigued, and slows down, feeling a sensation of heaviness in his legs. Yet after a while, our runner suddenly gets his "second wind." He starts running much more briskly, feeling light and free. His body has reached a higher state of organization. It has reorganized itself at a higher level of order, or coherence.

We can apply this concept of coherence to relationship. We are meant to live in harmony together, with a very integrated level of coherence. For example, we are meant to develop intuitive rapport with one another. It is meant to be a daily, breath-by-breath experience, not something remarkable. It happens first in loving relationships between any two people. Then the affinity expands to a third person, and then another, and on out through the entire soul group. Then soul groups join together in coherence, until we are one living, breathing, pulsing humanity, in accord with each other and with the loving impulse of this universe. Of course, this is very different from our current world of conflict and separation. Yet it is the undeniable path of spiritual evolution.

At a higher spiritual level, we can experience coherence by relating to our partner's deep spiritual heart through our own spiritual heart. In this way, our heart becomes an exquisite organ of perception. Through this, we can sense the true condition of our partner's heart. So for example, we can understand what our partner's deep heart is really expressing, even though the words spoken from the mind may be quite different. This enables us to offer profound understanding and support to each other, diving right to the core.

Our life together is a shared devotion. We are always helping each other, always supporting each other, in things both small and great. One of us physically tires at a task, the other gently comes and finishes. Almost like one person.

It is a constant willingness to be of service, of help, of blessing to one another. Like two urns, flowing into a trough that recirculates . . . one urn empties its water into the trough, and it circulates into the other urn, and on and on . . . a perpetual motion of giving . . . in things both small and great. But especially in the small things, the simple things, the everyday remembrances, for this is the fabric of which our life is woven.

This devotion is beautifully captured in the poem of the great Sufi master poet Hafiz, who lived in Persia during the 1300s:

*My dear,*
*How can I be more loving to you;*
*How can I be more*
*Kind?* [34]

Our souls are melded. This is something that can be felt far more easily than expressed. I would describe it as a mutual willing together, from a very deep level. Another facet of relating from the soul is that we share a profound level of lasting commitment.

We also feel our souls joined in a mutual caring for each other to the point of sacrifice. It expresses itself in a growing tenderness and gentleness, a very deep appreciation. It is the way you would feel if you knew that the one you loved were going to die tomorrow . . . a very reverential respect and cherishing. We see the deep beauty and belovedness of our partner.

Another way we experience our souls joined is that we were relating to each other before we met. As we look back, we can see several ways we were relating to each other long before we saw our faces. As Rumi says, lovers are in each other's hearts long before they meet.

One time, years before I ever met David, I was drawn to a wooded, very wealthy suburb of Chicago named Barrington to, as I told myself, "look for a home." It was absurd for me to think that this was possible, so absurd, in fact, that it took me several months to act on my inner urging. There was no possible way I could begin to buy a home there. But after a while, I drove out to Barrington several times, enjoying the wooded areas and, of course, never finding a home. What I didn't know at that time was that when I first felt the impulse to drive out there, David was living in Barrington for a few months.

Relating at the soul level allows us to travel deeper into our spiritual hearts, dropping into the Unity together, the state of being where we are one. There is no "other." This is the level of spirit. Here we know a reality beyond earthly duality and senses.

Here, we look into our partner's eyes and see One. There is nothing between, only Oneness. One, without another.

I would describe our marriage as almost like one body . . . almost like one heart . . . almost like one soul. One willing, one breathing, one moving, one pulsing, one shared yes.

Many longtime, lovingly married couples experience many of these affinities, I am sure. And I know that you understand that this affinity does not mean that we spend our days running slow motion through daisy fields into each other's waiting arms while a symphony of strings crescendos in the background.

We have the same life passages and inevitable challenges as anyone else. But they are gentler.

What this means is slipping into a deepening tenderness and love for each other, as we gaze at the deepening wrinkles on our faces. Years ago, afraid of turning forty, I never could have imagined that looking older would mean my husband and I would feel more tenderness toward each other. It means holding out a hand when we are being angrily accused by our partner, and saying, "It is safe here. I love you. There's only love here," relearning the harsh experiences of childhood. Only the love is real.

It means infinite listening to what one partner wants to say, until that partner grows into the sense of being heard and valued after years of not being heard or respected by family. It is being torn apart by family members' destructive behaviors, and determining that this will not tear us apart, and coming up stronger for it. It is facing a financial cliff and choosing to take a huge risk—and finding that it works in spades. Unity creates.

I am sure that being married by Sidi made our way much gentler, more graceful, and far more bonded. Our vow of "giving everything" is not a burden or restriction at all, but a natural flow of love between us. It feels effortless and good. Authentic love only knows giving. It only knows how to flow like a fountain.

All this leads to a remarkable capacity to create together. It began with righting the pieces of our lives, and bringing them into a constructive, supportive structure. I have told you the story of recreating our home, and that was only a symbol of the many aspects we righted, aligned, and brought together in our lives. In essence, we created an entirely new foundation—in both our home, and all aspects of our lives—to support our shared life.

When two people join with such full-hearted commitment, it does not matter what each partner is or has. If we seek our partners through that kind of a selection process, then we are missing the main point. What matters most in relationship is what we can create together, not what we individually have or don't have, be it in outer resources or inner capacities. In choosing a marriage partner, what matters most is how able we are to open our hearts and souls to each other. This allows the creative God presence to flow through us. The rest will follow.

And then something magical happens. A greater being is formed: an angel. When two are joined in the deep love, an angel of the marriage is formed. This occurs in all loving relationships. Any time two come together with the conscious intention for sacred relationship, an angel is formed. This angel holds the higher template of the relationship.

Though the creation of an angel may seem surprising, it is actually the way thought and intention work. Each thought is formed of light on subtle levels. And each thought is alive. It is a living being, actively creating. This is a tenet in Rudolf Steiner's work.

So we can realize that angels don't always come from outside ourselves. Sometimes, they are born in love.

As I was writing this chapter, I was drawn to a book about Emanuel Swedenborg, the Swedish scientist and mystic. I have never been attracted to Swedenborg, yet I was drawn to it for one purpose. To my surprise, I discovered that Swedenborg also experienced an angel of marriage. In his case, he perceived that those united in true love remain so after death, and appear as one angel.[35]

We can also gain perspective on this concept if we consider that every living being has its angel. A marriage is no different than a person, an animal, or even a blade of grass. As the Talmud says, "Every blade of grass has an angel that bends over it and whispers, Grow! Grow!"

As we learn to relate to this angel, we touch into deeper purposes of our union.

The angel of our marriage is very big and magnificent, a higher representation of us. It streams a very gentle, very powerful, very generous living force around us. When we contact it, our hearts glow, we feel expanded and stronger. It also offers guidance to us for our path together. This loving guidance from the angel is possible for all who join together in relationship that celebrates and honors the qualities of God.

But as wonderful as this is, there is one facet of our marriage that is most special to me. It is held within the phrase that flowed through me as I was writing the sacred love story:

> *Of themselves, they could give each other their hearts, their bodies, their souls. That was all. But when joined together, they became like two handles of one great vase, which, filled to overflowing, poured out in blessing to all.*

And so we find an even higher use of our creating, beyond creating such a beautiful life together. It is in helping people understand what love, and loving, truly is. And helping them to live this together. This is the dedication of our lives together.

And so we discover ourselves . . . two, joined in one harmony that the love and grace of God can pour through.

This is divine marriage.

# PART TEN

# LIVING IN JOY

*Joy occurs naturally. It is the inner essence of life.*

When we let go of what is not love within us,
we discover joy.

# 75 Being Held in the Heart of the World

### *Hawaii is like love*

There's a saying about Hawaii, that Hawaii is the heart center of the world. How could it be otherwise?

When people even hear the word "Hawaii," they light up. I remember calling my money center bank and talking with "Richard" in India. Finding out that I lived in Hawaii, he exclaimed, "Oh, tacos!" I answered, "No, that's Mexico. This is palms, pineapples, and surfing." Catching on, Richard laughed back through the phone, "Oh! Aluuuuha!"

When people enter Hawaii, their hearts open, they relax, they start to have fun. Lying on a beach and playing in its waves, eating fruit that dangles from an outstretched tree, or traveling within the island's embracing beauty—every part of Hawaii just invites you to open, relax, enjoy, and receive its abundance, so freely given.

You unwind deeper and deeper, and discover yourself held within a deep abiding goodness that just gives and gives and gives. Who can resist? Life slows down here to the beat of your heart, to the rhythm of the waves, to the flow of the moon and the stars. It slows down to trust. It slows down to harmony.

Guests arrive on our land, and their eyes well up in tears from the beauty, the love, the peace.

Their hearts open, and something very deep gives way.

Hawaii does that.

It is safe enough here to open your heart.

People come to our valley to stay for a while, moving away from whatever pressures them or troubles them. So often I hear them say they feel safe here. As they live here, their hearts open. They say it has been a spiritual experience for them, staying in the valley. They say that the valley is sacred. But it is also they who have become sacred to themselves, they who have come to know themselves in spiritual ways. For they have returned a bit more to their innocence, to the inner purity that was quietly within them all along.

For those who can receive Hawaii like this, Hawaii is a return to love.

Nature on the Big Island is still innocent. It holds the purity that must have been the way things were in the beginning. Here, nature moves in love's way, not humanity's. It knows a way from long before humanity invented its games of competition and war, its appetites for profit and greed, its nightmares of separation, lack, and fear.

In this loving abundance, there was no need for defense. Until recently, Hawaii's plants and animals had no defenses—because there was nothing to defend against. Plants had no thorns, insects no stingers. Even now, mint doesn't have as strong a flavor here for this very reason. And still today, we have barely anything that is threatening—no snakes, no bears or coyotes, no wandering cougars, no killer bees, no West Nile virus—our worst offenders are just bees and by the ocean heat, small scorpions and stinging centipedes.

Said even more simply, Hawaii is like love.

Love's way is gentle, so softly beckoning that you might not notice its call within your defenses and your fears. It softly beckons you to follow, and then you discover yourself falling deeper and deeper into its embrace.

Hawaii's way is soft and gentle, but it is very, very powerful. And that is also like love.

David says the whole island is like that. The island rain is gentle, steady, and warm. Yet it holds so much power that chartreuse duranta bushes in my garden have become trees, shooting up four feet after one week's rain. The trade winds are lighthearted, yet so invigorating they can lift you right up out of a sickbed and into the garden. The ocean is so soft, warm, and gently cradling that you can't help but jump in. Even just wading on its shores fills you with energy and strength for several days. The soil provides substance so deeply nurturing and sustaining—so powerful—that plants and shrubs grow to at least double the size they grow on the mainland, and in less time . . . twelve-foot poinsettias, twenty-foot-wide rosemary, twenty-foot, towering hibiscus, and four-foot-diameter impatiens.

The power of life here is stunning. Even in the most forbidding places, the power of life surges forward. In stark black lava fields, ohia trees twist their gnarly way upward through unforgiving rock, offering exquisitely beautiful lehua flowers, bright red puffs of delight in the grayed landscape. The bees will transform the essence of these flowers into the best honey on the island, lehua honey. From a stark black lava rock field, the sweetest honey.

The gentle softness is so profound here that it overpowers anything else. You can't push here, you can't rush, or things won't go right, they won't flow right. You slow down to the gentle lullaby of the endless rhythm of the waves and swaying palms, of balmy breezes and heady fragrances, of wispy clouds and soft island mists. It is a gentle persuasion. You fall asleep and discover yourself sleeping deeper than you ever have . . . held in a deep, abiding peace . . . as if falling into the arms of trust for the first time.

This gentle power is life. It is goodness. It is love made manifest.

# 76 Island Paradise

***The Big Island is like one very small continent— or one very big playground***

"Lucky live Hawaii" is what the locals say, and it is so true. The Big Island is a lot of fun. Though it's an island, it's actually like living on one very small continent there's so much diversity here. It's simply hard to get "rock fever" on this island.

Diversity is all around us here . . . so many cultures have created what the Big Island is today. There are always new people to meet from all around the world . . . with tons of creativity always brewing on the island, expressed in everything from lifestyles to art forms to houses. We can travel from ancient Hawaiian tribal sites to best-in-the-world resorts in minutes, and experience what living is like for the wealthiest people in the world or for those who live in Third

World conditions. Traveling around the island is always an adventure . . . the terrain and climates vary remarkably. And just the plants alone are awesomely varied. Literally, almost every time I travel the island, I discover a new flower growing.

And the Big Island is also like one very big playground. It offers a paradise of options every day, just waiting outside the door. There's so much to get up for with every new sunlit day.

Of all the Hawaiian Islands, the Big Island is known for being the wildest, most natural and free, with immense sweeps of breath-catching beauty. It's *natural* here.

Almost all the island is far away from touristy resorts and developers. That allows nature here to remain exceedingly diverse, with the greatest natural panorama of any island. From the highest waterfall, to the highest mountains, to the black and green sand beaches and world-class sandy-white beaches, to the incredible lava caves and the most brilliant night sky in the world, with the awesome rugged power of the world's most active volcano packed in for good measure, the Big Island shines as a place of adventure, romance, and just plain awesome experience. Here, you can still feel the ancient ways at many sites, sensing the deep power and gentle beauty of the aina while you relax on island time, far away from cares, crowds, and congestion. You can *breathe* here.

The mana, or spiritual power, of the island will fill you and lift you into greater reverence, greater happiness, and greater vitality. Where can you walk out of your grocery store and gaze out on palms and Hilo Bay, with a huge waterfall just a couple blocks away? Where else can you shop at Costco for coconut water, and then enjoy it at a world-class beach fifteen minutes away?

The Big Island still feels free and easy, just like an island breeze. Where do people say "Aloha," then hug and kiss you on your left cheek—when just meeting you? Where do guys give shaka to each other, the hang loose sign, 'cause they feel like "brahs"?

Far away from formula living and convention, the Big Island is still open and free and fun, always calling you to come out and play on another beautiful day.

# 77 And My Life Blooms . . .

***Into not just a flower, but a lovely garden***

Our lives hold metaphors, a poetry of meaning that weaves verses through our days, verses that begin to rhyme with one another over time. We are drawn toward the same experiences, and their metaphors echo and rhyme though our lives.

As we live these metaphors, their verses grow into stanzas. And eventually, with enough stanzas, we begin to see how it has all rhymed together into a meter of meaning, a pattern of purpose that defines our days and lives.

These life metaphors call us home. They are a breath of our soul's essence. As we are drawn to them, so they are drawn to us, sometimes in most surprising ways. They belong to us, for they are expressions of the seed pattern within our soul.

Whatever these metaphors are, they are in us always. Mozart and Beethoven's first compositions still echo in their mature works. It is as if there is one melody they were born singing.

And so it is with us all. We all are born singing one melody, the story, the song, the seed of who we are and what we are meant to be. And if we follow the highest within us, then we shall see these early metaphors blossom in fullness by the end of our years, the seed pattern within our soul reaching full flowering. If we follow what inspires us and gives us life, then a beautiful pattern gradually emerges into its fullness.

It is very much like the developing trays used to develop black and white photographs decades ago. Light was used to cast the film negative's image onto white photo paper. Then the photo paper was placed in a chemical solution in the developing tray. At first only the faintest outline of an image showed. Then gradually, the shape of the forms filled in, and the full range of grayscale color bloomed until finally, a complete image was revealed, embodied in its fullness.

We are all working to bring the light of spirit into full embodiment in the images of our lives.

In my life, one of my metaphors is flowers and color. They express the joy and beauty of the soul. And as they have woven their way through my life, they tell the story of my maturing into my true self, my soul.

In my early years, with the innocent freedom of a young child, free to be purely who I truly was, I delighted in color and flowers. I was drawn to them, helping myself to flowers out of a neighbor's garden as a toddler, and picking up a paintbrush long before kindergarten. I loved to paint flowers in watercolor.

Color and flowers always joined together for me. All through my young life, I placed colors of happiness, especially gold, the color of sunshine, on bulletin boards, with dried daffodils beside them. In high school, I painted my bedroom walls in flowers. Color simply made me happy. Color is a metaphor for the joy of the soul.

But then when I graduated from college and began working for a major Chicago corporation, I suddenly found myself in a drab world of corporate gray. Everything was gray. In our new flagship, solid black skyscraper, I had a little gray cubicle that matched everyone else's little gray cubicle. The walls were gray, and the carpet was gray. Huge windows ran along the outside perimeter of the floors, and when the day was gray, which it usually was, we were simply surrounded in drab. It felt stultifying. What a perfect metaphor for the repression I lived, how quashed I felt trying to fit into a place I did not truly belong.

Yet in my little gray cubicle, I sat with colorful pictures on my wall—of the Alps, flowers, and other most beautiful natural scenes. I wished that I could paint currents of color that swept in waves around the walls of my little cubicle. But of course, such expressions of color and individuality were disallowed. We all were decidedly corporate gray.

Yet even then, I always sensed that as my life bloomed, it would also bloom in flowers and color.

After a few years of this, I left for Colorado with my then-husband to live in nature. At a deeper level, and one I did not recognize at that time, I was moving to a place where I could come to know myself and feel free to express my deeper identity as it unfolded within me.

One day, I was at a beautiful little shop in Estes Park, high up in the mountains. It was a crystal morning, the air vibrant with bright sun, filled with the invigorating, clean fragrance of pines in the mountain air. And all around us were gorgeous flowers hanging in pots, dangling brilliant blue lobelia with spots of bright magenta pansies and little sparks of golden flowers. They were dazzlingly joyful little gems that sparkled in the sunlight and the crystal clear mountain air. Happiness itself.

Then I saw vibrant magenta-colored azaleas, just gorgeous, in a shop. But unlike the others, these were silk, a novelty at the time. Immediately, I was inspired by that moment of joy to start a business with silk flowers, expressed (and express-mailed) as gifts. They were gorgeous colors and flowers sent as little greetings of joy. I was filled with joy, fun, and happiness. I was so excited. It was a metaphor for beginning to come alive to my own soul and individuality.

A few years later I returned to Chicago and, by "chance", I moved near the very best silk floral designers in all Chicago, some of the best in the nation. I had the opportunity to create a business plan and seek investors to actually start a catalog of silk flowers delivered as gifts. And top direct marketing executives in Chicago were interested. It was very exciting.

So color and flowers were opening in my life, as was my soul. But the flowers, though beautiful, were not living. I knew that one day I would experience living with real flowers.

The metaphor rhymed again when I began seeing an English gentleman named Adrian. At that time, I was very ill, and Adrian, being deeply intuitive, had been waiting for the woman he knew was coming, a woman who would be ill when he met her. So he accepted my illness and shared his life with me.

Adrian owned a fine gardening business in Georgetown, a genteel suburb of Washington D.C., with many notable residents. He spent his time creating exquisitely beautiful gardens for his clients' garden parties. Having been raised in the garden-loving aristocracy of England, fine gardening came naturally to him, and inner guidance led him to make it his second career. His gardens were delightful little palettes of delicate and exquisite beauty, highlighting each fashionable home, many featured in the Georgetown Garden Tour each year.

Now, the flowers in my life were alive and enchanting, but I only observed them. I did not create the gardens, nor did I plant them or care for them, so they were not an expression that came from my center.

Later, Adrian even kindly planted a tiny, little autumn garden of mums for me around my townhome in the twenty square feet of earth available. And I began to plant impatiens there, and then veggies in garden boxes right on my townhome deck.

Something was coming to life. By this time, I had begun to consciously live from my soul far more deeply than before, and I was writing extensively about living from the soul. Yet the outer forms of my life did not allow my soul full expression.

Time passed, I met David and moved to Hawaii, and now, years later, my life is in full bloom and filled with joy.

And I have planted gardens upon gardens of flowers, over several acres, not just twenty square feet. We live surrounded by a paradise of beauty that graces our land. The flower gardens are filled with color—exotic beauties in rich and deep tropical colors, colors that come alive in the sun's radiance. Flowers are an expression of the soul's radiance. And all flowers are most beautiful when lit with the sun. And so it is with us—we become most beautiful, within and without, when filled with the radiance of spirit.

So flowers and color have been a poetic metaphor that has run through the verses of my life, growing as I have grown into the beauty and grace of the soul.

And so it will be for you. The beauty of your own life metaphors will blossom for you as you gradually mature into the fullness of your soul. Trust your heart, follow the highest within you, and you will also harvest a garden of radiant joy.

# 78 Growing Happiness . . . and Helping It Blossom for Others

### *We plant the gardens*

And so we planted gardens, glorious, bursting gardens in brilliant color, cascading, dancing with life, strewn with joy.

Lavender cascades of sandpaper vine dance joyfully in a riotous jumble while magenta plumes of justicia stand upright on their huge bush and chartreuse duranta bushes grow so tall they have become trees. Deep burgundy-red leaf plants provide a canvas for it all, along with all the green that luxuriates on the land. And all of this is accented with red, upright ti plants and gemlike canna lilies in yellow and orange, plus hibiscus in a riot of pinks, corals, yellows, and reds . . . all under a graceful canopy of drooping angel trumpets in yellow, pink, and white. It's exuberant!

We also planted a huge vegetable garden, a garden that just gives and gives and gives, like all our land. It's filled with basil and parsley, rich green leaves of red-ribbed chard, luscious lettuces, soft arugula, and radicchio. Anytime I go to the garden before dinner to gather an armful of greens, I feel such a sense of being filled. There is so much joy and happiness in the simple act of going to the garden and harvesting. There is such goodness in a garden. And isn't this what people have felt since time began? Isn't this why, since time immemorial, people have had such heartwarming celebrations at harvest time?

Cutting lettuce, picking tomatoes, gathering strawberries or tons of glorious greens, I always feel like this is the greatest wealth of all.

It reminds me of the time a man and his two young boys stayed in a cabin on our land. They were very healthy but had very little money, like many island people.

And so we offered to till the soil near their cabin, making a very large garden for them. I can still remember the day when David got out his tractor. It was bright and sunny, and the boys were jumping up and down with expectation, a very, very happy moment. They skipped and ran behind the tractor as David traveled across several acres for this great moment.

As David's tractor cut into the soil, tilling a large swath of land for the garden and carrying it a total of about five hundred feet—the garden suddenly emerging—the oldest boy, ten years old, jumped up and down for joy, happily exclaiming, "We aren't poor anymore! We are rich in vegetables! God has given us vegetables!"

His innocent joy, his simplicity, and his appreciation were a sheer delight for us. The children danced around the garden plot and around their father. It was a very special day.

This is what gardens do. They bring joy.

And gardens bring people together. People are naturally drawn to gardens, just as they are to kitchens. And so gardens become gathering places.

One very famous garden that gathered people together is Findhorn, the spiritual retreat in Findhorn, Scotland. Findhorn drew people. First they came for the spectacular produce, huge and bursting with vitality. Then they discovered something deeper: a garden of spirit, a place to nurture soul, and a way live from inner guidance, co-creating with nature, in service.

Findhorn's great pioneering work demonstrated the wondrous results of cooperation between humanity and the angelic kingdom's devas and nature spirits. Findhorn spearheaded a new way of living in harmony with all of life. And it all began with a garden.

And so it is with us. We may think of ourselves as gardeners of the soul. Our work is to bring forth the seed pattern within our soul. Just as a great oak is held within a tiny seed, so everything is held within us, in the center of our heart, the center which is God's alone, from which our life is guided. For we are creators, just as God. And our gift is life.

And as we grow in our ability to nurture that seed pattern within our soul, revealing the perfect pattern within, we give to all. We learn to become

the love that waters . . .  
the sun that blesses . . .  
the wind that guides . . .  
the earth that holds . . .  
for ourselves and others . . .  
through all the transformations of life.

As this divine template within us grows and flowers, it seeds new life . . . ever giving. We become wealthy, rich in spirit. We can't help but live in joy.

What great wealth, what great joy . . . just like a garden, endless in its bounty.

# PART ELEVEN

# CREATING HEAVEN ON EARTH

*As we end our journey together, I leave you with one thought:*
*Remember that the true art of manifesting is never done by us.*
*It is done through us.*
*The pure love does the work.*
*Our role is to surrender our limited self into this pure love.*
*This is how we create heaven on earth.*

The Gardens at Aina Lani

# 79 "Aina Lani" Means "Heaven on Earth"

### *A Perfect Place for Spiritual Retreat*

Well, by now you know that "Aina Lani" means "heaven on earth." And that's just the way we feel about the land. It holds us, and sustains us, and is infinitely giving. This is nature's gracious way when it is left free to be. Its grace is the same grace that is held within our hearts.

When people come to the land, their eyes light up and their hearts fill with a quiet, blessed joy. They immediately relax into a sense of great well-being and wonder. The remarkable purity here makes it a very powerful and sacred place. It is one of nature's pure cathedrals . . . spiritual, healing, sacred.

It is a perfect place for spiritual retreat. Ever since my mid-twenties, I knew that one day I would offer spiritual retreat for people in deep nature, with huge fields of green all around. And now, in the fullness of time, the dream that life dreams through me has been fulfilled.

But what to name the retreat? The name "Aina Lani" came to me spontaneously as we were traveling north toward Kohala on the highway facing the majestic, sweeping mountains that hold such a powerful presence. Immediately, it seemed perfect. It held the musical, rhythmic quality that captures the island's graceful beauty and flow. And I knew enough Hawaiian by that time to recognize that it meant "heaven on earth."

Immediately, I realized that this fit with a poem that flowed through me almost two years earlier. One day, as I awoke from a nap, this poem appeared, whole cloth, in my mind:

## *Let This Become Love*

*We are each*
*Healer and Healed,*
*Student and Teacher,*
*Forgiver and Forgiven,*
*Until all that remains is*
*Lover and Beloved.*

*Let us make a new earth together.*
*A Heaven.*
*Let This Become Love.*

The poem embodies the essence of Aina Lani. It is about taking the pieces of a life, the things that don't work, and surrendering them to the infinitely gracious capacity of the pure love right within the heaven in our hearts. Once we surrender to the pure love within our hearts, the God presence does the rest, and it does it beautifully. This is what I have learned in my life, and this is what I have lived. It is how I have been able to experience this heaven on earth.

And this heaven is always growing, for the deep love is always growing, just as we are always growing in our capacity to experience it. Can you imagine what we might create together if we could all live from within our deep hearts?

Our work together as a humanity is to remove the barriers within us to this sacred, holy way of living. Once we do this, everything changes.

For meeting life in this way allows us to live in the same physical world, but with an inner presence that enables us to experience living as an unfolding grace. This creates a new world, a heaven on earth.

# 80 Aina Lani is a Place of Heart Warming and Home Coming

***It is an experience of living in the pure love***

Every step of the way in creating Aina Lani has been led by inner guidance, attunement to the pure light within. Guidance said that Aina Lani is to be a place of teaching and sharing how to live within the deep love. These are the words that were given for Aina Lani retreat: "Aina Lani is a place of heart warming and home coming."

And so it is my hope that Aina Lani can be a place where we can take refuge from the outer world, and enter the inner presence of pure love that dwells within us, at the very core of our spiritual heart. Returning home. Home coming.

Aina Lani is to be a place where we practice living in relationship to the pure love, our truest relationship. From this grounding, we then learn how to remain in relationship with the pure love through all our other relationships, be they easy or challenging.

Aina Lani is a very special place of remarkably deep peace, serenity, and beauty in which we are held within the unity of nature. It is the ideal setting in which to practice living in the way of the pure love. Being in deep nature and gently observing how nature moves teaches us many facets of loving deeply.

So Aina Lani is a place of healing. Here, the pure love can make the rough places smooth, the torn seamless, and the hurt whole. Here, we can learn to take the tragedies of our lives and turn them to grace through the heaven in our heart. We allow the experiences of our lives, and our experience of ourselves, to become love.

And so we remember again, "Let This Become Love." It is remembering who we truly are.

Let us become love.

# 81 Living Aloha

***The deep, pure love waits for you, beloved***

The lyrics of "Bali Ha'i" lure us into a dream of paradise:

If you try,
You'll find me
Where de sky
Meets de sea;
Here am I,
Your special island!
Come to me, Come to me!

They evoke the dream we all have in our hearts of our "special island," our special dream to be who and what we truly are, and to express it in joy.

I hope my story of the deep, pure love of the Unity has shown you that life dreams a dream through you, a dream you are meant to bring to life for your good and the good of all. For when we enter the presence of the Living Unity within our hearts, we enter the stream of harmony that carries us through our lives. It opens the way before us, and makes our way graceful.

But most of all, I hope this story has given you a taste of the pure love within your own heart, and a longing to go deeper. For this is the greatest gift, the heaven in your heart, the kingdom of God within you.

This deep, pure love within your heart exists on its own, of its own. It really asks nothing.

And yet this pure love invites you to join it. All it requires is that you surrender anything less. This love is waiting for you, beloved. Your own special island.

This is the true love you can open your heart to. This is the enduring love you can trust, no matter what. This is the absolute love you can relate to through all your other relationships, for all are merely the Face of God, when we see truly.

Along the way, don't be fooled by a world that looks like something less than love. For every single experience in our lives—the easy and especially the difficult—is teaching us how to relate to the pure love deep within us, if we can surrender enough to see the gift in what we are given, and clear away all that is not love within us. This is true no matter how unloving and separate the situation seems. For ultimately, it must return to love. This is the story of humanity written through the centuries. What is not love must cease. Every conflict, every separation, must eventually become love.

And remember, in this world of wishing, that this deep, pure love, this goodness and Unity is all any of us really want anyway, no matter how much it might look like we want something from the outside world.

So begin to dream with me the dream your heart holds of your own special island . . .

*Let the pure love within your heart*
*carry you into a timeless now,*
*where all that exists is the beauty of this moment.*
*Let the deep love caress you, and gently carry away all that is not love.*
*Let the goodness of life penetrate you, warming deeply.*
*Breathe deep of this love and let it fill you,*
*Relax into its goodness . . . just bask.*

This is aloha. This is what you are, what I am, and what every one of us truly is: pure love.

It is always a journey, this deep love . . . always a deepening, a growing into more. It is a process of letting go, again and again, of what separates us from the pure love. Along the way are many veils that we let go, as we travel to the Unity within our hearts.

We must help each other along the way.

# 82 Aloha

***Let us touch foreheads and share breath***

In ancient Hawaii, the traditional greeting of Hawaiians was spiritual. They would touch foreheads together and share breath. In this greeting of shared breath, they were sharing spirit, touching essence, greeting each other at deepest levels. Essence to essence. Such a deep and authentic way to recognize one another.

The ancient Hawaiian word "Aloha" carries this same spirit, for "Alo" is the heart of the universe, the very heart of life itself. "Ha" is the breath, the loving spirit of the great Creator.

When we say "Aloha" from our hearts, we are allowing the heart of life to flow through our hearts. The very sound "ah" opens our hearts to life, to one another, and to ourselves. Take a moment and say "Aloha," emphasizing the "ahhh" sound, letting it penetrate your heart, and see if you can experience this.

As we say "Aloha," we are allowing the pure love to flow through our hearts and on to all of life. It fills our hearts and, at the same time, effortlessly radiates out. Saying "Aloha" is a practice of grace and loving spirit.

"Aloha" carries life. Every time we say it, people come to life. On the mainland, people light up and smile. Their eyes sparkle; they immediately relax and start to have fun. We become bonded by aloha. On the island, when we say it, we take it as an expression of loving kindness and caring.

"Aloha" is the spirit of life. It is the way we call forth the pure love at the center of our hearts, our souls, our spirits, the Unity in which we all are one.

And so we end as we began . . . with aloha. I wish you warm aloha . . . and I wish you the capacity to create, through the heaven in your own heart, a heaven on earth to bless you and others.

May it be so.

# APPENDIX:

# THE REMEMBRANCE, PRAYER OF THE HEART

## THE PRACTICE OF REMEMBRANCE

*Call words of light*
*into your spiritual heart,*
*words that carry you home to Unity,*
*the sacred spark of God within you.*

*Drop deeper and deeper into your heart,*
*purifying as you go,*
*until you come to experience the pure love*
*waiting deep within your heart.*

*Let it carry you deeper, and deeper*
*until the light of this love fills your awareness,*
*illuminating you*
*with the radiance of the soul.*

*Drop deeper and deeper still*
*until you fall into*
*the pure harmony that courses through all life,*
*no longer resisting, no longer separating,*
*surrendering into this ever-abiding grace.*
*This is Unity.*

*This is what is Real.*
*This is what you really are.*

*Welcome home.*

# INTRODUCTION TO THE REMEMBRANCE

For centuries, heart prayers have been used as a way of returning to God, a way to pray constantly. They enable us to hold a constant remembrance of God within our hearts as we go through the motions of life. At the physical level, a heart prayer is the repetition of a word or phrase that is repeated constantly within the physical or spiritual heart. At the spiritual level, a heart prayer is a method by which we gradually refine ourselves, gently releasing the hard-defended bastions of the limited personal self, and returning the self to God, to the pure love, to divinity. Heart prayers move through us as we pray them, enabling something greater to transform us in ways our conscious mind does not comprehend.

## Traveling through the spiritual heart to union with God

The heart is our pathway home. The heart is unique within us as the pathway to the soul, and through this to the Unity, or God. As we work with heart prayers, we travel deeper and deeper within the realms of the heart, naturally moving from outer personality to the inner realms of the heart itself, and we discover ourselves held in a deep, abiding love which always loves us. This is a profound and deeply moving experience. This love is beyond personal love. It is the love which loves always. It is the love which turns the universe. It is the love that is the very foundation of life itself.

As we move into this level, we become filled with a vast love not our own. We find our personality needs progressively disappearing into this burning warmth of love, while our authentic individuality is strengthened with the beautiful qualities of God. We naturally discover ourselves seeing with the eyes of the heart, opening the understandings that only the pure love can reveal. This experience moves from divine guidance all the way to illumination, revelation, and authentic prophecy. We might think of this as the level of the soul, with its light of knowing.

Then we naturally move deeper still, into an experience of the

Unity of life, where we are one with all. Ultimately, the soul disappears within this Unity, much as the outer personality has already been consumed in the pure love. This is a very deep state of being, rarely discussed or taught. The writings of St. John of the Cross[36] and St. Teresa of Avila[37] discuss this state. The Sufi teaching of the stations of the heart embody it, and the writings of Sidi al-Jamal[38] outline its twenty-eight stations. These descriptions surpass the comprehension of the conscious mind, and are to be read with the understanding of the spiritual heart.

## Heart prayers are practiced by both Christians and Sufis

In the Christian tradition, the heart prayer is the Jesus Prayer. It was practiced as long ago as the fifth century by the Desert Fathers and remains a very important practice today, especially within the Orthodox Church. It follows the exhortation of St. Paul to "Pray without ceasing."[39] We may also think of it as a way to "practice the presence of God," in the words of Brother Lawrence.

It uses the simple phrase "Lord Jesus Christ, Son of God, have mercy on me," or shorter versions of this exact phrase, such as "Lord Jesus Christ have mercy on me." "Lord Jesus Christ" is a sacred name, much as the sacred names used for the Sufi practice of Remembrance. The Christian practice and its powerfully transformative effects are beautifully described in the Russian spiritual classic *The Way of the Pilgrim*.[40]

In the Sufi tradition, the heart prayer is the Remembrance.[41] It, too, likely originated in the desert, and is actively practiced by Sufis the world over. It uses the name of God, "Allah." In Arabic, "Allah" means "The One." It can be prayed with other sacred names of God, such as "Alaha," which means "the Unity" in Aramaic, the language of the New Testament. "Alaha" was the word Jesus spoke.

The Remembrance heart prayer has remarkably transformative capacities because it uses words of light, sacred words with the power to invoke and evoke the living presence of the Living Unity within us.

These heart prayers are actually remarkably similar in both practice and result.

## HOW THE REMEMBRANCE CAN HELP US

Your heart is always praying. Down deep, it rests in pure love. It is always in pure love. That is its natural state, its constant prayer.

There is a point within the heart that belongs only to God. In the beautiful words of Thomas Merton, it is *"a point of pure truth, a point or spark which belongs entirely to God, which is never at our disposal, from which God disposes of our lives. . . . This little point of nothingness and of absolute poverty is the pure glory of God in us."*[42] We will call this the communion point.

But during our daily lives, we forget this communion. And when we do, we immediately fall into disharmony. This is separation. We forget. And our lives express this separation in many ways—rushing, striving, trying to get somewhere . . . doubting, questioning . . . feeling stuck . . . feeling unloved or unworthy . . . sensing we need to be doing something different. We feel in disharmony.

Heart prayers are a way of returning to the deep love, staying connected no matter what is happening. They provide the necessary bridge from outer life to inner communion. Through heart prayers, we remember. Heart prayers are very simple, yet exceedingly profound. Their results are immediate. They carry us into a deepening harmony with all of life: the Unity. This is called Remembrance. Remembering the deep love we truly are. As we practice them, we discover ourselves living in an ever-widening harmony.

The Remembrance is a heart prayer that can be done anywhere, anytime, while we are doing all the other activities of daily life. As we practice it over time, it gently transforms our experience of living, bringing blessing upon blessing.

## THE PRACTICE OF REMEMBRANCE

The goal of Remembrance is to learn to live from the pure love in your heart all of the time. It is to pray constantly, to be in constant attunement . . . to always remember the deep love, to always be experiencing it . . . to not believe what is expressing as less than love.

That is a very big order. But gradually and naturally, from the barest beginnings, the practice expands, day by day. The practice is very natural to the heart, and it is a place the heart wants to reside. We might think of it as taking refuge in the deep love within us. And so the practice grows of its own, because it consciously joins what is already within the deep heart.

When we begin practicing the Remembrance, we speak the sacred word aloud. As the practice grows, the Remembrance moves naturally from the lips to the heart, and words no longer need be spoken. The heart begins to pray the Remembrance on its own. It becomes something that comes naturally, for this is the natural prayer of the spiritual heart.

From here, the practice deepens into the soul. At this point, it becomes more and more constant, more and more steady, repeating even during sleep. It becomes a deep and abiding attunement with the divine within.

## LEARNING THE REMEMBRANCE STEP BY STEP

This appendix teaches how to practice the Remembrance. Ideally, this would be learned in person, but as with any prayer, it is the devotion within the heart, the surrender into the pure love, and God that ultimately guide the way.

Here is an overview of the steps by which we can learn Remembrance:

**Step 1: Baseline your spiritual heart.**

**Step 2: Chant the sacred sound "Ah" in your spiritual heart.**

**Step 3: Chant the sacred sound "Ah" as you gaze into the eyes of a partner.**

**Step 4: Understand ancient words of light, sacred words that carry you into an experience of the Unity within your spiritual heart.**

**Step 5: Pray the sacred words that evoke Unity: Alaha, Allah, Elohim, Elat. Experience each sacred word once, then chant it for a few moments, observing how it touches your heart.**

**Step 6: Determine which word your heart receives most deeply. Pray that specific word of light in your heart for at least five more minutes, observing how it affects you. Twenty minutes is ideal to receive what it offers.**

**Step 7: Baseline your spiritual heart once again.**

## NOW, LET'S LOOK AT EACH STEP IN MORE DETAIL

### Step 1: Baseline your spiritual heart.

Bring your awareness to your spiritual heart, in the center of your chest between your breasts. This is the heart chakra. Notice how this place feels. For many people, this is a new experience, something that they have not done before, so take your time and relax here a while.

Simply notice how your spiritual heart feels. There may be feelings here, emotions or physical sensations. There may be a sense of energy or color. Whatever you sense here is what you need in the moment, so please just allow yourself to be aware and accepting of it.

Now notice how open your spiritual heart feels. Bring your hands up in front of your heart, in a vertical prayer position, and allow them to gently open to express how open your heart feels. Notice this, because we'll use this as a baseline of how open your heart was in the beginning.

Notice also how warm or cold your heart feels, how light or dark, how light or heavy. It helps to create a scale of some sort, by assigning a number from one to ten, or making a mental image of it on a spectrum. Remember all these first impressions. You may want to write them down.

One way to open into this experience of heart perception more deeply is to begin with the awareness scan. The awareness scan brings you into harmony with yourself, by allowing you to relate with awareness to your physical body and your personality before moving into your spiritual heart. It makes you more present for the experience of joining with your spiritual heart.

## The Awareness Scan:

### Moving from outer physical focus to inner spiritual focus

1. Bring your awareness within. You may like to close your eyes.
2. Do whatever you need to get comfortable, to come into the present moment.
3. Now, just notice what you are aware of. Just observe. Spend a few breaths with this until you feel satisfied.
4. Bring your awareness to your breath. Notice how it moves through your body. Again, just follow your breath, just observe; don't try to change it. Spend a few breaths with this, until you have the sense of your breath.
5. Let your breath lead into your body. Notice the way it feels, what comes to your awareness, just observing. Spend a few more breaths with this.
6. Bring your awareness to your feelings. What emotions are you aware of? Simply notice your feelings as they move within you for a while.
7. Bring your awareness to your thoughts. What are you thinking? Allow yourself to observe your thoughts as if they were clouds rolling by; make no judgments.
8. Notice if you are aware of any intentions. Again, just observe.
9. Now bring your awareness back to your breath.
10. Do you notice any changes? Consider your breathing . . . your body . . . your emotions . . . your thoughts . . . your intentions.
11. Now, drop your awareness into your spiritual heart. And focus on how it feels.

**Step 2: Chant the sacred sound "Ah" in your spiritual heart.**

Begin to chant "Ah" aloud, while focusing within your spiritual heart.

Sounding "Ah" allows the spiritual heart to open. According to Neil Douglas-Klotz, the renowned scholar of ancient sacred languages, the sound "A" carries the sound-meaning of "pure Oneness and Unity."[43]

Keep repeating "Ah" over and over, and notice how your spiritual heart receives it. Notice what happens beyond your heart, to all of you. Focus on your body, your breath, your emotions, your thoughts, your intentions, and your energy field. What are you aware of?

It is important to begin with "beginner's mind," a lack of expectation or preconceptions. And it is equally important to accept that whatever you experience is right for you; it is what you need to be aware of in the moment. A few people will feel nothing at first. So be it. Over time, with application, the experience of the Remembrance grows.

After you have practiced "Ah," then read how others experience it, below.

I have taught this to hundreds of students, and there are some common perceptions that regularly occur. If we look at them on a continuum of deepening, here is what we see:

> Relaxing . . . "It's the sound of relaxing—this is what I do when I come home from the office."
>
> Calming . . . "I feel calm, at rest."
>
> Quieting the mind . . . "It's still, quiet . . . I'm no longer in my mind."
>
> Releasing . . . "I feel a complete release" . . . "Letting go" . . . "I feel like I'm letting a burden go."
>
> Warming . . . "My heart feels warm."

Lighter . . . "My heart feels lighter."

Deeper . . . "It drops me deeper in my heart."

Effortless . . . "It feels effortless."

Surrender . . . "I feel a letting go, a surrender" . . . "I feel emptied."

Filled . . . "And I feel filled at the same time—a paradox!"

Aligning . . . "I feel an inner alignment."

Coming Home . . . "This is coming home."

Notice if you shared these experiences or something different. Notice the power of the sound within your spiritual heart—how it can move you into a different quality of being, effortlessly.

**Step 3: Chant the sacred sound "Ah" as you gaze into the eyes of a partner.**

To expand your experience of how "Ah" moves through your spiritual heart, sit facing a partner. Move into the presence of your spiritual heart, and then chant "Ah" slowly as you gaze into each other's eyes. Do this until you absorb what is held within this experience.

You may need a moment to get comfortable with this—it's not a common thing to do, especially with someone new, but it will be worth moving beyond any initial hesitation.

This experience typically draws people into much deeper awareness of their partner. Some experience compassion for their partner, a much deeper relatedness than they usually experience with someone they just met. Others recognize beautiful soul qualities in their partner; this is easy when the heart is open, for the spiritual heart opens to the soul. Others receive intuitive understandings of their partner. For example, they may understand what their partner is learning in this lifetime; this is an expression of soul purpose. And still others go deeper still and experience a sense of there being no separation, expressed by one student as "there is no other." When we relate to others from the spiritual heart, all boundaries dissolve.

The sound "Ah" has the power to join, to unify, what felt separate only moments before.

**Step 4: Understand ancient words of light, sacred words that carry you into an experience of the Unity within your spiritual heart.**

As we experienced with sounding "Ah" in our hearts, sound has the power to transport us into an experience of sacredness within ourselves. We can extend this sound into words, sacred words of light. These are words whose very utterance evokes and invokes the state of Unity.

These words are sacred because they carry light. As they move within our hearts, they activate the light within us. They carry us into a much greater experience of our self.

## The spiritual meaning of light.

Light is a subtle concept that may need some clarification. We can briefly review some ideas to make this subtlety more observable.

Life and light are related. A ready example is the sun—its warming light brings life to all.

As we study this concept, we see that the more life something holds, the more light it holds. On the physical level, for example, the fresher a flower or fruit, the greater its luster and glow. On an emotional level, light is what lifts us up inside, filling us with the more life-giving emotions, like joy. Joy is expansive and enlivening to all around. On the mental level, a mind with more light, intelligence, is more active and alive with ideas than a mind with far less light.

Each of these examples shows experience coming more alive. We could think of light as enlivening, quickening, carrying more life force. So we begin to see that light correlates with life force.

We can go further and talk about our divinity and what light means in this way. Light opens many life-giving qualities within us. We can think of these as qualities of God, the Creator, the creative life force. These life-giving qualities take us into more of what we might be, they move us deeper into our experience of the Unity. And we begin to experience ourselves living with more of what makes life meaningful—more peace in our hearts, more love and joy in our lives, more understanding and wisdom.

To carry more light is to carry more life force, more ability to create. We acquire greater capacities. We grow in our capacity to love.

## Sacred words carry light. They bring Life.

How can a simple word do all this? To understand this, we need to think of words in a different way than we are accustomed to in our Western culture. In our culture, a word *describes* something—an experience, a person, or an object. It is a concept for the mind's understanding.

But with ancient words of light, the word itself *is* the experience, one and the same. As soon as we say a sacred word with awareness, its sound evokes the experience within us. The very sound of the word resonates within us, carrying us into an expanded experience of the quality that the word embodies. For example, many readers will have experienced the transforming effects of meditatively chanting "Om" or "Aum."

**The four sacred words of light: Alaha, Allah, Elohim, Elat.**

In our work with the Remembrance, we will start with four words of light that evoke the Unity, so that you can observe how your heart receives each one. These words are based on the work of Neil Douglas-Klotz, who uses them as a prayer, as a chant, and as a dance.[44]

The four sacred words each derive from a different ancient language. Below are their origins, meanings, and pronunciations:

**1. Alaha . . . The Unity (Aramaic) . . . (Ah lah' ha) . . . the language of Jesus**
Alaha is the Aramaic word for the Unity. This is the word that Jesus used when He spoke of the Unity, which we call "God" today. The word "God" did not appear as such in the Bible. It gradually evolved as the Aramaic word "Alaha" was translated from the New Testament into other languages. The word, God is derived from a German word meaning "good."[45]

**2. Allah . . . The One, Unity, or the One Being[46] (Arabic) . . . (Ah' lah') . . . the language of Muhammad**

**3. Elohim . . . The One that is also Many, Unity in Diversity[47] (Hebrew) . . . (Eh low eem') . . . the language of Abraham and Moses**

**4. Elat . . . The One that is Embodied, Here and Now[48] (Old Cannanite) . . . (Ay lat')**

**Comparing ancient words of light to modern English . . . Which holds more life and light for you?**

Let's do a simple experiment to dramatize the difference between modern English and ancient words of light.

In the physics of today, this Unity would share some qualities with the unified field. So we will use this phrase in our experiment.

Say "the unified field" in your spiritual heart slowly, and be aware of how it touches you. Repeat it as much as you need to. How does it feel? Where do you receive it—in your mind, in your spiritual heart? If you are like most people, it only touches your mind. It stays outside you. It does not really enter you at all. You are not moved by it.

Now, say one of the sacred words, "Alaha," "Allah," "Elohim," or "Elat," aloud while you focus within your spiritual heart. Say the word once, and stay with that experience, letting it deepen.

Then repeat the word aloud again and again, watching its effect on you. How does it feel? Where do you receive it? Everyone experiences these words far more deeply than the words "the unified field." They touch, they reach into deeper aspects of ourselves, and bring them to life, quickening them within us.

Ancient words carry light in a way the English language cannot.

Now, let's take a look these sacred words more closely and bring them to light and life within us.

**Step 5: Pray the sacred words that evoke Unity: Alaha, Allah, Elohim, Elat. Experience each sacred word once, then chant it for a few moments, observing how it touches your heart.**

We will focus on each of these words in turn. To begin, center yourself in the presence of your spiritual heart. Begin breathing in your spiritual heart. This is important, because breath brings consciousness. Breath and spirit are closely related. Spirit is held within both the words, the respiration of our breath moving through us, and the inspiration of spirit moving through us.

Now, say one of the sacred words, "Alaha," "Allah," "Elohim," or "Elat," aloud while you focus within your spiritual heart. Say the word once, and notice how it touches your heart. Stay with that experience, letting it deepen within you.

Then repeat the word aloud again and again, praying it within your heart. Observe its effect on you. Take time with this, and note carefully what happens progressively as you continue for several minutes, about one hundred repetitions.

Then, follow this procedure for each word in turn. Please be aware of any pre-existing bias within yourself that prevents you from opening fully to a word. You may be depriving yourself of an exceptional experience of the sacred that this one word can reach within you.

Some students start with such a bias, for instance, finding that only "Elohim" touches them because they are most familiar with it. Or some are uncomfortable using the word "Allah." What these students generally find is that, in time, all four words enable them to reach sacred space within themselves.

It is important to work with a sacred word that touches your heart. Occasionally, a student will find that none of these words touch their heart. In that case, please choose a word that does. For example, some people like to use the sacred word, "Yeshua," which is the name of Jesus as it was spoken in Aramaic during Biblical times. This word might also be seen as an interpretation of the Jesus Prayer of Christianity.

**Step 6: Determine which word your heart receives most deeply. Pray that specific word of light in your heart for at least five more minutes, observing how it affects you. Twenty minutes is ideal to receive what it offers.**

**Step 7: Baseline your spiritual heart once again.**

Now that you have completed the prayers, feel what is here. Can you feel a blessing in your heart? In the room?

Take a moment and check in with your heart again. Notice how open or closed, how warm or cold, how light or dark, how light or heavy your heart feels now. How does this compare with your first baseline?

If you are like most people, you will discover a significant difference. You will have begun the journey to the pure love within you. For now you have joined the prayer your heart is always praying, the deep love within your heart, the deep love that is who you truly are.

Welcome home.

## Deepening the Practice of the Prayer of the Heart

As you continue praying these sacred words as a practice, you will find that the experiences embodied in Alaha, Allah, Elohim, and Elat touch all aspects of your being. And when chanted or sung through your spiritual heart, they move you into something much greater. They make light of ourselves and our lives. They bring us to life, ever more life.

As you continue to pray this, you will find yourself living in an ever-greater love and well-being. This blessing of gentle love will keep radiating out, gradually refining you, releasing what is not love within you, ever purifying. It will radiate beyond you, to others and the situations you are in, changing them, making them graceful. For the pure love, the true love wants only to express. It wants only to love.

Along the way, this love will bring up what needs to be aligned and returned to love within you. Working with the deep love within your heart will bring up all that is not love until it is cleansed and released. If there is pain, and at times there will be, this is something in you that is seeking to be released. A way to work with what comes up is to physically locate it within your spiritual heart, and call the light of God into that area, using a sacred name for Unity. This progressively washes it, and allows you to see more deeply into the issue, and into what God is making here. This will progressively allow it to become love.

It will give you momentum toward abiding in this place always if you wake in your spiritual heart and go to sleep in your spiritual heart, using the Remembrance or the Jesus Prayer. The prayer works through you in ways we cannot know with our minds. The prayer of the heart moves us into Oneness, a goodness beyond our knowing or doing, a graceful harmony and deepening communion with God. We find ourselves given to something greater.

As you practice the prayer of the heart, you may discover, over time, that this one simple practice gently transforms your entire life, bringing blessing upon blessing. And as you continue, you may discover that you gently are transformed into a blessing for others, in ways beyond your knowing or doing, moved by the immense and gentle power of the pure love through you.

This is how we are supposed to live. This is what we are supposed to be: pure love itself, moving in harmony through all of life.

May it be so in your life.

# GLOSSARY OF HAWAIIAN WORDS

One of the big keys to pronouncing Hawaiian words is the glottal stop, when the word is abruptly halted within it, and then begun again. An example from English is "uh-oh." In Hawaiian, the glottal stop is represented by an apostrophe. So for example, the southern district, called Ka'u, is pronounced "Kah' ooh." If you pronounce it as normal English, as a friend did when they wanted to buy Ka'u coffee, it comes out "cow coffee," and no one understands what you want.

**Aina**: (ay' nah) Earth.

**Ali'i**: (ah' lee' ee') The Hawaiian tribal chiefs and chiefesses whom we call kings and queens.

**Heiau**: (hay' ow) Hawaiian temple. Used for offerings to the gods, and sacrifice.

**Ho Nau Nau**: (hoe now' now') Also called "Two Step," this great snorkeling beach gets its name because you take two big lava rock steps down into the water.

**Ka' Ano I**: (kah' ah no ee) Beloved.

**Kilauea Crater**: (kee-lou-ey'-ah) A volcanic crater within Mauna Loa volcano in Hawaii Volcanoes National Park. "Kilauea" means "spewing."

**Kilauea Iki**: (kee-lou-ey'-ah ee' kee') A pit crater near Kilauea Crater, and much smaller.

**Lani**: (lah' nee) Heaven, heavenly, sky.

**Lau lau**: (lahw lahw) "Lau" literally means "leaf." Lau lau is an original Hawaiian wrap, a delicious local favorite, where taro wraps around pork, fish, or chicken.

**Mahea**: (mah' hay ah) Hawaiians named each night of the twenty-eight moon phases. Mahea was the third night of the full moon and refers to the hazy moon.

**Mahealani**: (mah' hay ah lah' nee) Beautiful full moon in its hazy third night.

**Makai**: (muh kai') Ocean, used colloquially to mean "toward the ocean," as in "up half a mile makai."

**Mana**: (mah' na) Spiritual power.

**Mauka**: (mahw ka') Mountain, toward the mountain.

**Ono**: (oh' no) Delicious.

**Pakalolo**: (pah' ka low low) Marijuana, literally "crazy weed."

**Pali**: (pah' lee) Cliff.

**Pau**: (pow) Done, finished, as in "We're pau." "Pau hana" means "we're done for the day."

**Pono**: (poh' no) True, right, just.

**Pua'a**: (poo' ah' ah') Pigs.

**Puna**: (poo' na) Spring.

**Punalu'u Beach**: (poo' na loo' oo) Literally "spring dived for." Famous black sand beach on south of island.

# ENDNOTES

1 "Deliciousness Itself" is the phrase Mark Twain famously used to describe a cherimoya fruit.

2 "Kaulana, Kawaihae" is an exquisitely beautiful island song that captures the essence of the islands. It is available on YouTube, sung by Iz, Israel Kamakawiwo'ole, the legendary voice of Hawaii. It makes great background music for the introduction. YouTube video, 4:03, from *Facing Future*, compact disc, 2008, posted by sunsong23, February 10, 2008, https://www.youtube.com/watch?v=876MtdZJ-Lo

3 "Day-O (The Banana Boat Song)" is a traditional folk song from Jamaica, which banana workers sang in the fields.

4 I hasten to tell my friends and readers that our home is nothing like this today—it is beautiful and thoroughly comfortable—with indoor plumbing to boot!

5 "What is of all things most yielding?" Marc Lappe, *Of All Things Most Yielding* (New York: McGraw-Hill, 1972).

6 The Great Mahele of 1848 was a critical turning point in Hawaiian history. "Mahele" means "to divide or portion." This law allowed land to be divided and privately owned for the first time. Up until that time, it had been under the stewardship of the king and tribal chiefs. Many native Hawaiians were eventually disenfranchised from their lands through this legislation.

7 Since writing this, Pier 1 has arrived on the island.

8 Sabine Hendreschke, "Home of My Heart", 2010, accessed March 5, 2016, http://www.freestoriescenter.com/storyview.asp?entry=8384

9 Chronic fatigue syndrome (CFS) is also called chronic fatigue immune dysfunction syndrome (CFIDS).

10 I discovered in researching this chapter that the Tap and Growler was indeed about one hundred years old.

11 *The Holy Bible,* Deut. 6:4.

12 "Unity" is used in this book to mean God, Divinity, Oneness, spirit, the ever-abiding grace and harmony in which we are all one.

13 C.G. Jung, *Memories, Dreams, Reflections,* ed. Aniela Jaffe, trans. Richard Winston, Clara Winston (New York: Vintage, division of Random House, 1965), 293–294.

14 Rosalyn L. Bruyere, *Wheels of Light, A Study of the Chakras* (Sierra Madre, CA: Bon Productions, 1989), 25-29.

15 The Unity that we call "God." The Unity is very important in Sufism and represents the final stations of the heart.

"Unity" is the translation of the ancient Aramaic word "Alaha" which appears in the New Testament. This word has been translated as "God." The word "Unity" is truer to the original scripture, which is why I prefer to use it.

There are several other reasons I prefer to use the word "Unity".

First, the only way we can know God is through ourselves—through our perceptual and conceptual capacity. It follows that we cannot fully comprehend the Divinity. Yet we can grow in our understanding of it. This allows us to realize that there are many levels of understanding God.

To one person, God might be a man with a flowing white beard on a throne, a God in physical form. To another, God is love. For another, God is consciousness, an all-knowing intelligence. And for yet another, God is a state of being that we enter progressively more deeply as we develop. And still another way to understand God is as a creative force, the life force, or infinite life itself.

Second, "God" is a rather loaded word. People come to God with their wants and desires, their expectations, projections, and needs, and this leads to some very inappropriate perceptions and conclusions about what God is and how God should behave. For example, the expectation that "God should not allow that to happen" often leads people to separate from an experience of the divine.

16 When I refer to the heart in the text, it is not the physical heart. It is the spiritual heart, the heart chakra, called "anahata" in Sanskrit. The spiritual heart has many realms, and is unlimited in its expanse. I use the phrase "deep heart" synonymously with the spiritual heart center.

17 For a more complete explanation of the Remembrance and a way to learn it, please see the Appendix.

18 "If you are fire, I am wood." I have diligently sought to identify the source of this quotation, with no success. If anyone knows the source of this quotation, please contact anne@anneceleste.com so that proper acknowledgment may be made.

19 The Guide Sidi al-Jamal: "Sidi" means "teacher." It is the name by which beloveds call Shaykh Muhammad Sa'id al-Jamal ar-Rifa'i ash-Shadhuli. He passed away during the completion of this book, in November, 2015. He was the beloved Guide of the Shadduliyah way, the Guide to a remarkable number of Sufis around the world. From 1959 on, he lived on the Mount of Olives in Jerusalem. He was the Imam at the Masjid al-Aqsa, the Dome of the Rock on the Temple Mount, the golden dome that is so often photographed in Jerusalem. He was instrumental in preserving the Masjid al-Aqsa during many violent conflicts. Beginning in 1993, he began traveling to the United States and other nations to teach.

20 The Sufi path can be followed by Christians, Buddhists, Jews, Muslims, Hindus, and all faiths. This means that one can follow Sufi practices without being a Muslim in much the same way that a Catholic can practice yoga.

In my case, I have found a deeper understanding of Christian practices through Sufism. For instance, the Remembrance, the Sufi practice of Remembrance, a prayer of communion with the divine, is very similar to the Jesus Prayer, a profound prayer practiced by Christians. One dimension Sufism adds is the delineation of twenty-eight stations of the heart, a path of spiritual union with the divine, which I have never seen within Christianity.

There are various pathways within Sufism. Some are separate from Islam, and others are blended with Islam. It is my understanding that Muslims themselves do not embrace Sufism.

Within all the differing spiritual paths, it is wisest to see where spiritual paths agree rather than focusing on their differences. This leads to a deeper understanding of the divine, the life-giving creative force, rather than to conflict between doctrinal positions. Rumi said it very well when he proclaimed, "Not Christian or Jew or Muslim, not Hindu, Buddhist, Sufi, or Zen. Not any religion . . . My place is the placeless, a trace of the traceless . . . I belong to the Beloved . . ." Coleman Barks, *The Illuminated Rumi* (New York, NY: Broadway Books, 1997).

21 I say "normal person's head" because I perceive a richer, deeper, far more expanded, and articulated gold above the head of great spiritual leaders. The more developed a person, the more developed their auric field. There is actually no comparison between the field of a high master and normal people.

22 Recovery from severe CFS is rarely complete. Those who have had severe CFS usually continue with various compromises to the immune, nervous and digestive systems, as well as great sensitivity to many things, such as foods, medicinal drugs, and weather.

23 *Seraphine*. Directed by Martin Provost. 2008. France: TS Productions, 2009. DVD.

24 Eknath Easwaran, *Gandhi the Man*. 2nd ed. (Petaluma, CA: Nilgiri Press, 1978), 74.

25 Ritchie, George and Elizabeth Sherrill, *Return from Tomorrow* (Grand Rapids, MI: Chosen Books, 2007), 129-132.

26 I cannot locate a second source to verify the story of Wild Bill, yet the principle holds. Victor Frankl, psychiatrist and founder of logotherapy, was a concentration camp survivor, which he described in *Man's Search for Meaning*. In that book, he describes how some concentration camp prisoners gave away their last scrap of bread to others, making the point that we can determine the qualities by which we will live, regardless of our circumstance.

27 In my case, progressive deepening in Remembrance did this for me, but it could just as easily happen with the Jesus Prayer, prayed through the heart. See the Appendix for an explanation of the Jesus Prayer.

28 In Masuru Emoto's experiments, water is actively prayed over. Directed thoughts, such as "love and gratitude" are also used. The experiment is conducted with damaged water, for example, chlorinated city water, or polluted natural water. Under a high-precision microscope, it shows a significantly disfigured structure. After prayer, the water is transformed into hexagonal, crystalline structures of exquisite beauty. Masuru Emoto, *The Hidden Messages in Water*, (New York, NY: Atria Books, 2001).

29 From a scientific perspective, one could hypothesize that either the water changed, or the individual's perception of the water changed. Either would still be a valid outcome to the experiment since the experience of the water changed. However, I personally believe the water itself changes. I have done

this little experiment for years with wine. Long ago in the 1980s, before I gave up alcohol, I would do this with medium-quality wine. It always made the wine taste much finer, and at half the price!

30 Eknath Easwaran, *Gandhi the Man*. 2nd ed. (Petaluma, CA: Nilgiri Press, 1978), 114.

31 *The Bhagavad Gita*, trans. Eknath Easwaran (Petaluma, CA: Nilgiri Press, 1985), 164.

32 For readers who work with intuition, notice that this whole event is intuitive, and watch your own spontaneous impulses when your conscious mind is not aware of what is really happening. In this case, I did not have plans to visit with Joanie that summer, yet I spontaneously got an impulse to visit Jeanette without consciously knowing Joanie would be there. And, of course, Joanie held the key.

33 Alfred Lord Tennyson in his poetic tribute to her, "Kapiolani": http://www.public-domain-poetry.com/alfred-lord-tennyson/kapiolani-696

34 "It Happens All the Time in Heaven", *The Subject Tonight is Love: 60 Wild and Sweet Poems of Hafiz*, Trans. Daniel Ladinsky (New York, NY: Penquin Compass, 2003), 45.

35 Gary Lachman, *Swedenborg* (New York, NY: Jeremy P. Tarcher/Penguin, 2009), 166.

36 St. John of the Cross, *Dark Night of the Soul, A Masterpiece in the Literature of Mysticism*, Trans. E Allison Peers (New York: Image Books/Doubleday, 1959).

37 St. Teresa of Avila, *Interior Castle*, Trans. E Allison Peers (Mineola, NY: Dover Publications, 2007).

38 Shaykh Muhammad al-Jamal ar-Rifa'i as-Shadhili, *Music of the Soul, Sufi Teachings* (Petaluma, CA: Sidi Muhammad Press, 1994), 60–121.

39 *The Holy Bible,* Revised Standard Version (New York: Thomas Nelson & Sons, 1946), 933 (1 Thess. 5:17).

40 Anonymous, *The Way of a Pilgrim and the Pilgrim Continues His Way*, Trans. Helen Bacovcin, (New York: Image Books/Doubleday, 1978).

41 Shaykh Muhammad al-Jamal ar-Rifa'i as-Shadhili, *Music of the Soul, Sufi Teachings*, (Petaluma, CA: Sidi Muhammad Press, 1994), 172–177.

42 Thomas Merton, *Conjectures of a Guilty Bystander* (New York: Doubleday, 1966), 142.

43 Neil Douglas-Klotz, *Prayers of the Cosmos, Meditations on the Aramaic Words of Jesus* (New York: Harper San Francisco, 1990), 13.

44 I have found the chant from Neil Douglas-Klotz, "Alaha, Allah, Elohim, Elat" a beautiful way to pray and easy to sing throughout the day. To view more of his work, see http://abwoon.org/

45 Neil Douglas-Klotz, *The Hidden Gospel, Decoding the Spiritual Message of the Aramaic Jesus* (Wheaton, IL: Quest Books, 1999), 28.

46 Neil Douglas-Klotz, *The Sufi Book of Life, 99 Pathways of the Heart for the Modern Dervish* (New York: Penguin Compass, 2005), 2.

47 Neil Douglas-Klotz, *The Hidden Gospel, Decoding the Spiritual Message of the Aramaic Jesus* (Wheaton, IL: Quest Books, 1999), 28.

48 Ibid.

# ABOUT THE AUTHOR

**Anne Celeste is a spiritual counselor, teacher, and healer.** She uses her exceptional intuitive gifts, as well as her training in spiritual healing, energy healing, and psychological counseling to guide people as they integrate personality with soul.

**Her life work focuses on the spiritual soul.**

**She has made a lifelong study of the process of spiritual development,** integrating the inner, mystic paths of Christianity, Yoga, Sufism, and Tibetan Buddhism with the contemporary work of Alice Bailey, Rudolf Steiner, and others. Her research into hundreds of significant lives contributes to her understanding of spiritual development.

**Anne is an authority on intuition.** Since 1981 she has taught thousands of individuals, many in the caring professions, to live within the guidance of the soul. Her skills have been tested and highly ranked.

**Anne is a master teacher of the Sufi way,** appointed in 2003 by the beloved Guide Sidi al-Jamal of the Shadduliyah Way. This designation signifies that her heart is the earth on which others can travel as they journey into the Unity.

Previously, she had a twenty-year career in senior corporate management. A graduate of the University of Illinois, she did graduate study in Northwestern University's MBA program.

She teaches at Aina Lani, a six-acre spiritual retreat on the Big Island of Hawaii.

## WATCH FOR THIS COMING BOOK

**The Desert Wind: A Sacred Love Story**

*Just where can love take us?*
*And what might we be, together?*

*Imagine loving deeply, so deeply that*
*you could never be separate from love again.*

*That's just what happens to Estrella, as she travels into her heart,*
*learning to dissolve everything in the way of that love.*

*Listen as the Desert Wind tells the story of what we once were,*
*and what we can be once again.*

*It all happens the One Moment we choose to be only love.*
*For in that Remembrance, we come home.*
*Together.*

**For more resources and seminars, visit anneceleste.com**

Made in the USA
Columbia, SC
28 November 2017